Environmental Justice

About Island Press

Island Press is the only nonprofit organization in the United States whose principal purpose is the publication of books on environmental issues and natural resource management. We provide solutions-oriented information to professionals, public officials, business and community leaders, and concerned citizens who are shaping responses to environmental problems.

In 1994, Island Press celebrated its tenth anniversary as the leading provider of timely and practical books that take a multidisciplinary approach to critical environmental concerns. Our growing list of titles reflects our commitment to bringing the best of an expanding body of literature to the environmental community throughout North America and the world.

Support for Island Press is provided by The Geraldine R. Dodge Foundation, The Energy Foundation, The Ford Foundation, The George Gund Foundation, William and Flora Hewlett Foundation, The James Irvine Foundation, The John D. and Catherine T. MacArthur Foundation, The Andrew W. Mellon Foundation, The Pew Charitable Trusts, The Rockefeller Brothers Fund, The Tides Foundation, Turner Foundation, Inc., The Rockefeller Philanthropic Collaborative, Inc., and individual donors.

Environmental Justice

Issues, Policies, and Solutions

Edited by

Bunyan Bryant

School of Natural Resources and Environment
University of Michigan, Ann Arbor

ISLAND PRESS

Washington, D.C. • Covelo, California

Library of Congress Cataloging-in-Publication Data

Environmental justice : issues, policies, and solutions / edited by
    Bunyan Bryant.
        p.   cm.
    Includes bibliographical references and index.
    ISBN 1-55963-416-2. — ISBN 1-55963-417-0 (pbk.)
        1. Environmental policy—United States. 2. Environmental policy—
    Political aspects—United States. 3. Social justice—United
    States. 4. Sustainable development—United States. I. Bryant,
    Bunyan I.
    GE180.E585   1995   95-9316
    363.7'00973—dc20   CIP

Contents

Foreword

The country is now struggling to find answers to its toxic and hazardous waste problems. This struggle is deeply felt by people earning low incomes and people of color throughout the country as they engage in social protests to protect their communities against the inequitable impact of elevated levels of toxic and hazardous waste. A close examination of the waste problems points to a deeper, more fundamental problem. To solve the waste problem requires changes in how we produce and dispose of goods and services.

The ideas presented in this book should be viewed as a challenge. Since the Cold War is now over, we can turn our undivided attention to protecting and healing earth so that people can live and work in clean, safe, and nurturing environments regardless of the color of their skin or where they may live. We would be remiss in our responsibility if we refused to take this opportunity to make a difference. This book provides startling answers to our social and environmental problems and charts a course for action. We can follow that course to its destination if we all do our part.

In the interest of environmental justice and improved life chances for all people of color, I remain.

Charles D. Moody, Sr.
Executive Director and Vice Provost Emeritus for Minority Affairs
The University of Michigan

Acknowledgments

I wish to express my sincere thanks to Charles D. Moody, Sr., Executive Director and Vice Provost Emeritus for Minority Affairs, Lester P. Monts, Vice Provost for Academic and Multicultural Affairs, Sylvia Tesh, Ph.D., Gregory Button, Ph.D., Clarice Gaylord, Ph.D., Dorceta Taylor, Ph.D., Paul Mohai, Ph.D., Michel Gelobter, Ph. D., and. Charles Lee, Research Director for the Commission for Racial Justice of the United Church of Christ for their support during the editing of this book.

For editorial assistance I would like to acknowledge Kathy Hall, Kathy Nemsick, John Woodford, and Carol Kent.

Special thanks and appreciation also go to my wife, Jean.

Introduction

Bunyan Bryant

While greater attention is usually paid to development, little attention is paid to a damaging by-product of development—the pollution that is playing a major role in decreasing the quality of life for billions of people throughout the world. The questions facing us are: As we grow and develop at an exponential rate, depleting our highly cherished world resources, where will we find places to put our waste, particularly as we run out of land? Is it possible that shortages of places to dispose of our waste could trigger waste and race wars, as the United States and European countries make attempts to dump their waste in Third World countries?

Now that the Cold War is over, after almost fifty years of utilizing the lion's share of our nation's resources, the struggle now turns to the control of the heart and soul of this country; the struggle now turns inward in a quest for a new identity. Who are we since the Cold War has ended? Will we be able to resist environmental destruction? Will economic struggles among the European Common Market, Japan, and the United States become the basis of our new mission in the world? While the Cold War was used to justify weapons of destruction, it may also have served the purpose of defining a national mission, more so in terms of what we were against, rather than what we were for. Defeating Communism brought world peace and freedom from Communist domination, but it also left us without a clear mission. In the 1980s, even before the Cold War ended, signs of trouble on the political, economic, and environmental landscape were beginning to bode ominously for the future. While supply side economics was touted as the economic savior, it worked for the few—not the many. We were left with economic, political, cultural, and environmental woes that will not go away. While the rich get richer,

Although Bunyan Bryant's major faculty appointment is in the University of Michigan School of Natural Resources and Environment, he also has an adjunct position with the school's Center of Afro-American and African Studies. Professor Bryant has written a book called Environmental Advocacy: Concepts, Issues and Dilemmas, *and a manual called* Social and Environmental Change: A Manual for Community Organizing and Action. *He and Prof. Paul Mohai have edited a book entitled* Race and the Incidence of Environmental Hazards: A Time for Discourse *(1992). He is also co-principal investigator of the* University of Michigan 1990 Detroit Area Study on Race and Toxic Waste. *He was the co-facilitator of the Symposium on Health Research and Needs to Ensure Environmental Justice, 1994, and presently serves on EPA's National Environmental Justice Advisory Council.*

the poor get poorer; there are more street people, more unemployed, more underemployed, more single mothers, and one out of every five children is in poverty. Millions of people, particularly people of color and low-income groups, are located in the most undesirable sections of cities throughout the country; they are exposed to elevated levels of multiple pathways of pollutants that are persistent and dangerous. When the family farm went belly up, farmers could not stand the pain of losing their land—land which belonged to their family for generations; they committed suicide or became farm refugees and migrated to already overcrowded cities in search of menial jobs. In a land of plenty, corporate mergers resulted in dismissal of workers for the sake of higher profits as corporations engulfed and destroyed weaker ones by hostile takeovers; they raided pension funds and put together junk bonds to bankroll harebrained investment schemes. It was a time when union busting, which the country had not seen in recent memory, was at its height, forcing workers to make wage concessions while corporate executives increased both their salaries and benefits. It was a decade of avarice and unprecedented greed as the "Boeskys" on Wall Street took advantage of insider trading and made billions of dollars. It was the period of Savings and Loan (S & L) scandals, the largest in U.S. history, in which individual taxpayers were saddled with thousands of dollars apiece to bail out the failing industry and thus the economy. The 1980s were a time when James Watt, Secretary of Interior in the Reagan administration, handed over for private use our collectively owned clean air and water, forests, grasslands, coal, oil, and other resources. In the name of "getting government off our back," he gave away our national heritage at fire sale prices.

The economy was on the rebound in 1994 as evidenced by lower unemployment, a lower national budgetary deficit, and lower inflation. Within its first two years, the Clinton administration, with help from both the Senate and the House, passed more legislation than all other modern presidential administrations except for the Johnson and Eisenhower years. The Clinton administration was coming into its own in foreign policy (except for Bosnia and Somalia). But, despite all these successes, voters decided that was not enough. We have a change of the guard not based so much upon what candidates were for but what they were against. We have entered an era of politics of destroy rather than politics of winning or losing; we have entered an era of political "sound bites" rather than politics of substantive issues. We have entered an era of mean spirited behavior and greed that may surpass the greed and avarice of the 1980s. We are too quick to build jails rather than address the underlying issues of structural poverty, unemployment and underemployment, crime, and delinquency—even though we have the resource capability to make things better for people in need. Although Democrats were in control of both houses in 1994, the fact remains that this administration was not able to pass a national health insurance program. In addition, this administration had the worst environmental record in 25 years; they were unable to overcome the extreme pressures of conservative anti-environmental groups. The political reverberations of 1994 and 1995 and beyond may be the result of the defeat of Communism, leaving us adrift without a common enemy to provide the glue to hold us together.

At the international level, Miller (1988) states that global warming, deforestation (particularly of tropical rainforests), desertification and destruction of wetlands and coral reefs, and the extinction of species and plants at a rate of one every three days since 1975 (some put the rate even higher) are cause for unprecedented alarm. It was a time when developing countries not only found themselves overburdened (as they still are) with financial debt, but also found that each year their debt increased. As international monetary institutions such as the International Monetary Fund required austere money policies of the Third World countries seeking to rid themselves of debt, this often caused anti-inflation riots that threatened world equilibrium.

Meanwhile the economies of the European Common Market and Japan have gotten stronger over the last several decades and seem to be on a collision course with the economy of the United States. In many areas they are out-producing us and may already be getting a greater share of the world's market, which they now seem sure to do in future years. If this economic war that looms on the horizon should occur, it might become more threatening than any totalitarian Communist domination could have been; it could become more threatening because all three economies are gearing up to snatch not only greater shares of global markets, but to exploit more and more of the world's highly cherished human and natural resources. This would undoubtedly have a tremendous impact upon the world's ecosystems and levels of world pollution. The flip-side of economic development is poverty; can one exist without the other? While greater attention is usually paid to development, little attention is paid to a damaging by-product of development—the pollution that is playing a major role in decreasing the quality of life for billions of people throughout the world. The questions facing us are: As we grow and develop at an exponential rate, depleting our highly cherished world resources, where will we find places to put our waste, particularly as we run out of land? Is it possible that shortages of places to dispose of our waste could trigger waste and race wars, as the United States and European countries make attempts to dump their waste in Third World countries? We begin to get a glimpse of future conflict from the following statement:

> In May of 1988, the Organization of African Unity (OAU) passed a resolution declaring the dumping of toxic waste in Africa "a crime against Africa and the African people." In June of the same year, the Economic Community of West African States (ECOWAS) also passed a resolution calling for stiff penalties for those that dump toxic wastes. (Mypanya, 1992: 209–210)

Although African countries have been offered money several times their gross national product to accept foreign waste, they are beginning to refuse it; they lack both the knowledge, skills, and infrastructure to monitor the waste to make sure that it is safely stored (Mypanya, 1992; Alston and Brown, 1993). Therefore, to put the world on a path of sustainable development will require not only a reordering of our priorities, but also a quantum leap forward in the fundamental restructuring of the global economy and unprecedented international cooperation to head off an economic war and environmental catastrophes that will come from rapid growth and the wanton destruction of the world's resources. The 1992 Rio Conference was only a small yet significant step in the right direction.

A response to social and environmental issues at both the national and international levels is the environmental justice movement. Because this movement is much broader than the environmental or social movements, and because its issues are inextricably tied to one another, it touches upon every sphere of human endeavor. And although we have embarked upon an era of environmental destruction unprecedented in modern times, and although social conditions for many in this country and throughout the world have failed to improve to any significant extent, the environmental justice movement, drawing its strength from both the grass roots and academia, has the potential to change the way we do business in this country and throughout the world profoundly. If we fail to address environmental degradation, i.e., if we cannot sustain ourselves upon the planet, then what good are civil rights if we are not going to be around to enjoy them.

Little did we know that the struggle in Warren County, North Carolina, to resist the disposal of PCBs in a landfill in a predominantly African American area would gain national and international prominence. This struggle, having deep roots in the African American community, not only gained national attention, but it led to subsequent studies and conferences on the differential exposure of environmental hazards on communities made up of low-income households and people of color. A 1983 General Accounting Office Report found that in EPA's Region IV, landfills were distributed disproportionately in predominantly African American communities. In 1987, a United Church of Christ Commission of Racial Justice study found that the racial pattern of locating landfills in communities of people of color was national in character. More specifically, the Report stated that among a variety of indicators, race was the best predictor of the location of hazardous waste facilities in the United States. Scholarly writings by Beverly Wright, Michel Gelobter, Charles Lee, Bob Bullard, and by my colleagues Ivette Perfecto, Pat West, Paul Mohai, Dorceta Taylor, and Elaine Hockman (all here at the University of Michigan School of Natural Resources and Environment) basically support the findings of the studies listed above.

Several conferences and grassroots activities, described in later chapters, have been important in building the environmental justice movement. Of the several conferences held on this issue, two were organized at the University of Michigan

School of Natural Resources and Environment: *Race and the Incidence of Environmental Hazards and Issues,* which was the first academic conference to be held on this subject, although there were earlier writings on the academic landscape, and *Policies and Solutions for Environmental Justice.* During the former conference, which was held in 1990, the two significant outcomes were (1) a book of readings on *Race and the Incidence of Environmental Hazards* and (2) a series of high-level policy meetings with U.S. Environmental Protection Agency Administrator Reilly and his top aides and later U.S. EPA Administrator Carol Browner and her staff. Although these meetings started out predominantly with academics, they were broadened to include grassroots activists. These meetings were important in getting the EPA and subsequently other federal agencies to focus on policies for environmental justice. The outcome of the latter academic conference, held in 1993 at the University of Michigan School of Natural Resources, is this book of readings. While the first book focused on articulating the environmental justice problems, this book focuses on articulating not problems, but solutions.

Before proceeding further, however, I should define certain concepts. Although we use such concepts as "environmental racism," "environmental equity," and "environmental justice," the literature is conspicuously without definitions. While these concepts mean different things to different people, I have taken the liberty of defining them to serve as a common basis of understanding for reading the following chapters. Undoubtedly these concepts will be redefined as these issues are debated and as we become more knowledgeable about the impact of environmental racism, equity, and justice upon both institutions and individual behaviors. In any event, the following definitions are not meant to be carved in stone:

> *Environmental Racism*: It is an extension of racism. It refers to those institutional rules, regulations, and policies or government or corporate decisions that deliberately target certain communities for least desirable land uses, resulting in the disproportionate exposure of toxic and hazardous waste on communities based upon certain prescribed biological characteristics. Environmental racism is the unequal protection against toxic and hazardous waste exposure and the systematic exclusion of people of color from environmental decisions affecting their communities.

> *Environmental Equity*: Environmental equity refers to the equal protection of environmental laws. For example, under the Superfund clean-up program it has been shown that abandoned hazardous waste sites in minority areas take 20 percent longer to be placed on the national priority action list than those in white areas. It has also been shown that the government's fines are six times greater for companies in violation of RCRA in white than in black communities. This is unequal protection.

Therefore laws should be enforced equally to ensure the proper siting, clean up of hazardous wastes, and the effective regulation of industrial pollution, regardless of the racial and economic composition of the community.

Environmental Justice: Environmental justice (EJ) is broader in scope than environmental equity. It refers to those cultural norms and values, rules, regulations, behaviors, policies, and decisions to support sustainable communities, where people can interact with confidence that their environment is safe, nurturing, and productive. Environmental justice is served when people can realize their highest potential, without experiencing the "isms." Environmental justice is supported by decent paying and safe jobs; quality schools and recreation; decent housing and adequate health care; democratic decision-making and personal empowerment; and communities free of violence, drugs, and poverty. These are communities where both cultural and biological diversity are respected and highly revered and where distributed justice prevails

While environmental racism focuses on the disproportionate impact of environmental hazards on people of color communities, environmental equity and justice focus either on ameliorating potentially life-threatening conditions or on improving the overall quality of life for the indigent or people of color. Although environmental racism is based upon problem identification, the latter two concepts are based upon problem solving; we need to spend more time on doing something about the problem based upon our understanding of it. In most instances we have a pretty good idea of what needs to be done and we have the resources to make life better for people. The challenge is to overcome political and social inertia and make political and social change possible for a more equitable and environmentally just society. Some would argue that the 1994 election is a historic event that will in fact overcome political and social inertia. This may be true, but the issue is whether we are moving in the right direction for a just and humane society.

Over the last few years both scholars and activists have in most instances replaced the concept "equity" with the concept "justice." The former concept was too limiting for the job that needed to be done. By making the connections between environmental and social issues, environmental justice provides an opportunity for building broad-based coalitions in order to make profound changes to enhance the quality of life of people within this country. Obviously this will not be an easy task because those who are well served by the system will probably resist any meaningful change; in particular, this will not be easy because of the conservative politics in control of both the House and the Senate. But if we take environmental justice on as a challenge and if we keep our eyes upon the prize, we can make significant changes in this country that will positively effect the environment and millions of people across the land. I feel the following chapters are a step in the right direction.

Synopsis of This Book

In chapter 1, I give an overview of issues and polices for environmental justice. In chapter 2, Bailey, Alley, Faupel, and Solheim address the role of the professional in working with community groups on environmental justice issues. In chapter 3, Head questions the adequacy of our research paradigms for helping community people exposed to toxic and hazardous waste. Wright in chapter 4 focuses on the need for regional environmental justice centers at universities to help people affected by environmental hazards make informed decisions. In chapter 5, Ferris and Hahn-Baker present a paper on the history of the social justice movement and the need for an environmental justice policy. Bullard in chapter 6 addresses housing discrimination and the need for better housing for people of color and low-income people. Bezdek in chapter 7 states that funding for the pollution control and abatement industry will surpass that of the Defense Department by the year 2000 and will provide opportunities for lots of jobs. Hamilton in chapter 8 addresses the issue of an industrial policy that would seek to keep jobs here in the United States. In chapter 9, Wolcott, Drayton, and Kadri argue for using tax and expenditure policies as a way of reducing exposures and risk for all persons. In chapter 10, West et al. find that minorities have higher fish consumption rates than white anglers and they push for higher fish consumption standards. In chapter 11, Goldtooth speaks to the issue of the exploitation of native people and gives the rationale for sovereignty. In chapter 12, Ostendorf and Terry speak to the devastating impact of United States farm policies on the small family farm and the need to change them. Perfecto in chapter 13 describes organic farming in Cuba and cites it as an example of sustainable development that could be used here in the United States. And Buttel in chapter 14 presents environmental problems at the international level and ways of dealing with them. Appendix 1 is a copy of President Clinton's Executive Order 12898 on Environmental Justice, and Appendix 2 is a copy of the Executive Summary of the recommendations from the Symposium on Health Research Needs to Ensure Environmental Justice.

Based upon the above definition of environmental justice, this book is a response to the failure of public policy to deal effectively with social and environmental problems. It also grew out of the inability of professionals and the academic community to deal effectively with social and environmental problems we face today. While the articles are not necessarily a reflection of my own views, I am quite sure they are insightful enough to stimulate a meaningful discourse. It is critical that we start this discourse to help us chart a course for the future. Now let's take a deep breath and begin our journey.

1

Issues and Potential Policies and Solutions for Environmental Justice: An Overview

Bunyan Bryant

The control over research becomes manifested by who funds what and for what purposes. Why is more research money spent on nuclear power than on solar and alternative forms of energy? Why is more research money spent on large corporate agribusiness than on improving the economic efficiency of the small family farm? Why is it that more money is spent upon designing highways than mass transit systems? Through the influence of money, powerful corporate interests determine the character of scientific inquiry more so than those without money; powerful interest groups are not only in the position to define the problem to be researched, but they are in a position to benefit directly from its results—results and breakthroughs to help them gain a greater share of the market or in the accumulation of profits. If welfare mothers were given 100 million dollars to spend on university research, the political economy of inquiry would be radically different from that of government and corporate decision-makers.

While money moves upward, pollution moves downward (Odum and Odum, 1976); communities of color and low-income groups get less than their fair share of money and more of their fair share of pollutants. Communities of color and low-income groups not only get more than their fair share of pollutants (Bryant and Mohai, 1992; Bullard, 1983, 1984, 1990, 1993; Bullard and Wright, 1986, 1987a, 1987b, 1991; Burke, 1993; Gelobter, 1986; Goldman, 1991; Higgins, 1993; Lavelle and Coyle, 1992; Mohai and Bryant, 1992a, 1992b, 1992c; United Church of Christ, Commission for Racial Justice, 1987; Goldman and Fitton, 1994; Wernette and Nieves, 1991), but the working poor in particular (the unemployed are often protected by Medicare) are most likely to be unprotected by health care insurance, to suffer more from toxic- induced or -aggravated diseases, and to spend higher proportions of their income on medical health care as compared with more affluent groups. Another way of saying it is that if medical bills were subtracted from the accumulation of wealth, there may be less wealth for the wealthy and potentially better health care for the poor. The accumulation of wealth is thus created at the expense of someone else's health or quality of life, or even death, even though scientists argue that the number of people at risk from toxic exposure is very small. This struggle against toxic exposure resulting from the location of toxic and hazardous waste facilities in communities of color and low-income communities will undoubtedly increase in the future as the economy and by-products of production grow, and as more and more people become aware of the potential health effects of elevated levels of pollutants.

But there are those, mainly scientists and policymakers, who quickly point out that exposures are not necessarily linked to health effects. They maintain that people can be exposed to a variety of hazardous wastes or toxic substances and not suffer dire consequences. Until we can be sure of causality,[1] we will have a difficult time influencing policy; as professionals we would not be believable. The difficulty of proving causation is made clear in the following quote:

> The questions of what makes a given chemical dangerous to health and of why, how, and when dangerous chemicals may actually cause human illness are central to the matter of whether toxic waste sites such as Woburn's are the germs of a modern epidemic of environmentally induced disease. The waste sites that are toxic and potentially harmful are indisputable facts; more complicated is the matter of when and how this potential harm is unleashed to manifest itself in humans—whether in the form of rashes, nervousness, headaches, dizziness, nausea, birth defects or cancer. (DiPerna, 1985: 117)

Although we may not be able to prove causality due to confounding variables such as smoking, diet, indoor pollution, and synergistic and repeated effects of multiple exposures, this does not mean that cause and effect does not exist; it may mean only that we failed to prove it. Our inability to show causal relationships, which places us upon weak scientific ground, provides convenient opportunities for the paralysis of analysis; our inability to show causal relationships takes us down the slippery slope into a quagmire of confusion and entanglements and outright disagreements about levels of proof needed. At this point attempting to show causality, or that "A" causes "B," may be a no-win battle for most communities.

Given the complexities of causality, does the degree of risk to human health need to be statistically significant to require political action? Given the low numbers in cluster patterns (an apparent outbreak of disease clumped in time and space or both), do we need to show statistical significance, or should policy be based upon some other criteria? Given the complexities, should a 95 percent confidence level be adhered to for policy decisions? Should we err on the side of human health or on the side of conserving government resources? Given the complexities of causality, consistently debated in the academic community, should we just let people, most of whom are people of color and members of low-income groups, suffer and even die from toxic-induced and -aggravated diseases so that profits can be accumulated? Can we make policy decisions affecting the health of people who are differentially exposed to environmental hazards and toxic substance in the absence of conclusive data? The answer to the last question is yes, we have always done it, but not without being paralyzed in our discussions. How many studies or levels of "proof" do we need before we act in the absence of certainty?

To date, causality arguments or issues of certainty are often used to rationalize inaction, particularly when it has been economically or politically expedient to do so. "To call for absolute certainty and agreement among scientists before taking preventive action is merely a delaying tactic, effective only to the extent that people believe the myth that certainty characterizes science" (Tesh, 1990: 69). It is ironic that lead poisoning, cited by the Agency for Toxic Substances and Disease Registry (ATSDR) as the number one health problem among inner-city children, causes mental retardation or impaired mental abilities. Government policymakers, known to demand causality, have in turn known about the negative effects of lead poisoning on human beings for over fifty years—in fact we have known about the effects of lead since the Roman times—yet the government has basically refused to rectify this situation in any meaningful way, even though millions of inner-city children may suffer from lead poisoning and thus irreversible mental retardation. Despite failed attempts to demonstrate that smoking cigarettes causes lung cancer, we, after a quarter of a century of debate and countless amounts of money spent on research and litigation, were able to enact a policy warning the public that cigarette smoking may be harmful to human health. Meanwhile millions of people had died or became victims of cancer. Why did it take so long for the government to make a policy to protect human health? The issue is not that the cost will not be paid; the issue is who will pay the cost—victims or industry and/or government.

Today countless people across the country live in fear of hazardous waste facilities, polluting industries, and legal and illegal dumpsites. Critical to this issue of hazardous waste is the concept of certainty. Clearly, people of color and low-income communities or more affluent neighborhoods do not want to be the recipients of uncertainty. Because many toxic pollutants are invisible and because the incubation period of toxic-induced disease may extend over a number of years, how can they be certain that they are being exposed to an invisible contaminant? How can they be certain if a contaminant, known to be present, is actually being absorbed by their bodies? How can they be certain about the amount of contaminants absorbed? How can they be certain if the absorbed dosage is dangerous to their health? To evaluate dangers of invisible contaminants may be impossible even if scientific instruments are used to detect their presence (Vyner, 1988). To adapt to uncertainty can cause physical and psychological trauma. The issue of certainty has not only torn communities apart, but it has torn relatives and friends apart; people once in close relationships are no longer speaking to one another, because while some chose to believe the government or the scientific establishment in the face of inclusive data, others chose not to. The enormous psychological impact of uncertainty is indicated by the following statement:

There was a crisis situation with no specific reaction. There was no "grief" ritual. You don't know what to do. There are divergent emotions and reactions needed to cope. People prefer that this didn't happen. They can't see water pollution; they don't feel bad. They believe it, yet they can't cope, so they rationalize it. Even I had a point where I said, "Enough, I can't believe anymore." When the (neighbor's) child died, I reached my breaking point. I couldn't believe that he died from the water because I couldn't live here with the kids if I believed this. Other people shut off at the beginning. One person got an ulcer and the next didn't believe that there was anything wrong.... We didn't know what we were supposed to be doing! Are we paranoid, hypocritical crazies? (Comments from a community leader, Legler section of Jackson, New Jersey [Edelstein, 1982: 132; forwarded from Unger et al., 1992])

When immediate demands for certainty and solution are involved, the social and psychological impacts are not only evident, but so are the economic impacts. Housing stock, which is a life-long investment, begins to depreciate because few people want to buy in a neighborhood marked by conditions of uncertainty. In one working-class white community in Michigan, where a school was built on top of a landfill, a certain group of people chose to believe the school grounds were safe. Public knowledge of school ground contamination would depreciate the value of their land and housing stock, thus resulting in economic ruin.

While immediate demands for certainty and solution are characteristic of issue-oriented research, and while such research provides opportunities for community people to reclaim the democratic process, this has not been the case—i.e., for the most part. As more and more people make immediate demands, they will undoubtedly come in conflict with the well-established scientific community—a scientific community that feels threatened about democratizing scientific decision-making. Such decision-making may encroach upon their scientific domain of power and influence. Over the years, as the military, government, university, industrial, and scientific complex has become more powerful, so too have scientists. As scientists begin to obtain more answers to hypotheses through scientific methodology and the quantification of data, they will also continue to broaden their decision-making power, thus leaving communities of color and low-income groups marginalized with fewer democratic decision-making alternatives. This is clearly indicated in the quote below:

The shift from politics to expertise changes the rules for exercising power, as well as the structure of effective power. The result may entail a cost in equity, since it can well be argued that those most disadvantaged will be the people at the bottom of the system—those who are, through lack of education and of technical sophistication, particularly ill-prepared to deal with the presentation of issues in a technical framework, and still more so when it comes to dealing with those who speak the language of maps, diagrams, and statistical tables. (Peattie, 1968: 81)

This statement was made almost thirty years ago, and we feel today that community people demonstrate not only a greater environmental awareness, but are generally better educated. Also, community people are motivated to learn quickly if a situation is life-threatening to them, their children, and future generations. Nevertheless, even though several national surveys have indicated that the general public has become more environmentally aware, scientists have been unwilling to engage communities in the democratic process to help them make informed decisions. They make assumptions about the "smartness" of community groups, whom they see as too emotional and thus too irrational to understand complex scientific issues. These assumptions provide the rationale for the scientific community to shift more and more of society's decision-making power away from the community to themselves. As more and more community groups demand to be a part of the decision-making process to deal with environmental crises, they will undoubtedly experience resistance from the scientific community, as the following quote indicates:

> ...many scientists, economists, and government officials have reached the dismaying conclusion that much of America's environmental programs have gone seriously awry...that in the last fifteen years environmental policy has too often evolved largely in reaction to popular panics, not in response to sound scientific analyses of which environmental hazards present the greatest risks. (Schneider, 1993: 1)

While science has made tremendous contributions to humanity and the world, such as enriched diets, reduced infectious disease, improved transportation, shorter and more efficient work weeks, more leisure time activities, and improved communications, it has not been without blemish. While on the whole science has been better than no science, it has to stand up to criticism. While science has offered us a vision of total control of our environment through the understanding of natural laws, we are finding that such control is impossible. To a large extent the seemingly foreboding social and environmental problems we experience today, either directly or indirectly, are the result of science and technology. What has been thought to be a long-term solution often ends up not being a solution at all, but another long-term problem (Commoner, 1976). We seldom know the true results of the "technological fix" until we have traveled down the road a piece only to find that it may be too late to reverse catastrophic damages. And yet it is often community groups or victims of environmental crises and their ways of knowing who direct scientists in the right direction for testing hypotheses.

To make assumptions about people's "smartness," their ability to deal with scientific certainty, and their ability to become constructive partners in the problem-solving process only adds fuel to the flame of community professional/technical conflict. The need for certainty may be a motivating factor for people of color and low-income groups to be a part of a democratic problem-solving process.

Freudenberg (1984: 446) presents a compelling argument of why community groups should be a part of scientific decision-making processes. He states that "the vast majority of groups (environmental, health, public interests, citizen action groups) interacted regularly with scientists (89 percent) and health professionals (73 percent). Scientific experts were most frequently identified by these groups as the most valuable source of information." In their consultation with professionals, these groups proved their sophisticated understanding of complex scientific issues, such as toxic site remediation and the limits of epidemiological studies, Freudenberg showed. In other instances community or nonprofessional people have shown their capability of participating constructively in research or problem-solving or planning endeavors (Brown, 1992; Brown and Tandon, 1983; Carr and Kemmis, 1983; DiPerna; 1985; Gaventa, 1991; Nitcher, 1984; Stapp and Mitchell, 1990). For example, community people in Rocky Flats, Colorado, were able to conduct health surveys which played a role in leading to a campaign against nuclear poisoning, and in Love Canal in Buffalo, New York, such surveys led to the cleanup of toxic waste sites (Gaventa, 1991). In Woburn, Massachusetts, Harvard-trained community people collected information to substantiate the hypothesis of a housewife that childhood leukemia was associated with the city's drinking water (Brown, 1992; DiPerna, 1985). In India, after lay researchers received training, they successfully collected data on health behavior important to health planners, as well as on the health concerns of the community (Nichter, 1984). In Appalachia, people were trained to collect information from county tax rolls to identify under-taxed properties of absentee landlords, which put pressure on the landlords to pay their fair share of the taxes supporting social services and fire and police protection. Stapp and Mitchell (1990) successfully trained students to measure water quality as a step in the long-term process of restoring the health of the Rouge River in the Detroit area. These are only a few examples of nonprofessional people taking charge or being intricately involved in research endeavors across the United States and the world. It by no means diminishes the importance of the role of professional researchers to acknowledge that laypeople have the resources and capability to do a lot more than many professionals admit.

To use the resources and capabilities of community people in the problem-solving process, and thus enhance their cooperation, assumptions about their lack of "smartness" need to be challenged; they must be perceived as smart, concerned, caring, serious enough about being engaged in the problem-solving process, and able to follow through on responsibilities. If these assumptions fail to change, or if citizens fail to be included in the decision-making process, then citizens groups will continue to use confrontation as a tactic or as a medium for demystifying expertise in order to transfer problems from the technical to the political arena (Nelkin, 1985). If the community is not meaningfully involved in the decision-making process, it will most likely thwart or frustrate any attempts of policymakers to implement policy decisions.

When the burden of proof is on the community to demonstrate certainty, policymakers often want to hold them to the rigors of traditional research. Yet when policymakers initiate siting and remediation decisions, they often fail to apply that same level of rigor for certainty as they do for community groups. In 1985, for example, William Ruckelshaus, having stepped down for the second time as the Administrator of the Environmental Protection Agency, and having resumed his career in the waste management industry, stated that: "We assume that we have greater knowledge than scientists actually possess and make decisions based on those assumptions" (Blumberg and Gottlieb, 1989: 104). Even when Ruckelshaus, policymakers, and scientists recognized that policy decisions are based upon incomplete data, the community of those most affected by uncertainty is seldom a part of that decision-making process. For example, as the importance of risk analysis is elevated in policymaking, the need for substantive input from concerned community groups often declines. Thus, the outcomes of risk-analysis are more likely to favor industry than community groups (Blumberg and Gottlieb, 1989). Both siting and cleanup decisions get masqueraded as decisions based upon science and political resistance often takes precedence over scientific rigor.

While the traditional notion of research tends to wed scientists to causality, and while the causality paradigm often fails to help us deal with the immediate demand of certainty and solution, we need to find ways of protecting people until certainty is known or immediate solutions are feasible; we can no longer afford the causality debate to consume and engulf us while millions of people suffer and die; we can no longer stand by in silence for profits to be made at the expense of people's health and their very lives; we can no longer stand by while our environment is poisoned and while nonhuman life is destroyed by corporate and individual greed. Traditional research prevents us from addressing pollution issues in a timely manner. The constellations of needs bequeathed by decades of environmental exploitation and racial oppression are now demanding immediate attention. The role of academics and professional organizers becomes critical in the face of uncertainty. When there is an immediate call to action by those most affected, it is necessary for us to act even though it may be professionally risky, and even if in some cases we may have to jettison the cause and effect research paradigm much more in the future than we do now.

While the production of chemicals may be useful to us in the short run, we do not always know the long-range effect or the long-term synergistic effects of these chemicals upon the environment and indeed upon our health. However, classical research paradigms are the backbone of academia, particularly with respect to satisfying the thirst of curiosity for the sake of knowing, or with respect to embarking upon scientific missions such as putting a person on the moon or exploring our solar system. Because both curiosity and mission-oriented researchers have more control over immediate factors regarding research, they can become proactive; they can, without pressures of responding to immediate demands, design research projects more in accordance with the storybook model; they can generate their own hypotheses, test them, and publish their findings with fewer immediate demands. Yet, issue-oriented researchers often have less control over external factors because of immediate demands of community. Because issue-oriented research is often born out of crisis conditions, immediate demands place researchers in a reactive rather than a proactive position (Anderson, 1985). Researchers are thus at a disadvantage because of events beyond their control. While issue-oriented research is crisis driven, curiosity and mission research are more storybook driven.

The issue of certainty regarding the extent of human risk factors involved makes it difficult to find immediate solutions in time to save lives—sometimes thousands and even millions may become ill or even die before corrective answers can be found. Because of immediate demands for certainty and solution embodied in issue-oriented research, scientists often find themselves in a position of not knowing more than those most affected. As we grow and produce more toxic and hazardous waste, and as the potenial for issue-oriented research becomes more prevalent, we must make a paradigm shift in order to view community people most affected by environmental hazards as co-partners in research and problem-solving. This practice will lead to informed decisions based upon the best information available. Issue-oriented research will continue to profoundly alter the role of professionals who expect to make significant problem-solving contributions. The conflict between professional and scientific bureaucrats does raise some interesting questions, such as: What is the role of the scientist in issue-oriented research? What is the decision-making role of the public regarding issue-oriented research? Is there a balance between the utilization of scientific knowledge where decisions are made by professionals and the utilization of the democratic process where decisions are made by the people? Although these questions are beyond the scope of this book, they need to be answered if a working relationship is to be crafted between community people and professionals.

The Political Economy of Inquiry and the Crisis of Confidence

Although the common notion is that scientific inquiry is value-free and objective, "its relation to what it 'observes' is never unmediated: that is, the economic, political, and social environment in which people 'do' science and technology intervenes between cognition and its object" (Aronowitz, 1988:16). Scientists, like everyone else, bring presuppositions, values, and emotions to observation; they seldom stand apart from the world to view it dispassionately. While scientific inquiry is never carried out in a vacuum, the pretense of ethical neutrality gives such inquiry its legitimacy; it allows knowledge to be treated as a commodity (Dickerson, 1984) to be purchased by the highest bidder. While scientists are concerned about maintaining their professional autonomy and freedom, they nonetheless succumb to social controls of powerful forces to use science in a discourse to narrate a certain political and economic reality. The requirements posed by powerful interest groups become the basis of a fundamental critique of scientific inquiry and technology; they are not neutral instruments separable from the context in which they occur.

The control over research becomes manifested by who funds what and for what purposes. Why is more research money spent on nuclear power than on solar and alternative forms of energy? Why is more research money spent on large corporate agribusiness than on improving the economic efficiency of the small family farm? Why is it that more money is spent upon designing highways than mass transit systems? Through the influence of money, powerful corporate interests determine the character of scientific inquiry more so than those without money; powerful interest groups are not only in the position to define the problem to be researched, but they are in a position to benefit directly from its results—results and break-throughs to help them gain a greater share of the market or in the accumulation of profits. If welfare mothers were given 100 million dollars to spend on university research, the political economy of inquiry would be radically different from that of government and corporate decision-makers.

Because the majority of grassroots organizations seldom have equal access to prestigious universities for their research interests, they must force temporary and sporadic changes in the political economy of inquiry by taking to the streets or to the political arena (e.g., Agent Orange, AIDS, and toxic and hazardous waste). Through protest they educate the general public to broaden the sphere of influence by attracting large numbers of people to lend emotional and political support to their issue, and thereby move the government from indifference to allocating research money for science and technology as defined by activists. These suc-cesses have required incredible amounts of resources and political pressure on decision-makers in order to make them accountable. Because it is difficult for community people to define the research agenda, and because they have to take to the streets to publicize their issues, they find themselves growing more angry and more distrustful of government and institutions of higher learning—a distrust that has grown since the 1960s. While the political economy of scientific inquiry has resulted in mounting profits, people of color and low-income groups have often lost confidence in both government and universities; they feel the political economy of inquiry is bent toward resolving profitability problems of corpora-tions—corporations that are already notorious for failing to pay their fair share of taxes or for being up to their necks in scandals. Communities often feel that institutions of higher learning could spend more time solving public health and safety problems. They have lost confidence in government and corporations because of cost overruns on government contracts that number into billions of dollars. They have lost confidence because the concentration of wealth continues to increase in this country, and because too many people are unemployed or underemployed, and because too many people go malnourished and live in deplorable conditions. They feel, correctly or not, that institutions of higher learning and government regulatory and scientific agencies have not responded to their call for toxic cleanups or research; they often feel they live in sacrifice areas for toxic and hazardous waste. Because professionals are an integral part of the political economy of inquiry, their role has been questioned both as researchers and as practitioners (Becker, 1967; Brown, 1992; Chambers, 1983; Cloward and Piven, 1975; Freidson, 1971; Funnye, 1970; Gouldner, 1968; Haug and Sussman, 1969; Mitroff, 1974; Wolf, 1970). To receive tenure, faculty tend to ask research questions that lead to tenure and not necessarily to find helpful answers for community groups living in polluted areas. A colleague of mine jokingly made this statement at a recent conference. But joking aside, the statement may have merit in that community groups in particular often feel that research done by scholars has been less than helpful. Even though this may be a misperception, people often behave as if perceptions were in fact real.

Often research findings and health care policies assign blame for sickness at the individual rather than at the institutional level.[2] Health care policies are intended to help people make the right choices in order to live healthy lives despite the fact that they may live in contaminated communities. Disseminating information for people to make informed health care choices is part of the rugged individualism that grew out of the pioneering spirit of this country. The ideology of individualism blames the victims—not the polluting institutions. If a person becomes ill, it is because they made bad choices or failed to take care of themselves. The ideology of individualism not only blames victims for their toxic-induced and -aggravated illnesses, but also keeps people from confronting institutions that may have created the condition for their illness in the first place. To require industry to cleanup its act or to practice pollution prevention strategies would cost corporations billions of dollars. Individualism is at the heart of pollution control policies.

Let me explain why. This country has a population of about 230 million people. Let us say that with pollution control technology 1 in 10,000 people a year will die or get sick because of a given toxin—about 23,000 people a year. But what is implied in this country is that there is something inherently wrong with the 23,000 individuals who became ill or died, suggesting that their deaths were their own fault, or that they were inherently too weak to survive exposure to toxins. But if the companies stopped producing toxic substances, there would most likely be a substantial reduction in morbidity and mortality rates. How does this relate to the political economy of inquiry? If most research dollars go to inquiries about pollution control, this will require industry to make few changes in production by adding pollution control technology, and thus protect their profits, even at the expense of people's health. If most research dollars, on the other hand, were allocated to pollution prevention, industry would have to spend a considerable amount of money gearing up to use nontoxic materials and technologies, thus cutting into their profits. We can expect concerted resistance to the latter alternative even if pollution prevention saves thousands of lives. In more subtle forms the political economy of inquiry becomes evident in the following analysis of two questions: "Will I get sick if this stuff is in the air?" sounds like a value-free question. On the other hand, "Should this stuff be in the air?" appears political. But the first question is as political as the second; it just hides its acquiescence to the status quo (Tesh, 1990:162-63). Those who ask questions that support individualism are often viewed as scientific researchers. While those who ask questions about institutions are often viewed as political or even extremists.

Although there will always be interest groups competing for or buying resources from universities, universities can do a better job in granting access to community groups in order to help them solve critical research questions in the surrounding community. To do this will require that universities change their reward system, such as tenure, promotion, and merit structure, to encourage faculty to become more involved in solving local community social and environmental problems. Although some research of this kind is done, it pales in relation to what is done for powerful outside interest groups. We also feel universities should do more to embrace alternative research methodologies in order to satisfy other research interests as well. There are different and valid ways of knowing that should be highly cherished within the university.

To solve environmental justice problems we need professionals to work not only across disciplines to solve environmental justice problems, but also with community groups; we need them to interact with community groups with the assumption that they are "smart" and knowledgeable about environmental hazards affecting their lives; we need them to view community groups as allies rather than adversaries in working to solve environmental problems; we need them to stake their claim to the community rather than to the whims of powerful interest groups. This will require researchers to: "(a) discard the scholar's arrogance, learn to listen to discourses conducted in different cultural syntax, and assume the humility of those who really wish to learn and discover; (b) break the asymmetry of the relations generally imposed between interviewer and interviewees in order to exploit the latter's knowledge; and (c) to incorporate people at the base as active and thinking individuals in their self-investigation" (Fals-Borda et al., 1982: 36). Although our professional training goes against the first requirement, we must nonetheless take on the challenge of finding new ways of relating to and involving laypeople in what is often life-or-death research.

Similarly more and more community groups should keep professionals honest by making them accountable. One of the best ways to hold professionals accountable is for community groups to become informed enough to challenge them on the issues; wherever possible, citizens should question professional researchers by consulting other professionals with different opinions and by consulting their own knowledge. The role of both the university and the professional is critical if we expect to provide meaningful solutions, even if it means going against well-established university and professional conventions

General Cleanup Policies:
The Issue of Certainty and the Immediacy of Solution

The debate on causality and the role of universities, professionals, and grassroots activists is an interesting one that needs to continue, but not at the expense of action against pollution or at the expense of people's health or their very lives. Grassroots activists, having lost patience with agencies for not responding to their concerns, have demanded that these agencies respond to environmental health needs. The frequent inability of scientists or policymakers to respond to high risk populations demand for certainty and immediate solutions regarding contaminated air, water, and land only adds to their frustrations and oftentimes anger. Today communities across the country are faced with an environmental crisis that stems from contaminated landfills, incinerators, and polluting industries. As crises become more numerous, we can expect community groups to use confrontation as a means of communicating their deeply felt concerns about environmental risks and exposures. We can expect them to communicate risks from a position of power. Decision makers often listen from a position of power—not from a position of weakness. Krimsky and Plough (1988: 2) put it most aptly when they state that "citizen groups, less concerned about formal theories, have become increasingly aware that getting a message across to government in disputes over health and environmental hazards is essentially a political activity." Risk communication becomes more than just a research agenda, but a political one, as people or special interest groups organize to exercise power to satisfy immediate demands. To deal with immediate environmental crises, we need effective policy guidelines. The formulation of those guidelines should grow out of participatory research, where professional/technical people work collaboratively with community activists on various projects.

Both professional and community activists should attempt to break from the confines of the traditional research paradigm of causality, the scientific backbone of certainty, even if it calls forth consternation and ridicule from the professionals' colleagues. In many cases both laypeople and professionals have good hunches about where to start the clean-up process based upon laboratory tests and chemicals known to be carcinogens. To sidestep the argument of cause and effect requires us to cleanup contaminated areas (particularly where we observe the presence of certain toxic chemicals and patterns of illnesses), until the effect becomes oblivious or nonexistent. If the effect disappears, then we know we have probably dealt with the cause, even though we may never be certain of the specific cause. If environmental justice is to prevail, public policy must be based upon prudence and the outcome of citizen participation and/or participatory research, and not necessarily upon the traditional scientific research paradigm. More and more public policy will have to be based upon judgments of what is just and fair.

But isn't that expensive? Yes, but so are the lives of those most affected. Cleaning up our cities would create jobs ranging from recycling materials and waste, which created 14,000 jobs in California alone (see Bezdek, chapter 7) to cleanup of Superfund sites. Rebuilding roads, bridges, housing stock, schools, public buildings, parks and recreational facilities, public transit systems, water supply systems, waste-water treatment, and water disposal systems are all possible and much needed. While some feel that rebuilding inner-city infrastructures will make us more competitive on the global market, others feel that it is necessary for sustainable development and the survival of our urban areas. Such jobs would be consistent with President Clinton's National Service Program in which over 150,000 students may participate, many of whom can devote time for environmental cleanup. Such jobs are consistent with the highly successful Detroit Summer Program, where, in the spirit of the students who went south to work in the civil rights movement, students are asked to come to Detroit to help cleanup and refurbish housing stock and participate in other neighborhood projects. Although this does not make for "good science" in the traditional sense, it may reduce both the number of exposures and risks, and simultaneously provide jobs. Since our communities are long overdue to be refurbished, we need to spend money to cleanup and rebuild our cities across the nation to make them more livable and nurturing. The alternative is to spend untold billions of dollars on toxic-induced and -aggravated diseases, while also losing billions of dollars on depreciated land values, housing stock, and worker absenteeism. This is an expense our country can no longer afford.

Recycling, Reduction, and Reusing (3Rs) Policies and Issues of Certainty

Despite the fact that establishing causality may be viewed as the best way to make policy decisions, many environmentalists refuse to wait until scientific certainty has been established. They have taken action by organizing and setting up successful recycling programs in cities throughout the country; they have been fairly successful in making people aware of the need to conserve energy and to reduce their wastestream. While recycling, reduction, and reusing (3Rs) policies have been relatively successful in getting people to alter their wastestream from landfilling and incinerating, this process has become part of a pollution-prevention policy—a policy that positions itself between production and final incineration and/or landfilling. It attempts to get people to curtail their wastestream by encouraging the 3Rs of products and materials. Although these strategies are popular among environmentalists, they are also becoming popular among communities of color; waste reduction may take the pressure off building new incinerators or landfills in communities of color or low-income neighborhoods. The 3Rs are driven by at least three major forces: First, between 1950 and 1975 six billion tons of hazardous waste have been deposited on or under land throughout the United States. The EPA estimates that there are about 26,000 sites where hazardous material was dumped before the passage of present laws to regulate their disposal. Each year more than 292 million tons of hazardous waste is produced in the United States, an average of 1.1 ton for each person in the country (Miller, 1988). The production of such large amounts of waste at such an alarming rate has reached epidemic proportions. Where do we dispose of it? Second, population growth and a corresponding rise in consumerism increase the average use of nonrenewable and renewable resources per person. While the average resource-use per person in affluent countries is expected to rise sharply in the coming decades, developing countries are hoping to become more affluent too. With this fast rate of growth and development, scientists are predicting worldwide shortages of resources. To stem the tide of resource consumption, recycling, reusing, and reduction seem to be a feasible strategy. And third, there is the assumption that if we pollute less by using the 3Rs, then we will do less damage to the environment and thus less to ourselves. Perhaps there will be less morbidity and mortality. In addition, post-production recycling strategies would provide a number of jobs for people and thus help an ailing economy.

Pollution Prevention Policies and Issues of Certainty
Of the two policies mentioned above, none is as effective as pollution prevention. The best way to deal with immediate demands of certainty and solution is for both professionals and community activists to emphasize the prevention of fugitive emissions that are dangerous, fat-soluble, and persistent. Barring toxic substances from the production process would provide certainty that neighborhoods would be safer. These harmful substances include many of the organochlorines, 11,000 of which are now used in the commercial sector; some of them have been banned or severely restricted, such as DDT, PCBs, chlordane, mirex, dieldrin, heptachlor, and chlorofluorocarbons (Thorton, 1991). Even if we could reduce the escape of these harmful chemicals in smokestacks by 99 to 100 percent through incineration, which is almost impossible to do economically, the continued by-production of bottom and fly ash would still present a danger to health through increased concentration of those toxic wastes. Millions of tons of ash each year would still find their way into the air or potentially leaky landfills even if we used the best available technology. Many of these landfills or ashfills may become Superfund sites for the next generation

But prevention strategies of certainty—i.e., of using nontoxic materials in the production cycle—may place communities of color and low-income groups on a collision course with professions that are wedded to risk management, risk assessment, and other pollution control strategies. Pollution control strategies, backed by the professional/technical class more so than grassroots activists, are

Table 1.1. Significant Improvements in U.S. Pollution Levels Emissions

Pollutant	Time Period	Change	Remedial Measure
Lead emissions[a]	1975–80	–95%	Removed from gasoline
DDT in body fat[b]	1970–83	–79	Agricultural use banned
PCB in body fat[b]	1970–80	–75[c]	Production banned
Mercury in lakes[b]	1970–79	–80	Replaced in chlorine production
Strontium 90 in milk[b]	1964–84	–92	Cessation of atmospheric nuclear tests
Phosphate in milk[b]	1971–81	–70	Replaced in detergent formulation

Source: Environmental Quality, 22nd Annual Report, The Council on Environmental Quality (forwarded from Commoner, 1992). This table does not include the thousands of toxic chemicals that have not been banned or removed.
[a]Measured as amount emitted per year.
[b]Measured as concentration.
[c]Changes in percentage of people with PCB body fat levels greater than 3 ppm.

limited in their corrective effects. The basic task of pollution abatement and control devices is to progressively reduce concentrations of fugitive emissions as they pass through technological systems that extract or destroy them. If systems can remove 90 percent of pollutants, then how much monetary resources would it take to make technological systems efficient enough to remove 99.9 percent of the fugitive. emissions? The limitation is that to go from 90 percent efficiency to 99.9 percent efficiency raises costs exponentially, thus cutting into profits to an extent that companies say that it is not worth the cost to go the last mile. As pollution controls are made more efficient and as their cost escalates, further environmental protection is blocked. But reduction of emissions by even 90 percent is not good enough because it fails to eliminate the bioaccumulative effects of certain pollutants that are dangerous, persistent, and fat-soluble, particularly as they move up the food chain and cause major health problems (Commoner, 1992).

Citizens groups and public opinion, more than professional/technical people, have embraced pollution prevention strategies and have demanded that DDT and PCBs be banned. Similarly, phosphate became a target of public concern over eutrophication. Due to the outcries of children organized by the Citizens Clearing-house on Hazardous Waste, McDonalds abandoned the use of polystyrene ware to package food; the widespread boycott of apples caused Uniroyal to discontinue the use of the insecticide Alar; a number of incinerators have been closed in favor of recycling centers as a result of strong local opposition; public concern about strontium 90 eventually played an important role in the passage of the Nuclear Test Ban Treaty between the United States and the former USSR (Commoner, 1992). It is interesting to note that many of the pollution prevention strategies came to the public's attention as a result of community activism rather than scientific recommendations. Emphasizing pollution prevention strategies basically eliminates the causality argument.

An emphasis on prevention, however, will require considerable economic change in this country; it will cost industries, particularly the chemical industry, billions of dollars. To recoup their monetary loses, chemical firms should be supported by federal aid to help them make the economic transition from producing and using chemicals such as the organochlorines to producing more environmentally benign chemicals. Other industries will not be hit as hard economically in making this transition, but they will also need support for an economic transition on a scale our country has never seen. And since the world is relatively free of the destructive competition between the former Soviet Union and the United States, this economic transition we have embarked upon can be seen as the peace-time conversion we so badly need to get this country on track and moving forward again. Undoubtedly, some critics will disagree with this proposal. They believe that the chemical industries, having made billions of dollars, should be left to fend for themselves. But it is unrealistic for them to do so given the order of magnitude of change we are asking them to make.

Toward Conclusive Policies and
Solutions for Environmental Justice

Thus far the discussion has been on the issue of causality and immediate demands for certainty and solutions to environmental crises. Critical to the discussion have been general cleanup strategies, the 3Rs, and pollution prevention. We now turn to a more comprehensive discussion of environmental justice. This discussion is necessary if we expect to reverse the perilous trend of environmental destruction and the disproportionate impact of environmental hazards on low-income people and people of color. This discussion is necessary, too, if we are serious about crafting new policies to ensure that environmental justice will be served. What is meant here by "environmental justice?" We define environmental justice as those institutional policies, decisions, and cultural behaviors that support sustainable development, that support living conditions in which people can have confidence that their environment is safe, nurturing, and productive, and that support communities where distributive justice prevails. Distributive justice is important because the market system gives rise to both the organization of American society and the unequal distribution of wealth and patterns of toxic exposure and disease.

Because the market system gives rise to the organization of American society and its distribution patterns, microbes and viruses may be the last agents—not the first—to examine for causality. The first place to look is at the social structure in which wealth is accumulated. If the social root of health and disease is the way society is organized, then community cleanup, pollution control, and preventive measures are only temporary stopgaps. If we want to deal effectively with health risks and exposures, we must also deal with the structural components of poverty and racism.

The current movement in minority communities is focused on environmental issues and distributive justice—justice that addresses decent and safe jobs, decent housing, decent schools, and decent and safe neighborhoods. While social and political movements have basically failed to make environmental connections, the mainstream environmental movement has failed to make social connections with oppressed groups. The environmental justice movement, however, brings together the social, economic, political, and biophysical connections in ways that are unprecedented in this country. This movement has begun to profoundly affect the way we think, behave, and govern ourselves.

To make environmental justice a reality, we need to focus on several comprehensive policies to help eradicate poverty, racism, and disease. While these policies may overlap with one another, they are listed separately to emphasize their importance. We can begin the process by launching a national health care program.

National Health Care Policy

Unless we have an effective national health care policy, we cannot achieve environmental justice. Because thousands of new chemicals enter the market each year—and eventually enter the air, water, and soil—those who already suffer disproportionately from noxious pollutants will probably suffer more and/or in greater numbers. It is shameful that 38 million Americans lack health insurance. We hypothesize that a considerable number of them live in places that make them vulnerable to disproportionate amounts of toxic waste. They may suffer in greater percentages to toxic-induced and -aggravated diseases than those living far away from polluted sites. Therefore it stands to reason that those exposed to greater numbers or higher levels of toxic or hazardous waste should have health care protection. Not providing medical treatment to those who have no insurance may, in the long run, be even more expensive than guaranteeing treatment to all. What could have been a simple and relatively inexpensive treatment at the outset could triple or quadruple in costs because of the progressive worsening of the disease. To continue without a national health care program that protects all citizens equally against want and need is not sound economic policy. Even though special interest groups will resist a single payer national health care program sponsored by the federal government, such a program is more likely to provide better protection for the majority of people in this country than any other system. To bring health care costs under control would also benefit our economy. Government or industrial policies should no longer force people of color and low-income groups to subsidize growth and development by burdening them with exorbitant medical health care costs.

A National Energy Policy

To address environmental justice we need an effective energy policy. The amount of energy we waste in this society is staggering. And as long as we are dependent upon sources of energy from other nations, we must also depend upon military might to defend international corridors for the safe transport of energy supplies. We run the risk of losing the lives of thousands of young men, with people of color experiencing a higher percentage of casualties than their white counterparts. We can prevent the likelihood of killing fields by becoming less dependent on foreign sources of energy and by conserving our own. Hayes (1976: 7) stated that "we annually consume more than twice as much fuel as we need to maintain our standard of living. We could lead lives rich, healthy, and fulfilling—with much comfort and with more employment—using less than half the energy now used." It is ironic that during the Great Depression and World War II, our country had innovative and successful conservation and recycling programs that saved money and created jobs. But following the war, we became a throwaway society—not a conserving society. We refused to heed Rachel Carson's (1960) warning, in *Silent Spring*, about the harmful effects of chemicals and Vance Packard's (1960) warning, in *The Waste Makers*, where he describes our wastefulness as a society.

Through improved energy conservation we could not only become less dependent on international energy supplies but we could create more jobs. In fact, evidence suggests that a sustainable energy economy based upon alternative sources of energy would produce more jobs than one based on nuclear power or fossils fuels (Flavin and Lenssen, 1990; Grossman and Daneker, 1977; Hayes, 1976; Jordan, 1978; Lovins, 1976). Flavin and Lenssen (1990: 41) report that a study in Alaska found that "weatherization created more jobs and personal income per dollar than any other investment, including the construction of hospitals, highways, hydroelectric projects." Weatherization alone could create a number of different jobs for workers, carpenters, sheet metal workers, and others. The solar industry will need photovoltaic engineers, solar architects, plumbers, and carpenters. Also a vast number of jobs will come from recycling, recovering, reusing, and reducing our wastestream. Although the jobs may be numerous, we need to make sure that they are safe and decent paying ones.

A National Environmental Education Policy

To eradicate environmental illiteracy, we need an effective environmental education program. Although more Americans are becoming aware of environmental problems, the majority remain environmentally illiterate. We need environmental education programs in every public school from K through 12th grade. Through our schools, churches, and programs such as Boy Scouts, Girl Scouts, and Boys Clubs, we need to provide environmental educational programs to enhance people's knowledge of their surroundings and to help them become environmentally effective citizens. To launch policies that support sustainable communities where distributive justice prevails requires an environmentally educated citizen— a citizen who understands the importance of, and connection between, our environment and our social, economic, and political institutions. An environmentally educated citizen is a prerequisite for social and environmental change. As people become more environmentally literate, they may be in better position to protect themselves against toxic chemicals and live healthier lives.

A Policy for Sovereignty for Indigenous People

Over the years, in fact ever since the inception of this country, Indigenous people have been exploited for their resources and their land. Even now the lands of indigenous people are being sought after because many reservations contain coal, oil, and uranium as well as timber and other mineral resources. In other instances, Indigenous people must struggle to maintain fishing rights guaranteed them by treaty. Today indigenous people control only a fraction of the land and resources they did at the time of first contact with Europeans. The lack of control of their land relegates them to a state of dependency, leaving them unable to solve rampant unemployment, poverty, and attendant social problems. To address environmental justice also requires us to address sovereignty issues of Indigenous people. This issue will not go away; Indigenous people have been unjustly wronged and deserve a redress of their grievances; they want control over their land in order to make decisions affecting their lives, their culture, and their natural resources. The U.S. government has signed more than 400 treaties with Indigenous people, all of which have been broken (Zinn, 1980: 515; also see Goldtooth's chapter in this book). Although the issue of sovereignty is a complex one that extends well beyond the boundaries of this book, we need to define it within its present context. What would the sovereignty of Indigenous people mean today for Indigenous people and for the U.S. government? The issue of the sovereignty of Indigenous people should be dealt with. Because many of them over the millennia have provided good stewardship of the land, we can learn from them; they can help us reconnect to the land and teach us how to have more reverence for nature.

A National Industrial Development Policy

Critical to an environmental justice policy is an effective industrial policy. We need to take a holistic problem-solving approach to environmental justice. Environmental justice has to go beyond ameliorating disproportionate environmental impacts upon people of color and low-income groups; people need decent paying jobs as well. We cannot speak of environmental justice unless we address the need for an industrial policy—an industrial policy to get America working again. To date, the United States is probably the only industrialized country in the world without such a policy. The effects have been devastating for millions of people who have lost their jobs due to plant closings and layoffs. Automotive workers in Ypsilanti, Michigan, lost out to workers in Arlington, Texas, because Arlington workers were willing to make more concessions. Powerful industries are forcing states to compete with one another by marketing anti-labor or anti-environmental packages in order to attract them. Unemployment brings with it an array of social problems such as lowered self-esteem, drug and alcohol dependency, and child abuse and family violence. Since people of color are often the "last hired and first fired," we are deeply concerned about the disproportionate number of African- and Hispanic-American workers who have joined the ranks of the unemployed, and we are deeply concerned that the General Agreement on Tariffs and Trade (GATT) and the North American Free Trade Agreement (NAFTA) may have a harmful impact upon American workers—at least in the short run. Not only does the United States need an industrial policy, the whole world does as well, particularly as the European Economic Community, Japan, and the United States continue to compete for world hegemony and economic dominance. We need policies that lay out rules of both international fairness, environmental protection, and just policies for workers.

A Housing Development Policy: The Core of an Urban Policy

Much of the urban infrastructure of roads, bridges, housing stock, schools, job centers, public buildings, parks and recreation, and public transit is eroding and underfunded. Because a viable urban infrastructure directly relates to the quality of life of inner-city residents, it is important to rebuild, revitalize, and recivilize our inner cities. Segregated urban housing patterns supported by government policies, lending patterns of private banks, and decisions of industry to move to other parts of the country or the world and leave cities with eroding tax bases all help undermine urban infrastructures. Poverty, crime, and health problems abound in the nation's decaying cities. Thousands of inner-city youngsters are hooked on drugs, babies are having babies, black homicide is the number one cause of death among young black males, and more black males on a per capita basis are incarcerated in our prisons than in South Africa's, even though South Africa has fewer constitutional freedoms. Forty-four percent of inner-city youngsters are exposed to lead poisoning from lead-based paint chips or dust, or from drinking from leaded water pipes—lead poisoning that causes irreversible mental retardation and impaired muscular control. Housing discrimination has shackled people of color to the inner cities, where they experience first hand decaying infrastructures, chronic unemployment, abject poverty, polluting industries, landfills, incinerators, an overloaded and demeaning health and welfare system, and shoddy police and fire protection. Housing development policy should include not only new, improved, or refurbished housing stock, it should also be the focal point for building the decaying infrastructure. Improving the nation's housing stock without improving its decaying infrastructure would only spell failure in the long run.

Toxic Fish Consumption Policy

People use rivers of inner cities and rivers and lakes of wilderness areas and reservations for their livelihood and recreation. Many waterways are polluted by industrial discharges; nevertheless people of color use them for subsistence fishing. Native people in particular fish both to eke out a living and for certain cultural traditions. The increasing contamination of fish has alarmed all who use these waterways, but especially people of color, because they consume a lot more fish than the average citizen. While whites often use catch-and-release methods, people of color are apt to catch and eat. Heavy reliance upon fish consumption advisories to protect consumers of fish should be viewed only as a stopgap measure until toxic fish consumption standards are tightened, our rivers and lakes cleaned up, and industry and government barred from poisoning our waterways. Fish consumption advisories also place a hardship upon people of color because fish are a main source of their protein. What is needed is a policy that is fair and just, one that will keep, improve, and maintain high standards of cleanliness for our waterways.

A Sustainable Development Policy

Environmental justice cannot exist without a sustainable development policy—one that requires business, industry, and individuals to embrace a new environmental ethic to ensure our survival here on the planet earth. Such a policy cannot depend upon the short-sighted use of nature, but such a policy must depend upon achieving a harmonious working relationship with nature. A sustainable development policy would require us to conserve energy, to produce and grow our food in safe ways, to use nontoxic materials in our production cycle, and to give up the chemical war on pests—a war that has poisoned and killed migrant farm workers, destroyed organic materials in soils, created hundreds of resistant strains of agricultural pests, and contaminated our underground water supplies. Sustainable development would require us to change from a consumer-oriented society of conspicuous consumption to one of environmental ethics. We need to work hard not only to address the issues of global warming, destruction of the ozone layer, extinction of plant and animal species, the depletion of our soils of vital nutrients, and the systematic destruction of our rainforests, but also to sustain and improve upon race and class relations. We need to bring both rampant consumerism and population growth under control because *both* of them contribute to the destruction of the biophysical environment and threaten life here on earth. We need a sustainable development policy to deal with problems of inner cities, a policy to guide policymakers and community groups interested in improving the quality of their lives.

A National Farm Development Policy

The farm crisis of the 1980s, fueled by government economic policies, uprooted thousands of people from their land. It has left once-viable rural communities destitute. As the 1990s began, it become clear that the farm crisis was taking on different dimensions as evidenced by the increased concentration of corporate economic control of the land, food production, and distribution systems. The new dimension of the farm crisis manifests itself in the concentration of power that comes from an increased reliance on biotechnology. Agribusiness has been purchasing seed companies, while agrichemical and animal health businesses have been merging, adding a distinctly new dimension of corporate control of our food production. Through genetic engineering and cloning we can produce animals and plants with uniform characteristics. It appears genetic engineering will increasingly be used to circumvent natural processes that affect land, labor, and weather. If we can cultivate orange juice from orange cells, then why bother tending to trees? New farm policies are needed to curtail the power and influence of agribusiness and to protect family farms; we need reform of land tenure laws to make it easier for people to return to the land; and we need policies to protect people and jobs. We need policies to protect migrant workers and people working in the meat-packing and other farm industries from brutal exploitation. We need policies to help revitalize rural America so that it can again be the backbone of community values.

Land Trusts Policies

Land trusts or land banks[3] are strategies to be applied in any country, developed or undeveloped, and in urban or rural areas. Land use in cities or in the countryside is determined by who controls the land. The land trust is not a new idea; it was first applied to wilderness areas over 100 years ago. By restricting land use, these trusts protect land against unwanted development. Millions of dollars have been spent by the Nature Conservancy to buy land to place in trust in order to save wilderness areas from commercial development.

Land trusts are planning tools to help control both the rate and the direction of development. By using these tools, communities can ensure that land is leased—not sold—to small business enterprises, or they can set land aside for greenbelts, urban parks, or urban gardening; or land can be leased to farmers or to citizens for private housing sites. The houses or buildings would belong to private owners—

with the stipulation that the trust has the right of first refusal and that owners would be allowed to recoup money from improvements on homes and buildings, plus a modest profit—but the land would remain in control of the trust. Thus, housing would always be affordable because the land would be freed from speculation. By curtailing speculation, we could prevent urban sprawl and all its negative effects. While eighty percent of the land would remain in private hands, the trust or bank could trade or purchase land to position itself for more control over long-term development. Land trusts are nonprofit corporations that are democratically controlled. In this case the by-laws of the trust should clearly require support of environmental justice.

Banking Policies

Depressed municipal areas should be able to create banks and use profits from investment to rebuild local infrastructures in order to provide much needed services, such as mass transportation, recycling stations, city composting programs, and city parks and recreation facilities.

While this idea may not be suited for every community, we feel it does have promise for large bankrupted urban and rural areas; city- and rural-owned banks may be viewed as temporary systems to be in operation for twenty years or so until cities and rural areas can regain enough financial resources to meet the needs of their citizens. City and rural banks could use profits from investments to retrofit local government buildings for increased energy efficiency, to build small hydroelectric dams, to cleanup rivers for subsistence fishing and other recreational activities, to invest in eco-community development corporations, and to build cogeneration facilities to increase energy efficiency. Profits could be used to purchase solar technology (such as photovoltaic cells and/or active and passive solar systems) for government buildings, to build recycling stations, to weatherize government buildings, to support business incubators as an aid to small businesses, and to improve fire and police protection. Capital to operate these banks would come from city taxes, municipal bonds, various funded government programs, and tax abatements (tax abatements to businesses would be considered as a direct investment in local businesses). To capitalize the banks for such activities, citizens could be attracted to make socially responsible investments. The banking investments would create jobs for carpenters, plumbers, electricians, and unskilled laborers. Private banks would also be encouraged to make loans to enhance environmental justice projects in local communities.

An International Development Policy

To support an international environmental justice policy requires commitment to a new vision of society. Certain toxic chemicals are banned from disposal in the

United States. Nevertheless, industry is shipping them to developing countries. In Africa, which is in dire need of foreign exchange, over fifty percent of countries have been contacted by various companies seeking hazardous waste disposal sites. It is interesting to note that while local and county officials of predominantly Third World communities in the United States have been attempting to attract hazardous waste in exchange for jobs, heads of state in Third World countries have been been attempting to attract hazardous waste in exchange for dollars. In fact, dollars earned from hazardous waste disposal exceed the GNP of most Third World countries. The question is whether government officials or heads of state should sacrifice long-term health for short-term economic gain. However, resistance is growing to the siting of hazardous waste facilities in people of color communities in the United States and in countries abroad.

Another area of grave concern is the destruction of the rainforest. We cannot continue to place a disproportionate amount of the blame on Third World countries for rainforest destruction as a tactic to force them to heed international agreements unless we in industrialized countries first establish our own effective energy conservation program. An effective energy conservation program could reduce greenhouse gases significantly. Yet we blame Third World countries for the production of such gases through burning of their rainforests to clear land for local and international interests. And, at the same time, gases derived from combustion of industrial fossil fuels in industrialized countries have been understated. The hypocrisy here is obvious: the developed world attempts to get Third World countries to surrender their sovereignty over natural resource policies by giving them in turn insignificant amounts of foreign aid, technical assistance, and debt-for-nature swaps in which debt is reduced in exchange for unspoiled land. In chapter 14, Buttel states that a substantial amount of money to alleviate poverty or for debt forgiveness might do more good for environmental protection than would biodiversity or the forest-conservation documents prepared for ratification at UNCED.

A Policy for Pollution Abatement and Control: Jobs and the Environment

When the emphasis is upon pollution prevention, what value does pollution control technology have? The emphasis on pollution abatement control should not be on the control of fugitive emissions that result from immediate production processes, but on the cleanup of pollutants already persistent in the environment. These would include slowly biodegradable pollutants such as DDT and other chemical pesticides, and nonbiodegradable pollutants such as toxic mercury, lead compounds, and some radioactive substances. Pollution abatement control can be developed to cleanup our underground water supplies, landfills, superfund sites, oil and radioactive waste in the oceans, wasteheat in bodies of water, sewage disposal sites (animal and plant waste), photochemical smog, and other hazardous waste. If, however, pollution abatement control is used to control the amount of fugitive emissions into the atmosphere, it should be viewed only as a short-term intervention for controlling toxic chemicals until nontoxic substitutes can be found.

In chapter 7, Bezdek states that:

> Since the late 1970s, protection of the environment and abatement control of pollution have grown rapidly to become a major sales-generating, profit-making, job-creating industry. Expenditures in the U.S. for PABCO and related environmental protection programs have grown (in constant 1992 dollars) from $27.7 billion per year in 1970 to $169.8 billion per year by 1992—increasing much faster than GDP over the same period.

Pollution abatement control industries will undoubtedly make a significant contribution to job creation and environmental protection. Because such technology is needed here and abroad, thousands of jobs could be created, stimulating the economy and helping to lessen our budgetary deficits. Although pollution abatement control is a growth industry that will surpass the defense budget by the year 2000, such jobs need to be decent-paying ones; we should not expect people to work for poverty wages while others live in affluence. While the policies mentioned above would mark some progress, they would still fail to achieve environmental justice. One can live in a clean and pristine environment while still being locked in poverty or being subjected to multiple forms of racism, or both. Therefore we have to go beyond saving the environment. We have to save ourselves from one another.

Regional Environmental Justice Centers

University environmental justice centers could be used to help various levels of government work out general cleanup and pollution prevention policies and strategies. University regional centers could be established to deal with problems of environmental justice. It will require the expertise of many disciplines to solve current environmental problems. It will require unequivocal support from universities, governmental funding agencies, and community groups. It will require the support of faculty and students from different professional backgrounds working in participatory research projects with local citizens. We need these justice centers not only to work on prevention and control, but also to help make the necessary peacetime economic transition. We must make the production cycle more compatible with the environment and at the same time render decent paying jobs for people who need or want them. Billions of dollars will be involved as we reshape industries to change their production patterns to be compatible with the biophysical environment. The concept of an environmental justice institute originated at the

University of Michigan must take hold in other universities. Further, we hope universities throughout the country will find creative ways to organize multiracial centers to work with affected communities.

To solve problems of toxic exposures and disease, we must also focus on the cleanup of neighborhoods, particularly since our neighborhoods need cleaning up anyway. To do otherwise will engulf us in years of debate while people continue to suffer from toxic-induced and -aggravated disease. More immediate policies need to involve community groups in the decision-making or participatory research projects related to their well-being. Such projects should be supported by the 3Rs and pollution prevention strategies, with the latter being by far the most effective. These policies or solutions, however, are only temporary. To effectively deal with issues of disease and exposures, we must change political and economic determinants; the issues of hunger, unemployment, poverty, and distributive justice will have to be dealt with. Environmental justice attempts to deal with such determinants by designing and implementing policies to focus on health care, energy, education, sovereignty for Indigenous people, industrial development, sustainable development, housing development, farm development, and international development. These policies, although not conclusive, may overlap. We cannot expect to solve the world's environmental and social problems by just dividing the world into little specialized segments for understanding and solution. We need to take a holistic approach if we expect to solve the most pressing social and environmental problems confronting us today. Both universities and professionals need to make a paradigm shift in order to view exposures and disease from a different framework. This is not to underplay the important role of traditional research; it is important, but so are people's lives.

Responding to these social and environmental problems gives us a chance for a new identity—one that is grounded in respect for nature and for one another. This new identity is not based upon war or environmental destructiveness, but upon a society where everyone is environmentally literate, where schools are exciting places to learn, where our cities are safe, livable, friendly places to be, and where diversity is celebrated; where no one is in poverty, and where everyone is protected against hunger and has a decent place to live. Our new identity comes from building new and sustainable communities where participatory research, democratic decision-making, and other ways of knowing are just as important as conventional research. Isn't this a risky thing to attempt? You bet it's risky! But life will be far riskier if we fail to create our new identity of caring, of being certain about the safety of our environment, and of hope.

In order for policy decisions to make fundamental change, we must change the role of the professional, science, and universities. Additional discussion that addresses these roles and their limitations can be found in the following three chapters. However, we must be prepared to make other structural and political changes in which scientific communities are embedded.

Notes

1. Certainty seldom exists because of too many indeterminacies in life. But surely one of many jobs of society is to encourage or promote certainty—yet it is a struggle that is never won. People want to live with a sense of certainty that they live in toxic free or safe communities. People demand certainty. The demand for certainty comes from their fear of the unknown and of the potential impact of multimedia exposure on their health.

2. A good share of the information related to the political economy of inquiry came from *Hidden Arguments*, by Sylvia Noble Tesh, a faculty member at the University of Michigan School of Public Health.

3. Land banks operate from the same principles as land trusts; however, the former are governmentally controlled.

2

Environmental Justice and the Professional

Conner Bailey, Kelly Alley, Charles E. Faupel, and Cathy Solheim

Professionals often have a trained incapacity to look beyond their areas of expertise. Engineers and scientists (including social scientists) tend to develop expertise in relatively narrow subfields within their disciplines. The process of specialization contributes to the power of the scientific enterprise and the ability of engineers to solve increasingly complex problems. Greater specialization, however, increases problems of communicating across disciplinary or even subdisciplinary lines.

Introduction

There is no doubt that risks associated with environmental hazards disproportionately affect minority populations that are least able to defend themselves due to poverty and political powerlessness (Bryant and Mohai, 1992; Bullard, 1990). Hazardous and solid waste disposal sites, as well as petrochemical and other sources of environmental pollution, typically are located in poor neighborhoods, far from the comfortable suburbs where the captains of industry live. Risks associated with these sources of pollution include the intensely personal danger of cancer or respiratory ailments from exposure to industrial pollution, as well as the psychological and social disruption caused by fear of an industrial accident or the chronic threat of pollution from a landfill or incinerator.

Conner Bailey is an associate professor of rural sociology at Auburn University. Since joining the Auburn faculty in 1985, Dr. Bailey has focused his attention on public participation in environmental decision-making. Together with Charles E. Faupel, he has been studying the social and political impact of the nation's largest hazardous waste landfill, located in Sumter County, Alabama, the population of which is seventy percent African-American.

Kelly Alley is an assistant professor of anthropology at Auburn University. Since joining the Auburn faculty in 1990, she has been involved in the study of grassroots responses to problems of solid waste landfills and other environmental controversies in Alabama.

Charles E. Faupel is an associate professor of sociology at Auburn University. Dr. Faupel has been working with a team of researchers at Auburn on a study of grassroots environmental organizations in Alabama.

Cathy Solheim is an assistant professor of family and child development at Auburn University. Recently, she has been focusing her research on how involvement in grassroots environmental organizations affects family life.

The purpose of this chapter is to discuss appropriate roles which professionals can and should play in promoting environmental justice. The term "professional" here is used broadly to encompass individuals who typically have one or more university degrees and are employed in some supervisory position that requires the regular use of their training and experience. The term professional also carries with it a strong connotation of autonomy, "the right to determine work activity on the basis of professional judgment" (Haug and Sussman, 1969: 153). However, this autonomy is limited. Most professionals are employed by bureaucratically structured organizations (i.e., regulatory agencies, corporations, universities) which shape and constrain the roles which individual professionals are able to play when addressing issues of environmental justice. It is important, therefore, that we begin our discussion by analyzing the nature of these organizations and their impact on professionals in their employ.

The Technocratic World View

Scientists and engineers perform key professional roles in environmental management. For the most part, scientists and engineers have been socialized into a technocratic world view characterized by formal rationality and confidence in their ability to solve problems. This technocratic world view has powerful institutional roots in universities, private and public research laboratories, and in such important government agencies as the National Science Foundation, the Department of Defense, the National Aeronautics and Space Administration, and the Environmental Protection Agency (EPA)—to name but a few. Corporate support is no less strong and may be the crucial element in terms of promoting the technocratic world view to the general public through advertising of wondrous new products. News media frequently act as willing promoters of the technocratic world view by seeking out expert commentary on the latest "gee-whiz" development in the world of science and technology. The public often are willing adherents to the technocratic world view, which represents the contemporary expression of "can do" social values.

Central to the promotion of the technocratic world view is the notion that experts are in the best position to make important decisions for society as a whole. This is especially true for complex issues (e.g., environmental pollution), concerning which the average lay person has limited familiarity. The problem with this view is that most technical experts are enmeshed in organizational structures that influence, and in some cases dictate, the types of solutions considered (Wolfe, 1970). The process of becoming educated is more than simply the accumulation of knowledge and skills, it is also the process of becoming socialized. Scientists and engineers have experienced these dual processes of education and socialization at universities and, subsequently, in their professional careers. For example, an engineer considering the problem of solid waste management is more likely to concentrate on improving the design of a landfill than on means of reducing the volume of waste generated in the first place. He or she may also consider it somebody else's business to be concerned about the impact of such a landfill on minority communities. The point here is not to diminish the importance of technical experts in solving environmental issues. Rather, we must realize that most experts have been effectively socialized during years of university training and occupational experience to respond in certain ways.

Professionals often have a trained incapacity to look beyond their areas of expertise. Engineers and scientists (including social scientists) tend to develop expertise in relatively narrow subfields within their disciplines. The process of specialization contributes to the power of the scientific enterprise and the ability of engineers to solve increasingly complex problems. Greater specialization, however, increases problems of communicating across disciplinary or even sub-disciplinary lines. Perhaps more importantly, specialization makes it less likely that technical experts will be equipped to consider alternative solutions to specific problems or to the larger picture within which the specific problem is but a part.

Professional myopia is an important factor explaining the persistence of environmental injustice. The siting of hazardous waste facilities presents difficult problems for risk managers, who understandably seek to minimize the number of people who could be exposed to accidents. Among the criteria used in siting such facilities is low population density (see U.S. Environmental Protection Agency, 1974). Taken alone, this criterion makes good sense as a means of minimizing public health risks. Siting a hazardous waste facility in the middle of a major city or even in a thickly settled non-metropolitan area would represent more of a risk to human health than siting the facility in an area where the population is relatively sparse. In practice, consideration of demographic characteristics has been limited to population density, a simple measure of numbers of people per square mile. The problem is that low population density correlates highly with rural poverty (Bailey and Faupel, 1992). In the South, sparsely populated rural areas typically are poor and have a high proportion of African-American residents. In the Southwest, poverty and low population density are associated with minority populations of Native Americans and Mexican-Americans. As a result, the criterion of population density has the unintended effect of targeting certain communities to act as hosts to solid and hazardous waste landfills. The effects of these policies have been well documented (Bullard, 1990; Bryant and Mohai, 1992; U.S. General Accounting Office, 1983; United Church of Christ, 1987). Three out of the four largest commercial hazardous waste landfills are located in the South (United Church of Christ, 1987), and three out of four of the largest hazardous waste landfills in the South are in minority communities (U.S. General Accounting Office, 1983). Nationwide, three out of the four largest (and six out of the nine largest) commercial hazardous waste landfills are located in minority communities (United Church of Christ, 1987). Even the EPA has belatedly recognized the disproportionate impact of environmental pollution on minority communities (U.S. Environmental Protection Agency, 1992).

Issues of environmental and public health have become contentious and thus litigious within our society. Disputes over environmental issues can be costly and time consuming for all parties involved. Regulatory agencies and industrial interests attempt to protect themselves from legal actions by basing their decisions on objective criteria and the rational logic of risk assessment. However, scientific criteria and logic often systematically ignore the disproportionate burden of environmental and human health risks imposed on minority communities. Lawyers, scientists, engineers, academicians, and other professionals can play important roles in challenging current policies and practices, but to do so they must cast aside professional blinders and critically examine the consequences of their actions.

Professional Roles in Promoting Environmental Justice

Regulatory agencies and industry interests control enormous human and financial resources. These resources are what give bureaucratically structured organizations such enormous power in our society. In contrast, citizen interests typically lack comparable organizational or financial resources. Further, and critically, citizen groups often do not have access to technically trained professionals who can hold their own against those in the employ of agencies and industries. This is especially true in the case of poor, rural communities. This is not to imply that people from these communities are ignorant or lack intelligence. To the contrary, people in these communities often possess detailed knowledge of local ecosystems and are painfully aware of threats posed by hazardous waste facilities in their midst (Bailey, Faupel, and Gundlach, 1993). What these communities lack is access to the decision-making process that is dominated by technocrats working within bureaucratic structures. To compete effectively in the policy arena, these community groups often are in need of assistance from lawyers, academicians, and other professionals.

The political nature of environmental policy underscores the need for professional involvement in the struggle for environmental justice. Access to the legal and political process in this country is unevenly distributed. Mr. Wilfred M. Greene of Wallace, Louisiana, the head of an African-American community group fighting the establishment of a large industrial facility, was quoted as saying, "We could organize and meet all we wanted, but we only really started moving things when we got expertise on our side" (quoted in Suro, 1993: 12). Such professional assistance can come from a variety of sources. For present purposes it makes sense to distinguish between two kinds of professional roles: those played by individuals who work for regulatory agencies and corporations actively involved in environmental management; and those played by other professionals.

Working within the Belly of the Beast

As noted above, regulatory agencies and major corporations bring substantial human resources to the field of environmental management. Indeed, the passage of environmental legislation since the early 1970s has led to creation of a powerful and profitable new industry that increasingly has become dominated by a handful of large firms such as Chemical Waste Management Inc. and Browning-Ferris Industries. These and other corporate actors generally take the lead role in decisions regarding siting of landfills, just as corporations in manufacturing or other industries make their own decisions about where to site their facilities. The role of professional staff within state and federal regulatory agencies is to ascertain whether or not the proposed site meets technical requirements mandated by law. In other words, regulatory agency staff generally play reactive roles to decisions made by the private sector.

This does not mean that professionals within regulatory agencies have no role to play in assisting citizen groups and supporting the cause of environmental justice. Quite to the contrary, regulatory agency staff can provide valuable assistance to citizen groups in a variety of ways that involve openness and information exchange. Citizen groups often start out starved for information on regulatory procedures, wastestreams, and health risks associated with environmental pollution. Regulatory staff have within their power the ability to facilitate or complicate the flow of information to citizen groups. The latter course is taken all too frequently. This is so, we believe, because regulatory agency staff see citizen groups as adversaries rather than allies.

This unfortunate state of affairs is built into the process of environmental management in the United States and is an outgrowth of our nation's adversarial legal system. Regulatory agencies are constantly defending themselves in court from suits brought by citizen groups and corporate interests. As a result, these agencies often adopt a defensive posture, determining not to act beyond the narrow confines of their legislative mandates. Interactions between professional staff of regulatory agencies and the general public all too often are restricted to formal public hearings that are limited in scope to discussions of the technical merits of a proposal. For example, in Alabama all published notices of public hearings held by the Alabama Department of Environmental Management (ADEM) contain the following phrase: "The ADEM is limited in the scope of its analysis to environmental impacts. Any comments relative to zoning or economic and social impacts are within the purview of local zoning and planning authorities and should be expressed to them" (Alabama Department of Environmental Management, 1993).

The result of this technically driven hearing process is that many opportunities for interaction are missed, reducing the ability of these agencies to make important information available to the general public. Further, attempts to limit discussion of the social and economic impacts of a proposed facility all but guarantee that many members of the public will come away from such a meeting convinced that the regulatory agency really cares very little about their immediate concerns.

Not even the most enlightened regulatory agency will be able to avoid conflict with some public interest, but there are ways of channeling such conflict into constructive energy. A key component of this approach is the willingness of agency staff to listen and pay attention to what the public is trying to tell them. Ideally, this attitude should be pervasive within any agency that serves the public interest. Realistically, however, a more practical approach is for environmental regulatory agencies to employ community relations coordinators who serve as two-way translators of community concerns to the agency, and of agency perspectives and technical proposals to the community (Black, 1991:9). Some states (e.g., Illinois) have professional staff who perform such ombudsman-like roles, but most do not.

An alternative role for professionals within regulatory agencies and corporations is that of "whistleblower." This role often carries with it considerable risk of harassment and threats to professional advancement. Considering the possibility of official sanctions and social ostracism within the workplace, potential whistleblowers must carefully weigh any decision to speak out publically against what they believe is wrong. An alternative approach to whistleblowing is to mount a campaign for internal reform within the agency or corporation. This approach entails its own risks to the initiative of being tagged as a malcontent who "isn't part of the program." For obvious reasons, the prevailing agency culture operates to still such voices, both through the threat of sanctions and ostracism, and through the process of socialization that influences professional attitudes (Wolfe, 1970). Despite this tendency to uphold the *status quo*, agencies and corporations are capable of transformation when confronted by organized groups able to combine effective strategies and moral persuasion (Korten and Siy, 1988). The moral issue of environmental justice and the determination to work with people rather than do things to people might prove to be the right combination for working within "the belly of the beast." The reality is that regulatory agencies and private sector corporations are key actors in environmental management, and success in making these actors more responsive and responsible can have far reaching positive consequences in the arena of environmental justice.

The Outside Consultant

Citizen organizations involved in the struggle for environmental justice face many obstacles to gaining a hearing for their concerns. Technically trained experts within regulatory agencies and private corporations often consider citizen activists to be driven by irrational fears and emotions. Technical requirements for effective opposition to proposed facility siting or permit modifications may be beyond the competence of community-based groups. Under such circumstances, the group may decide to bring in outside assistance. Such assistance can take the form of an individual consultant or a professional organizer associated with an organization within the environmental movement.

A number of groups within the environmental movement actively work with grassroots community groups in providing technical assistance and advice on strategy and organization. Notable among these organizations are Greenpeace, National Toxics Campaign, and Citizen's Clearinghouse for Hazardous Wastes (CCHW). CCHW, founded by Lois Gibbs (who organized the Love Canal Homeowner's Association), publishes a regular newsletter containing columns on legal and technical advice. In addition, CCHW publishes technical reports on such issues as incineration and corporate misconduct geared to community activist needs. All three of these groups serve to facilitate networking among community groups, a process that is further encouraged by regional and statewide environmental organizations throughout the country.

These and other national environmental organizations (e.g., the Sierra Club) can provide valuable assistance to local organizations, but there is a danger that local agendas can be overshadowed by the agenda of the national organization. Professional organizers can provide valuable assistance in organizing campaigns, devising strategies, and sharing experience gained by other groups. Outside organizers, however, need to build on local expertise and an understanding of what is important to local residents without taking charge of a campaign. The organizer's role is to build local capacity for self-sustaining action. This is not compatible with a take-charge approach by experienced outsiders. The outside organizer needs to be a facilitator, not a leader. Similarly, private consultants hired by community-based organizations need to remember that they are working for a group of citizens, and not the other way around. Lawyers, engineers, geologists, and other professionals can provide valuable assistance to community groups, but they need to do so in a manner that does not usurp community interests.

A recent example of local and outside agendas being in conflict occurred in Mississippi during the first months of 1993. A regional organization representing progressive labor, civil rights, and environmental interests was invited by a community-based group to assist in organizing a rally held in opposition to siting of two hazardous waste facilities in a predominantly African-American community. The local organization had over ten years experience in successfully fighting attempts to site hazardous waste facilities in its county. The outside organization willingly agreed to provide the local group with assistance and funding, but sought to dictate the agenda for the rally itself. The outside organization wanted to use the local forum to publicize its broader set of social and economic concerns. In the eyes of the local organization, the introduction of other issues (e.g., workers rights) would have deflected attention from its immediate struggle and would have resulted in the loss of important local support. After lengthy discussions, the regional group backed off and let the local organization set the agenda.

In this case, a strong local group was able to maintain control. In another recent case, however, a long-established community-based environmental group involved in the struggle for environmental justice collapsed in large part due to involvement of two key members in a national organization. One of these individuals became a member of the national organization's board of directors while the other was hired as a community organizer. Financial difficulties in the national organization later caused a shift in priorities and structure, resulting in the community organizer essentially being fired by the board of directors. This created friction between this individual and the friend who was on the board at that time. One result was that these two people, the heart and soul of one of the South's most visible community groups, no longer speak to each other. As a consequence, to all intents and purposes, the group no longer exists. In this case, linkage of local actors to a larger organizational agenda diminished local capacity to address issues of environmental justice.

The Academic Observer

Academic researchers involved in the issue of environmental equity are all but inevitably torn between two strong forces. On the one hand, they are trained to be objective, rational, and generally skeptical. As researchers, they depend on funding sources that may have vested interests in the outcomes of their efforts. Nonetheless, as humans they may be drawn to the moral issue of environmental justice and the emotional appeal of those who struggle for this cause. Maintaining objectivity regarding an emotional issue like environmental justice requires more than ordinary discipline and may be unrealistic.

Nonetheless, academic research that respects scientific conventions of objectivity represents a powerful tool for influencing public policy. The current debate on environmental justice has been fueled largely by the work of academicians such as Beverly Wright, Bunyan Bryant, Robert Bullard, and others who are represented in this volume. Their work has provided an important source of legitimacy to those who claim that the history of environmental policy in the United States is one of injustice. The record supporting this view is so strong and clear that the EPA finally has had to face the issue, producing a two volume report on "environmental equity" (U.S. Environmental Protection Agency, 1992).

The dissemination of scholarly research usually is limited to professionals within academia. Researchers concerned with issues of environmental justice need to make special efforts to present and distribute their findings to a wider audience, including academics from other disciplines, professionals in regulatory agencies, and the far larger public audience of citizens concerned with social and environmental justice. This does not mean academic researchers should limit the sophistication of their techniques, models, and theories. But good research dealing with issues of fundamental importance like environmental justice needs to reach a broader public of concerned citizens and policymakers. Academic researchers working with grassroots organizations need to share their insights and their data with these organizations. This can be accomplished through an "action research" approach involving community residents in research design, data acquisition, and analysis so that the community group effectively "owns" the research (Littrell, 1985). Action research promotes enhanced organizational capacity to identify and act on problems that members of a community or group perceive to be important and represents a fundamental reorientation of the research enterprise away from control by the outside professional. This approach brings with it some important difficulties for many academic researchers, who are expected to produce research for discipline-oriented journals read by their academic peers. Much if not most of this material is of little use or interest to the general public. Academics who choose these more traditional outlets for their research still can make their findings available to broader audiences, but they must make a conscious effort to do so.

Beyond research, academicians also advise government agencies. In Alabama, for example, attention to the canons of academic objectivity led to the asking of one of the present authors to serve on a legislatively established task force charged with recommending long-term environmental policies for the state in the field of solid and hazardous waste. Fellow task force members initially were surprised to see a social scientist on the panel and uncertain that someone with this background would have anything to contribute to policy. After two years of meetings they had a somewhat clearer perception of social science perspectives on environmental issues, and many recommendations on public involvement in the policy process were incorporated in the final policy recommendations. Taking the stance of an objective academician was essential for gaining access to the policy process and for introducing a new perspective on public involvement.

Similarly, our status as competent researchers focusing on issues of environmental justice created an opportunity for two of the present authors to become involved in a legal suit that may have far-reaching national implications. The state of Alabama was sued by Chemical Waste Management Inc. (CWM) over several restrictions placed on CWM's hazardous waste landfill in Sumter County. Sumter County is home to CWM's Emelle facility, the nation's largest hazardous waste landfill. The population of Sumter County is over 70% African-American, while the community of Emelle is 90% African-American (Bailey, Faupel, and Gundlach, 1993; see also Bullard, 1990). Research we conducted on this case involved a critical examination of CWM's safety claims. The case made state and national newspapers and significantly raised public awareness of hazardous waste issues in Alabama. During June 1992, the U.S. Supreme Court allowed Alabama to set a limit on the volume of wastes coming from other states.

Conclusion

Academicians concerned with environmental justice need not check their moral codes at the door of the scientific enterprise. All scientists bring to their endeavors a set of fundamental values that guide their work. The scientific approach itself is a classic example of such an ideology. Academic researchers should make no apology for being drawn to their work by concern for social and environmental justice.

Both causes and solutions to problems of environmental equity are political in nature. Low-income rural minority communities have become targets for those who generate and dispose of the nation's industrial wastes. In this political struggle, professionals can play key—but not central— roles in providing technical assistance and credibility. The heart of the movement towards environmental equity, however, must remain within the movement itself. The emotional appeal of environmental justice gives the movement enormous political potential for forcing change. In the process of assisting grassroots groups to promote progressive change, technical experts, scientists, lawyers, and other professionals can help increase the credibility of grassroots groups in the eyes of regulatory agencies. In the final analysis, however, regulatory agencies are guided by politicians and politicians can be swayed by a mobilized public. Professionals who desire to promote the cause of environmental justice need to realize that the struggle is a political one. Legal and technical debates are the forte of the professional, but are of secondary importance to strengthening the voice of affected communities.

3

Health-Based Standards:
What Role in Environmental Justice?

Rebecca A. Head

Health or toxicity data for particular chemicals can be unavailable or inadequate. Current health assessment models may also not be capable of using all the possible variables, and therefore can be unreliable in predicting and proving potential disease or injury due to environmental contamination. Risks or dangers associated with exposures to chemicals are especially problematic in communities hosting multiple facilities that may be, albeit legally, emitting various chemicals into the air, water, or soil. There, the chances are increased that residents will be exposed to many different chemicals simultaneously.

Introduction

Total cases of injury, disease, and death due to exposure to pollutants are difficult to estimate, though there are many reports that correlate the relationship between pollution and human health effects. Data from the 1980s indicate that the same pollutants that can cause damage to the ecosystem or its components (e.g., forests) can also adversely affect human health. Pollutants, such as those resulting from fossil fuel use, may result in as many as 50,000 premature deaths every year in the United States (U.S. Office of Technology Assessment, 1984). One potential consequence of repeated human exposures to pollutants can be the onset of cancer. Cancer is of major concern because one in four individuals in the U.S. will have cancer sometime in their lifetimes, and one in five will die from cancer, the second leading cause of all deaths in the United States. Estimates of 60–90% of all cancers[1] have been attributed to environmental causes. However, these studies may define

Rebecca A. Head is currently director of Washtenaw County's Department of Environment & Infrastructure Services (EIS) in Ann Arbor, Michigan. Dr. Head received her Ph.D. in toxicology in 1983 from the University of Michigan and was awarded certification by the American Board of Toxicology in 1989. She is a past chair of the American Public Health Association's Environment Section, and serves on the Michigan Air Toxics Scientific Advisory Panel and on the Michigan Emergency Response and Community-Right-to-Know Commission. She holds the position of adjunct professor in the University of Michigan School of Public Health's Environmental Health Sciences Program.

environmental exposure as any external exposure or extrinsic factor (e.g., contaminated food, water, air, soil, diet, and smoking) versus those attributed to inherent genetic or other characteristics (Starke, 1994; Nadakavukaren, 1990; U.S. Office of Technology Assessment, 1981). According to the National Institute of Occupational Safety and Health, exposures to any of about 60,000 studied chemical compounds produce toxic effects such as eye or skin irritation, immunological toxicity, reproductive problems, birth defects, neurological damage, carcinogenicity, or death (The Conservation Foundation, 1987). Standard protocols have not been developed nor are comprehensive studies required to determine the potential of every new chemical or chemical use, to elicit adverse reproductive, developmental, neurological, or immunological effects. Additionally, it can be difficult to assess the human exposure effects of chemical contamination even when only a single chemical component is detected. Often exposures to multiple chemicals occur (Starke, 1994). This compounds the complexity of establishing a cause-and-effect or causal relationship.

Toxic substances appear to be almost ubiquitous. By 1987, more than eight million chemical substances had been registered by the Chemical Abstract Service. Of these, at least 63,000 have been listed under the Toxics Substances Control Act (TSCA) as being in commercial use. Approximately 7,000 other substances in commercial use are not subject to TSCA regulation. New chemicals are introduced at a rate of about 1,500 per year.

The Conservation Foundation reports that every year the United States generates approximately 50,000 pounds of air, water, and solid wastes *per each of the estimated 240 million U.S. residents.* Manufacture and distribution of goods and services yield most of these wastes, with only three percent being produced by household activities. These figures are presumed to be underestimates, due to the method of calculating wastes based on their dry weights and because they do not include waste estimates for imported products that may then be added in some form to the wastestreams (The Conservation Foundation, 1987). In fact, industry in the United States generates more than 12 billion pounds of waste per year (Allenby and Richards, 1994).

Available emission data illustrate the potential magnitude of the pollution problem. Toxics emitted in the air pose dangers because the pollutant medium (air) is difficult to sequester, and therefore exposures are difficult to prevent. Other media (water or soil) holding contaminants pose similar challenges because reliable and available methods to measure and control exposures are difficult to assess and implement. Additionally, clear data and consensus may not exist regarding the effects that these exposures may elicit.

Many chemical substances are legally permitted for release into the air, water, or soil. For example, the federally mandated 1989 Toxic Release Inventory (TRI) showed that regulated manufacturing facilities reported the environmental release of 5.7 billion pounds of the toxic chemicals that are required to be reported (U.S. Environmental Protection Agency, 1991). The 1992 TRI Report indicates that some decrease has occurred but still shows a release of 3.182 billion pounds (U.S. Environmental Protection Agency, 1994). The TRI list includes about 300 chemicals, so it is clearly not comprehensive in its monitoring of commercial chemical substances that are emitted to air, water, or soil. Most of these emissions are planned or permitted under specific federal laws (e.g., the Clean Air Act). Others are unplanned releases. Spills and other releases of hazardous materials occur in U.S. communities almost 500 times per week, or 25,000 times per year (National Center for Small Communities, 1990: 1). Often this kind of contamination has not been discovered and categorized or, if known, the degree is not determined. This information may be available only to those experts who assess site or media contamination.

Problem Identification
Environmental racism occurs because both racism and pollution are widespread (Head and Guerrero, 1991). In the United States, people of color are not inherently more or less susceptible to toxic substances but often live in areas where potential exposures are more likely than in primarily white communities (United Church of Christ et al., 1987). Exposures can occur many times to the same chemical (multiple exposures) due to occupational circumstances in the workplace, to product use in the home, and to ambient levels or unplanned emissions in the community. Additionally, exposure to different chemicals or complex mixtures serves to complicate actual exposure assessment profiles. How can current health and environmental standards be used to protect such populations? What new approaches, criteria, and programs are necessary for protection?

This chapter discusses two perspectives. First are circumstances where scientific information is sufficient to determine a potential causal relationship that can result in injury—the causal component is due to exposures to environmental contaminants. In this situation, a relationship exists and low-income and communities of color should be able to benefit from the application of good science. Second are those existing conditions where available scientific information or protocols are not adequate or cannot be applied sufficiently—as defined by current regulatory criteria—to support the thesis that potential causal relationships do exist. This lack of officially decisive evidence can occur even with the knowledge that exposures to known or suspected toxic chemical substances may be taking place. Further examination of these issues will focus on some of the insufficiencies inherent in certain scientific data processes and how these problems may be compounded through flaws in regulatory processes.

Issues Related to Health-Based Information
There is a widely held belief that a cause-and-effect relationship must be established prior to utilizing health-based data for regulating chemicals to control

exposures. First it is important to examine the idea of causality. As described by Plutchik (1968: 144–57), the 18th century philosopher David Hume determined three conditions necessary for identifying one incident as the cause of another. These are as follows: that the events resulting in a cause-and-effect relationship are "contiguous" in some manner; that the causal incident must be a precursor of the effect incident; and that a "necessary connection" exists between the two events.

Plutchik further explains that "necessary and sufficient conditions" must occur in order to precipitate the cause-and-effect situation. It is often not possible to prove completely that the conditions surrounding the two events are those that verify, without ambiguity, cause and effect. To reach conclusions regarding causality, methods involving interpretation of the data and events must be established. Although these interpretations may be appropriate, given the current scientific models, they inject uncertainties into the process. Uncertainties add more subjectivity to the results. Issues related to scientific uncertainty are examined later in this chapter.

Several issues exist when linking the cause of exposure to a particular environmental chemical contaminant or injury, or disease, or death. The first is determining whether exposure to the chemical can damage an organism. Next, that effect has to be associated with a specific injury in humans following exposure to such a chemical. In the absence of any human data, certain animals are tested and act as physiological models for humans. Correlations are then based on a variety of factors such as existing toxicity data for similar chemicals tested in animals, or for which human exposure data are available, or any new data related to the toxicity of the chemical in question. The degree of toxicity depends on the damage or disease caused by the chemical once at the site of the effect (e.g., alcohol in the liver) and what dose or concentration causes the effect. An acute effect occurs after one exposure following a short duration. Chronic toxicity is attributed to injury occurring after repeated exposures over a long period of time. Any contaminant that can cause a toxic effect is deemed more serious if it continues to persist in the environment (as PCBs) and if it increases in concentration as it passes up the food chain (as occurs with certain pesticides or other organic compounds).

Current criteria for potential causal relationships are based on complicated assumptions and assessments of available data because, as explained, the absolute cause-and-effect relationship is often difficult to establish. Hence, scientists may seek data associations that suggest a correlation as the basis for inferring a causal relationship. It is interesting to note that this absolute relationship of causality may have been less of a factor when combating past public health epidemics than in current efforts related to investigating and responding to environmentally induced disease. In those past epidemics, unequivocal cause and effect was not necessarily determined prior to action being taken to mitigate the disease (e.g., malaria).

Once enough data are in hand to suggest a correlation between the exposure and the effect, or a potential causal relationship, limits are set for the allowable environmental concentrations. These same data sets are used to determine whether the chemical is too risky for its associated use versus the benefits gained with use. Criteria may differ for the same chemical because legislative measures set the criteria and guidelines based on the relevant law. This is particularly true of workplace or Occupational Health and Safety Agency/Act (OHSA) standards versus EPA regulations (Amdur, Doull, and Klaassen, 1991).

Scientific exploration is approached from a rather piecemeal perspective, that is, breaking the problem into minute controllable portions, often called variables. Hence, even when variables are known, they may be spread among scientific disciplines and thus require a concerted effort to piece back together again all the data needed to explain the effects in an integral manner. Recently, a multi-disciplinary group of twenty-one scientists met regarding the hormonal effects of environmental contaminants that are, primarily, synthetic chemicals and heavy metals.[2] They concluded:

> A large number of man-made chemicals released into the environment, as well as a few natural ones, have the potential to disrupt the endocrine[3] system of animals, including humans. . . . Many wildlife populations are already affected by these compounds. . . . Unless the environmental load of synthetic hormone disrupters is abated and controlled, large scale dysfunction at the population level is possible. . . . Banning the production and use of persistent chemicals has not solved the exposure problem. . . . Impacts on wildlife and laboratory animals as a result of exposure to these contaminants are of such a profound and insidious nature that a major research initiative on humans must be undertaken. The scientific and public health communities' general lack of awareness concerning the presence of hormonally active environmental chemicals. . . must be addressed. . . . The effects of endocrine disrupters on longer-lived humans may not be as easily discerned as in shorter-lived laboratory or wildlife species. Therefore early detection methods are needed to determine if human reproductive capability is declining. This is important from an individual level, as well as at the population level, because infertility is a subject of great concern and has psychological and economic impacts. (Colborn and Clement, 1992: 1–6)

These statements are consensus findings and recommendations of academic scientists, rather than those proposed by a policy-focused group or an environmental advocacy organization. This kind of comprehensive assessment is a critical first step in gaining more complete information about current and future issues of concern associated with such chemical exposures.

Besides acquiring more complete data sets, scientists must develop more sophisticated models for data assessment and effect determination. Experts who examine whether a situation or chemical actually may result in harm must subject data to interpretations, as discussed previously. In fact, scientific experts can often disagree with one another and each may present her/his findings as the appropriate conclusion. Certainly, various detailed steps and systems have been developed by experts to determine the causes of cancer, birth defects, or harm to the immunological system. Detailed protocols and experimental designs test the structure of the chemicals, the routes of exposure, and the exact interactions of chemical molecules once inside an organism. The focus is on discovery of new toxicological or biochemical information, not necessarily on prevention of adverse effects.

When systems and designs fail to consider the prevention of exposure, they also fail to address the prevention of injury or disease. If we had approached microbial contaminants, such as smallpox and cholera, in the same manner, we would still be measuring (or attempting to measure) the exact response any organism (human or other) would exhibit to a challenge from a microbial attack. The current AIDS epidemic illustrates what can happen when public policy relies too long on examination or study of a situation before federal preventive action is taken.

Perhaps the issue also lies within the scientific method that requires scientific proof of causality. The public health expert or regulator (vs. the laboratory scientist) has the added obligation to act, even with mixed or inconclusive data, in order to protect the public health. Waiting for positive causal data to emerge may mean disease, permanent injury, or even death to many persons. It is imperative that public officials focus on prevention, as that is the key to protection.

Klapp (1992) discusses the role of scientific uncertainty in public health and environmental standards setting. She examines how, when dealing with regulatory agencies, uncertainty can be used to advance alternative perspectives or to obtain opposing litigated judgments. Three cases and related challenges are highlighted: the 1977 Food and Drug Administration's (FDA) ban on saccharin; the 1984 New York City Department of Sanitation's proposal to site a municipal waste incinerator, despite concerns about dioxin emissions and the risk of cancer; and the 1976 Federal Power Commission's (also the Federal Energy Regulatory Commission's) push to develop the existing Everett, Massachusetts, terminal for the temporary storage and then shipment of liquefied natural gas despite public fears of explosion. She notes that with scientific uncertainty:

> Science becomes a resource for citizens and industrialists when they use the uncertainties in the evidence to question decisions proposed by regulatory agencies.... Citizens and industrialists attempted to use such uncertainties as resources in bargaining. (Klapp, 1992: 5)

The Use of Health-Based Information:
Are Communities of Color Protected?

What is the political context in which we apply scientific data, information, or criteria to make health-based policy decisions? As indicated, society often approaches assessment of hazards, including pollutants, from the perspective of the dangers they may pose. Douglas and Wildavsky (1982) indicate that risks[4] are inherent in our society and that these risks can be categorized on the basis of how various groups weigh different information, perceptions, and concerns. They further state that:

At the level of public policy the main dangers can be grouped into four kinds:

1. foreign affairs: the risk of foreign attack or encroachment; war; loss of influence, prestige, power;
2. crime: internal collapse; failure of law and order; violence versus white collar crime;
3. pollution: abuse of technology; fears for the environment; and
4. economic failure: loss of prosperity (Douglas and Wildavsky, 1982: 2).

Interestingly, the risks related to environmental racism draw from several of the above categories: the second category creates risks because the current legal system fails, as a result of an internal collapse of the system, to address pollution situations in an equitable manner; and the third category creates risks because of the evidence of inappropriate facility siting and operating procedures that result in contaminated air, water, or soil. The longer-term effects can yield risks, related to the fourth category because contaminated land, as with polluted Superfund sites, may jeopardize the economic stability of an area unless massive economic resources are supplied to clean up the sites.

Siting and operating criteria are based on federal, state, and local laws and regulations. Development of those siting and operating criteria is left to regulators and interested parties with access to the regulators and other decision makers. Criteria are often presented with the explanation that they are based on technological methods and available data. However, criteria selection is conducted within the realm of public policy, which is inherently political and subjective. Criteria may also be identified as necessary and important based primarily on what data are presented, to whom, and in what format. If the risk of exposure to a particular chemical of a specific concentration is deemed high, then criteria will be developed to assess and control exposures or to set the acceptable level of that chemical contaminant in the environment.

Developed criteria and the perceived situational dangers or risks are interrelated. Douglas and Wildavsky (1982) conclude that judging risk is based on perception: the collective constructs of what is acceptable. They maintain that:

Ranking dangers (which is what risk assessment[5] requires) so as to know which ones to address and in what order, demands agreement on criteria. . . . Because no one knows it all, there can be no guarantee that

the very dangers people seek to avoid are those that actually will harm
them the most. (Douglas and Wildavsky, 1982: 3)

Governmental cleanup programs often seek to deal with only the technical
issues of cleanup versus those related to exposures and health-based concerns
raised by community residents living near the contaminated sites. This occurs even
when the mission is to protect the public health, as with the federal Superfund
cleanup program. Communities of color may find that a potential causal relationship can be demonstrated but that enforcement and cleanup do not occur in the
same timeframe, or to the same protective degree, as in white communities.
According to Lavelle and Coyle (1992), cleanup of toxic Superfund sites takes
longer to occur and the level of cleanup is less rigorous in communities of color
than in white communities. Those who pollute are likely to pay significantly lower
fines if they pollute in communities of color than in white communities. Lavelle
and Coyle report that the *National Law Journal* staff after analyzing the past seven
years of U.S. environmental lawsuits and data related to all the Superfund
hazardous waste sites in the United States, found that

- Penalties under hazardous waste laws at sites having the greatest white
  population were about 500 percent higher than the penalties at sites with
  the greatest minority population, averaging $335,566 for the white areas,
  compared to $55,318 for minority areas.

- The disparity under the toxic waste law occurs by race alone, not income.
  The average penalty in areas with the lowest median incomes is $113,491,
  3 percent more than the $109,606 average penalty in areas with the
  highest median incomes.

- For all the federal environmental laws aimed at protecting citizens from
  air, water, and waste pollution, penalties in white communities were 46
  percent higher than in minority communities.

- Under the giant Superfund cleanup program, abandoned hazardous waste
  sites in minority areas take 20 percent longer to be placed on the national
  priority list than those in white areas.

- In more than half of the 10 autonomous regions that administer EPA
  programs around the country, action on cleanup at Superfund sites begins
  from 12 percent to 42 percent later at minority sites than at white sites.

- At the minority sites, the EPA chooses "containment," the capping or
  walling off of a hazardous dump site, 7 percent more frequently than the
  cleanup method preferred under the law of permanent "treatment," to
  eliminate the waste or rid it of its toxins. At white sites, the EPA orders
  treatment 22 percent more often than containment. (Lavelle and Coyle,
  1992: S1)

These reports indicate that causal data or health-based assessments are of little value if the community cannot get adequate response and action from government officials. Hence the process used to protect public health can become the goal versus actual health protection and exposure prevention (Krimsky and Plough, 1988).

Inadequate Health-Based Information: What Are the Consequences for Communities of Color and Poor Communities?

Health or toxicity data for particular chemicals can be unavailable or inadequate. Current health assessment models may also fail to be capable of using all the possible variables, and therefore can be unreliable in predicting and proving potential disease or injury due to environmental contamination. Risks or dangers associated with exposures to chemicals are especially problematic in communities hosting multiple facilities that may be, albeit legally, emitting various chemicals into the air, water, or soil. The chances are increased that residents will be exposed to many different chemicals simultaneously.

Current exposure, risk, and safety assessment models only examine and set limits for the "safe" concentration of a *single* chemical. Usually, exposure situations include the workplace or community or home, but all three or even two combinations are not considered. Certain regulatory criteria may not require all exposure assessments to the same chemical, as when an individual or a population is exposed or may be potentially exposed to the same chemical contamination in the water, air, and/or soil. Exposure to other products in the home that may also contain the chemical, or in the surrounding environment of the community, is not usually included in exposure models. Certainly, workplace exposure and home and/or community (i.e., nonworkplace) exposures are almost always viewed as separate exposures. Community residents could be exposed on the job to a particular solvent, then in the home to the same solvent as a component of a cleaning agent, and yet again to that chemical as an emission because the workplace facility releases it into the air or other media. Hence, total potential exposures to the chemical, as contained in various products, wastes, or emissions, may combine to reach a level that can pose health risks, while measurable amounts in discrete situations may never reach a level warranting regulatory concern.

Appropriate protocols do not exist in the regulatory arena to determine what the consequences may be for an individual or population exposed to more than one chemical at a time. These multiple chemicals may each be present at low levels, yet in combination may pose health risks. Thus, the potential effects (additive, potentiating, synergistic, or antagonistic) due to exposures to multiple chemicals or complex mixtures will be undetermined (Schoeny and Margosches, 1988; DeRosa and Dourson, 1988).

Other associated exposure issues depend on population or assumptions used by the various models. For example, usually the exposure and resultant "safe dose" are derived from a model that uses a healthy adult white male as the criterion. Assumptions based on exposures to sensitive populations of children, women, the elderly, the poor, those who are sick, the homeless, or others are not usually considered. To begin to rectify these omissions, scientists and policymakers are starting to propose the inclusion of sensitive populations, such as children, as necessary for public health exposure assessments and other health-based models (National Research Council, 1993; Jackson, 1992).

Communities with people of color may be especially at risk because they are more likely than those in white communities to live near hazardous waste sites or facilities that emit toxic chemicals. They also are less likely than white communities to receive timely relief from these unwanted chemical exposures because government agencies can be slow to respond.

Conclusion

Site-specific environmental pollution as a consequence of racial discrimination and its consequences in communities of color has been described in recent media and professional publications and at various professional and community-based conferences, such as the 1990 Conference on Race and the Incidence of Environmental Hazards, the 1991–1994 American Public Health Association Annual Meetings, and the October 1991 First National People of Color Environmental Summit. Preceding and following the Summit, regional networks have held conferences involving community-based groups to continue discussions and organizing around these issues (Head, 1994; Head, 1992). These issues have attained federal recognition evidenced by sponsorship of and subsequent discussions during the 1994 National Symposium on Health Research and Needs to Ensure Environmental Justice[6] and by the issuance of the executive order on environmental justice (The White House, February 11, 1994). Solutions proposed to end the injustices in environmental risk include prevention, which is often related to a community's right and power to prohibit siting of polluting facilities or to curb the facilities' health-threatening polluting activities.

Short-Term Measures

Policies must be established that will eliminate structural and systemic roadblocks to real change. Often, the final decision-making power in the siting of facilities falls outside the community. These facilities may discharge toxic chemicals into the surrounding air, water, or soil and present danger to community residents. Criteria regarding siting facilities and regulating the kinds and amounts of emissions, planned or unplanned, may be known only to those who regulate or propose such facilities. Hence, a strong argument exists that selective criteria must be set for communities of color to protect them against the public health threats known to be prevalent in these areas.

Current regulatory models must be adjusted to include relevant exposure criteria, in order to protect communities and to compensate them for increased exposures. Because the models often cannot be readjusted to incorporate all relevant variables, certain safety factors must be applied as immediate protective measures. These special safety factors should be established for those communities of color and poorer communities that experience more toxic exposures of longer duration and exposures to multiple (different) chemicals. Since situations are never exactly the same, separate safety factors must be developed for each situation. Likewise, children, women, the elderly, and other individuals require additional safety protection.

Communities must have the right to develop specific siting and operating criteria, to monitor facilities, and to review all permit, emission, and release data. The right to adjust the levels of discharges must be included with inspection and monitoring programs. Since the facilities draw resources from the communities, they must also provide funding for communities to hire their own experts and inspectors. Preventive health care, monitoring, and reactive care must be provided as necessary and needed.

Longer-Term Measures

Comprehensive reports, such as the one edited by Colborn and Clement (1992), can provide an assessment of current environmental and health effects. These should be regularly compiled by governmental health agencies. This kind of study can present a more complete picture, making available critical information on toxicity issues.

Elimination of unwanted discharges and cleanup of contaminated sites are necessary longer-term measures, but mitigation and planning programs must be initiated immediately.

Pollution prevention or toxic reduction programs are important longer-term measures for which planning can be initiated now.

Community participation and confirmation of these and other measures are essential so that "solutions" are practical and reasonable for those most affected.

Notes

1. Cancer consists of multiple diseases (at least 200) that are put into one category due to similar growth processes inherent to the diseases (Nadakavukaren, 1990; U.S. Office of Technology Assessment, 1981).

2. Examples include "pesticides and industrial chemicals such as DDT and its degradation products; DEHP [di(2-ethylhexyl)phthalate]; HCB (hexachlorobenzene); kelthane; kepone, lindane and other hexachlorocyclohexane congeners; methoxychlor; octachlorosytrene; synthetic pyrethroids; triazine herbicides; EBDC

fungicides; certain PCB congeners; 2,3,7,8-TCDD and other dioxins; 2,3,7,8-TCDF and other furans; cadmium; lead; mercury; tributyltin and other organo-tin compounds; alkyl phenols (nonbiodegradable detergents and antioxidants present in modified polystyrene and PVSs); styrene dimers and trimers; soy products; and laboratory animal and pet food products" (Colborn and Clement, 1992: 1–2).

3. The endocrine system includes glands associated with the reproductive system.

4. The use of "risk" here does not refer to the concept of risk assessment, a probabilistic model that is used as a regulatory tool by federal and state environmental agencies to predict possible cancer and, sometimes, reproductive toxicity cases after lengthy exposure to certain concentrations of harmful chemicals or energy (e.g., benzene and UV radiation, respectively). The risk assessment model, like other health assessment models, incorporates various exposure-time, dose, and other assumptions to calculate the risk or chance of getting cancer (or reproductive toxicity) from exposure to a specific chemical.

5. To state these risks is not to endorse quantifying the dangers of pollution with the tools of cancer risk assessment or to assume that risk assessment is an appropriate health-based tool to be used when studying situations involving contamination, in conjunction with environmental racism.

6. February 10–12, 1994, Crystal Gateway Marriot Hotel, Arlington, Virginia. Sponsors: National Institute for Environmental Health Sciences, National Institute of Health (NIH); NIH—Office of Minority Health Research; U.S. Environmental Protection Agency; National Institute for Occupational Safety & Health; Center for Disease Control (CDC); Agency for Toxic Disease Registry; U.S. Department of Energy; National Center for Environmental Health, CDC; Community Groups/Environmental Justice Networks.

4

Environmental Equity Justice Centers: A Response to Inequity

Beverly Wright

One could conceive of a number of center models developed to fit the geographic needs of communities. The Deep South Center for Environmental Justice, based at Xavier University in New Orleans, is one model developed specifically for the Deep South, although it is applicable to other geographical regions as well. The center is called a "Communiversity" because the model emphasizes a collaborative management or partnership between communities and universities. The partnership promotes bilateral understanding and mutual respect between community residents and academicians. In the past, collaborative problem-solving attempts that included community residents and academicians were one-sided in terms of who controlled the dynamics of the interaction between the two, who was perceived as knowledgeable, and who was benefited.

Environmental justice, equity, and racism are words that evoke different meanings and strong reactions from diverse groups. These concepts, with their differing interpretations, have brought the issue of disproportionate burden of environmental pollutants of certain segments of the population to the forefront of environmental concerns.

While recent studies provide strong evidence to support the charge that minorities and the poor suffer disproportionately from toxic exposures, this has always been the case. Minorities and the poor have always known that they suffer

---

Beverly Wright is the director of the Deep South Center for Environmental Justice. She is the recipient of the Deblois Faculty Fellow Award for Outstanding Research in the quality of life issues from the University of New Orleans. Two other particularly significant awards are the Environmental Justice Award from the Tulane University Chapter of the Black Law Students Association and the Urban League's Outstanding Achievement Award. Her areas of specialty are environmental policy, environmental equity, grassroots and people of color environmental organization, and occupational health. Dr. Wright has also served on various boards and panels. She has a Ph.D. in sociology from the University of New York at Buffalo. Dr. Wright has several publications to her credit, both as an author and a co-author.

pollution in greater amounts than their white, generally more affluent, counterparts. Neighborhoods of the poor and minorities historically have been the prime targets for most nondesirable but "necessary" by-products of an industrial society. These neighborhoods are generally seen as paths of least resistance, and thus more likely targets for polluting facilities or industries.

The evidence is quite conclusive in regard to such pollutants as lead, toxic substances in the air, and pesticides, and compelling and oftentimes controversial in other areas such as hazardous waste sitings, but in general there are large gaps in the research due to a lack of data collection by race, class, and other categories.

A review of the literature shows that for at least 40 years, American children have been poisoned by lead. However, African-American children living in central cities, the suburbs, or rural areas suffer greater rates of poisoning than their white counterparts.

Lead poisoning is also correlated with income. Among African-American families earning less than $6,000, 68 percent of the children are lead-poisoned, compared with 36 percent of white children of similar family income. In families with incomes exceeding $15,000, more than 38 percent of African-American children suffer from lead poisoning compared with 12 percent of whites. Thus, even when income is held constant, middle-class African-American children are three times more likely to be lead-poisoned than their middle-class white counterparts (see Agency for Toxic Substances and Disease Registry, 1988).

It is estimated that under the new 1991 standard (10 μ/dl), 96 percent of African-American children and 80 percent of white children of poor families who live in inner cities have unsafe amounts of lead in their blood—amounts sufficient to reduce IQ somewhat, probably harm hearing, reduce the ability to concentrate, and stunt physical growth. Even in families with annual incomes greater than $15,000, 85 percent of African-American children in cities have unsafe lead levels, compared with 47 percent of white children (Florini et al., 1990).

What Has Been the Government's Response to Such Compelling Scientific Evidence of Disproportionate Exposure?

In the spring of 1991, the Bush administration announced an ambitious program to reduce lead exposure of American children, including widespread testing of homes, certification of those who remove lead from homes, and medical treatment for affected children. Six months later, Center for Disease Control (CDC) officials announced that the administration "does not see this as a necessary federal role" to legislate or regulate the cleanup of lead poisoning or to require that homes be tested, or to require homeowners to disclose results once they are known, or to establish standards for those who test or clean up lead hazards (Hilts, 1991: 14).

It seems that the National Association of Realtors pressured President Bush to drop his lead initiatives because they feared that forcing homeowners to eliminate lead hazards would add $5,000 to $10,000 to the price of those homes, further harming a real estate market already devastated by the aftershocks of Reaganomics (Hilts, 1991: 14).

These events also stand as a warning to all of us who believe that "scientific evidence" alone is sufficient to resolve environmental health problems. These issues are complex, in that responses to scientific information are often compromised by socioeconomic and political factors. Their resolution will require organized responses that will entail the development of a mechanism to facilitate the collaboration of agencies and other stakeholders needed to find solutions that involve not only scientific but also political and economic interventions.

How Do We Reconcile This Inherent Conflict between Costs vs. Benefits and Human Health?

In the area of air pollution, studies have found that minorities and the poor are being significantly exposed to more elevated levels of air pollution than whites (see Gelobter, 1988, 1990; Wernette and Nieves, 1992).

The research reveals similar findings in the area of hazardous waste siting. Studies show race to be the most salient demographic characteristic for the siting of commercial hazardous waste facilities (United Church of Christ, 1987; U.S. General Accounting Office, 1983; Bullard, 1983; Bullard and Wright, 1985, 1986; Wernette and Nieves, 1992). The pervasiveness of this unethical if not illegal disregard for the health and welfare of certain segments of our population (i.e., minorities and the poor) was dramatically revealed by the 1984 Cerrell report. That report, commissioned by the California Waste Management Board in 1984 to advise the state on how to overcome political obstacles to siting mass-burn garbage incinerators, found low-income neighborhoods suitable or politically safe for the siting of garbage incinerators. Specifically, in one chapter of a lengthy technical series, the report concludes that "the state is less likely to meet resistance in a community of low-income, blue collar workers with a high school education or less."

According to the report, "All socioeconomic groupings tend to resent the nearby siting of major facilities, but the middle and upper socioeconomic strata possess better resources to effectuate their opposition. Middle and higher socioeconomic strata neighborhoods should not fall within the one-mile or five-mile radius of the proposed site" (Cerrell Associates Inc., 1984: 43). The report targeted particularly vulnerable sectors of the population, especially minority communities, for these sitings.

The Cerrell study has lent strong support to the contention of many researchers that minorities and the poor are singled out for disparate treatment in the siting of environmentally hazardous facilities and are disproportionately affected by pollution.

Moreover, a recent study by researchers at Yale University School of Medicine and the New York Department of Health gives greater urgency to the need for more attention to these issues. The study reviewed infants born with a birth defect who lived near inactive hazardous waste sites. The data suggest a small but statistically significant increased incidence of birth defects in babies born to mothers living near toxic sites (Geshwind et al., 1992).

In the arena of pesticides the same scenario appears. Racial minorities, especially Latinos, are more likely to be employed as migrant farmworkers and are at increased risk of exposure to dangerous pesticides. Farm work not done by farm families is done primarily by ethnic minorities. Eighty to ninety percent of the approximately two million hired farmworkers are Latino, followed by African-Americans, Caribbeans, Puerto Ricans, Filipinos, Vietnamese, Koreans, and Jamaicans (Wasserstrom and Wiles, 1985; Moses, 1989). It is estimated that as many as 313,000 farm workers experience pesticide-related illnesses each year (Wasserstrom and Wiles, 1985; Perfecto, 1990). Not surprisingly, Hispanic women generally show higher levels of pesticides in their milk than white women do.

There are also nearly four million public and subsidized housing units in the United States that are frequently treated with toxic pesticides to exterminate insects and other pests. These units house millions of people, including a disproportionately high number of people of color and those who are most vulnerable to pesticide exposure—young children and the elderly.

Exposure to lead poisoning, air pollution, pesticides, and hazardous waste sitings is of great concern to minority and poor communities. The problem, however, is greatly aggravated by differences between the opinions and interpretations of data by the groups affected by pollution and the governmental agencies that set and implement policy. Presently, it seems regulating agencies believe that they must produce "acceptable scientific evidence" to justify the allocation of funds to equity issues. Equally pervasive is the opinion the affected communities hold toward traditional scientific methods and government scientists. It is their belief that traditional science and traditional government will never be communities for environmental justice. A major discrepancy exists between community and government perceptions of what determines acceptable evidence. What can we glean from the history or other cultures to help us understand this dilemma?

In recent years policy analysts have come to recognize cross-national comparison as a technique for illuminating noteworthy or desirable elements of decision-making in certain national contexts. This approach has proved especially fruitful in studies of science-based regulation. Comparisons between countries have helped identify institutional, political, and cultural factors that condition decision-makers' use of scientific knowledge. This research has demonstrated, for example, that the analysis of evidence, especially in fields characterized by high uncertainty, can be influenced by the participation of differing classes of professionals in the

administrative process, the composition and powers of scientific advisory committees, and the legal and political processes by which regulators are held accountable
to the public. As a result, it is by no means uncommon to find decision-makers
interpreting the same scientific information in different ways in different countries
(Jasanoff, 1992).

Cultural variation appears to influence not only the way decision makers select
among competing interpretations of data, but also their methods of regulatory
analysis and their techniques for coping with scientific uncertainty (Jasanoff,
1992: 29).

When knowledge is uncertain or unambiguous, as is often the case in science
bearing on policy, facts alone are inadequate to compel a decision. Any selection
inevitably binds scientific and policy considerations, and policymakers are forced
to look beyond science to legitimate their preferred reading of the evidence. A
number of forums on equity issues have been conducted and represent a step that
can impact policy, especially in situations of scientific uncertainty. For the first
time (1) high-level professionals in the administrative process are becoming
sensitized to equity issues; (2) the composition and powers of scientific advisory
committees now include academicians, grassroots organizers, and scientists interested in equity issues; (3) the legal and political process by which regulators are
held accountable to the public is also reflecting equity concerns. This was
exemplified by the Waxman hearings on lead and the recent out-of-court settle-
ment in *Matthew V. Coye v. the State of California*. The case involved the state's
not living up to the federally mandated testing for lead of some 557,000 poor
children who received Medicare.

These are historic times and some progress has been made; however, there are
issues that need immediate attention and long-term solutions. There is great
concern for communities referred to as "hot spots." These communities are
painfully experiencing delays in the determination of "acceptable evidence"
before their problems can be remediated or redressed.

It is easy to put numbers into a statistical model to determine that a particular
risk to a certain group is statistically insignificant, but it is another thing to find case
after case, for example, of cancer in one block of a small black community along
Louisiana's "Cancer Alley," to smell the stench of Alsen, Louisiana, and listen to
the stories of death due to cancer, cases of asthma, rashes, awful smells that cause
nausea at night and insomnia, to name a few. Towns like Reiveilltown and Sunrise,
Louisiana, no longer exist because the chemical plants built up to their backyards
caused so much sickness, death, and overall human misery that the communities
were finally bought out. But industry did not escape without a lawsuit! And in the
case of Reiveilltown, vinyl chloride was found in the blood of children.

It is painful to listen to the people of Texarkana, Texas, and Columbia,
Mississippi, talk about their community buyout with polluting facilities and EPA,
or recite their unbelievable litany of health complaints.

Then there are the cases of West Dallas, Texas, East St. Louis, Illinois, and the South Side of Chicago to name a few. The communities that I have mentioned are mostly African-American. These citings are in no way meant to diminish the human sufferings of Latino, Asian-American, Indigenous-American, and poor white communities, but only to represent my personal experiences.

In California, the mostly Latino East Los Angeles and Kettleman City are overrun with companies trying to site hazardous waste incinerators in their communities. Kettleman City is a rural farmworker community of about 1,500 residents, of whom 95 percent are Latino. It already has one hazardous waste landfill.

Native American lands have also become prime candidates for waste disposal proposals. More than three dozen reservations have been suggested as sites for landfills and incinerators.

Disproportionate exposure is a serious problem for many communities and presents a serious challenge for regulating agencies, health providers, and environmental researchers. The question that must be answered is: *What has been the impact of disproportionate exposure from environmental pollutants on minority and poor communities?*

This question cannot be answered yet by the agencies whose duties are to protect the health and safety of the citizens of this country, because research data have not been collected by race and/or class. We presently find that government agencies, including EPA, may require investigation of exposure by race or class in the future. Because studies by race and class are conspicuously absent from most analyses related to environmental health exposure, scientific determination by government agencies along racial and class lines is still nearly impossible.

Many of the impacted communities are exposed to many toxic facilities. This of course means that residents are exposed to many different chemicals at one time. However, we have very little scientific knowledge on the cumulative or synergistic effects of exposure to chemicals. Enforcement regulations do not take this fact into consideration. For example it is possible for one small community to have many facilities releasing toxic chemicals on its citizens, but each individual facility may fall within the allowable federal limits for toxic releases. The important question of cumulative risk is absent from the equation. Moreover, what impact do the "safe" limits of exposure for individual facilities have on a community with multiple polluting facilities that are in close proximity to residents?

Regulatory compliance and enforcement are at the heart of many community environmental problems. How can the federal government ensure regulatory compliance by state and county governments? Has EPA evaluated the degree to which states or local governments are complying with environmental regulations? The experiences of many polluted communities suggest that this has not occurred. Methods for ensuring state and local government compliance must be developed.

These communities want and need an *action plan* from the government. The citizens who suffer from elevated levels of pollution are seldom interested in technical risk assessment probabilities or explanations of cost effectiveness, biomarkers, biological susceptibilities, etc. What they want is protection under the law by the agencies that are charged with the management and regulation of environmental health. These communities have lost faith in the government's ability to protect them from environmental harm.

Ineffective responses to environmental problems by government have resulted in serious distrust by communities of those agencies responsible for the health and safety of the public. This distrust of government regulators is based on numerous factors, the most pervasive of which is the perception that the government acts only in the interest of the polluting industry. Moreover, government agencies responsible for regulating industry are seen as inappropriately biased in favor of particular industry risk management policies or approaches. Communities believe that government staff are not competent to deal with chemical risk issues; that government officials are deficient in skills to communicate risk information and to interact with citizens; that government officials have mismanaged regulatory programs and made highly questionable regulatory decisions; that experts and officials have lied, presented half truths, or made serious errors; and that equally prominent government experts have taken diametrically opposed positions on chemical risk issues. Also, reports of various risk numbers based on quantitative analysis of risk customarily do not match the public's perceptions of risk. This disagreement between experts and others may often be due to the public's reactions to risk statistics (Slovic, 1991). This phenomenon has created serious difficulties in the ability of policymakers to manage risk in a way that is acceptable to communities in the wake of previous ineffective responses to environmental problems.

Meeting the Challenge

The government must develop a mechanism to efficiently redress community grievances. Several academicians and grassroots environmentalists have proposed the development of regional Environmental Equity Justice Centers across the nation as a means of expediting government response to community grievances and effecting change. For example, it would appear that historically black colleges and universities (HBCUs), and other minority (Hispanic, Indigenous) institutions would represent a natural link between impacted communities and government regulatory agencies. This linkage between community groups, HBCUs, other minority institutions, and the goverment has not evolved due to perceptions and some real "experiences" of unequal treatment from, and access to, government agencies. Regional Environmental Equity Justice Centers housed at institutions in close proximity to impacted communities would facilitate the connection between communities and the government agencies mandated to deliver environmentally protective services to citizens. Such centers could increase the agencies' capacity to equitably deliver services.

It is important to note that these centers must function in ways that are decidedly different from traditional organizations. Remember, the centers' scientists must develop a trusting relationship with communities that have grown weary with the bureaucracy and its nonresponsiveness and are even more disenchanted with scientific studies, researchers, and their research findings. These centers should be designed to address:

1. Regulatory compliance and enforcement problems related to disproportionately high contamination of communities of color and to the unequal protection of those communities;
2. The impact of disproportionate exposure on the health of communities of color;
3. The environmental education and training needs of disproportionately exposed communities; and
4. The economic impact of disproportionate exposure on minority and poor communities.

The Deep South Center for Environmental Justice

One could conceive of a number of center models to fit the geographic needs of communities. The Deep South Center for Environmental Justice, based at Xavier University in New Orleans, is one model developed specifically for the Deep South, although it is applicable to other geographical regions as well. The center is called a "Communiversity" because the model emphasizes a collaborative management or partnership between communities and universities. The partnership promotes bilateral understanding and mutual respect between community residents and academicians. In the past, collaborative problem-solving attempts that included community residents and academicians were one-sided in terms of who controlled the dynamics of the interaction between the two, who was perceived as knowledgeable, and who was benefited.

The model represents an innovative approach for understanding and assessing environmental issues with emphasis on specific problems that exist due to the disproportionate exposure of minorities and the poor to environmental pollutants. The approach is unique in that it fosters collaboration with, and equal partnership between, communities and universities.

The essence of this approach is an acknowledgment that for effective research and policy-making, valuable community life experiences regarding environmental insult must be integrated with the theoretical knowledge of academic educators and researchers. Either group alone is less able to accomplish the goal of achieving environmental equity, but the coming together of the two in a non-threatening forum can encourage significant strides toward solutions.

The Deep South Center for Environmental Justice is a consortium of four universities—Xavier University, Dillard University, Southern University of New Orleans, and the University of New Orleans—in collaboration with community environmental groups and other universities within the region. The Center strives to achieve three objectives: partnership between university and community, interaction between program components, and legacy. It has three activity components for reaching its objectives: (1) research / policies (2) community assistance/ education, (3) primary, secondary, and university education.

Through its various programs of research, education, and community partnership, the Deep South Center for Environmental Justice will produce (1) paradigms to address environmental injustices, (2) a curriculum that can be replicated, (3) demonstration of an integrative approach to research and policy, and (4) an effective model of a community/university partnership, all to address environmental equity in a region of the country that has disproportionately borne the burden of environmental degradation.

Recommendations

1. The government must develop a mechanism to quickly redress community grievances. Administrative policies to appropriately service "hot spots" or high-risk communities should be a top priority. The Environmental Protection Agency (EPA) should be applauded for its present effort to establish an Environmental Equity Office. But this office should be adequately funded to service the needs of special populations. The last thing that this problem needs is another disadvantaged minority office with insufficient funds to address the needs of the disadvantaged.

2. Regulations should be developed to prevent this human tragedy from recurring. Federal standards should be enacted and enforced that make it unlawful to so unmercifully burden a community with environment pollutants.

3. Synergistic effects of pollutants should be the subject of major research.

4. Regional Environmental Justice Centers should be developed around the country to investigate problems of equity and impact.

5

Environmentalists and Environmental Justice Policy

Deeohn Ferris and David Hahn-Baker

Broadening the environmental movement would signal the importance of social issues and the strength of diversity, and would allow it to draw upon different traditions, such as the animism of indigenous people and the variety of cultural perspectives and skills found in people of color communities. Broadening the movement would also increase the political power of such groups as the Hispanic Congressional Caucus and the Congressional Black Caucus, which have the best historical voting record on environmental issues in the United States Congress.

Introduction

The struggle to redress disproportionate exposure to environmental hazards in this country or globally is defined by environmental justice activists as a life-and-death struggle. The principles of the environmental justice movement include not only equal protection from environmental risks, or life and health issues, but also the right for people to live in communities that are environmentally safe, regardless of their race or income. Spearheaded by community-based grassroots activists, this movement has embarked on a campaign to develop and implement comprehensive solutions to this most critical human and environmental problem.

To remedy disproportionate pollution exposures on low-income and people of color communities, both domestically and globally, requires allocation of significant resources from public and private sectors. While the environmental community has demonstrated its ability to progressively influence public policy and

Deeohn Ferris, a 1978 graduate of Georgetown University Law Center, has spent fourteen years specializing in environmental law and environmental public policy. Her tenure includes nearly eight years with the U.S. Environmental Protection Agency, and as the director of environmental quality for the National Wildlife Federation and as the director of the Environmental Justice Project for the Lawyers' Committee for Civil Rights under Law. Presently, she is the executive director of the Washington office on Environmental Justice.

David Hahn-Baker is on the faculty of the Gradute School of Political Management at George Washington University and also has taught in the School of Natural Resources and Environment at the University of Michigan. His major focus is on the disproportionate impact of pollution on low-income and people of color communities. He has worked extensively with both national environmental and civil rights organizations.

redirect both public and private resources to environmental problem-solving, it must now use its power and influence to expand the green agenda to encompass the principles of equal environmental protection and to build sustainable communities that are both environmentally sound and just. To do this, the environmental community must join forces with grassroots activists in order to bring about meaningful and productive action that enhances the quality of life in high-risk populations.

Overall, this nation is far from achieving the goal of equal protection from pollution. To promote the equal protection or the environmental justice principle as part of a holistic green agenda is wholly compatible with the traditions of protecting wildlife and conserving habitats. Between environmentalism and environmental justice, there is at least one compatible goal: pollution prevention to protect human health and to preserve the environment. Toward that end, a partnership between mainstream environmental groups and environmental justice advocates has considerable potential for success.

In partnership with environmental justice advocates, environmentalists can build upon the resources, strategies, and tactics in order to propel the environmental movement to the forefront of this nation's agenda. With mutual interests in environmental protection, advocates can work together for changes in both government and private sectors.

To build a meaningful relationship based upon mutual goals requires expansion of the customary green definition of what constitutes an environmental issue. Because environmental justice activists target unequal control of pollution and other institutional barriers to equality, such as unfair employment, unequal access to jobs and job training, and inadequate housing and education opportunities, this struggle for environmental parity for all races is inextricably linked to an aggressive overall social justice agenda.

The Environmental Justice Movement

Born out of a struggle for social justice, the environmental justice movement visibly emerged in the late 1970s. Yet even before the '70s, people of color recognized the linkages between social justice and environmental protection issues. For example, the Rev. Martin Luther King Jr. often noted the connection (Commoner, 1987).

To highlight environmental concerns important to people of color, the federal government in 1978 produced a brochure on the disproportionate impact of pollution on people of color, entitled *Our Common Concern*, which published comments on the special importance of environmental issues to blacks from civil rights activists such as Vernon Jordan, Coretta Scott King, and Bayard Rustin (U.S. Environmental Protection Agency, 1978).

Portending future alliances, the National Urban League and the Sierra Club jointly sponsored the 1979 City Care conference in Detroit. The conference was notable for two reasons: it initiated a short-lived dialogue on a broader definition of the environment, beyond wilderness and wildlife issues; and it brought together two organizations with interests heretofore considered divergent—civil rights and the environment.

Activism continued into the early 1980s, when citizens of Warren County, North Carolina, were arrested while opposing the siting of a PCB disposal facility in the poorest, most African-American area of the state (despite the fact that the area also contained the state's shallowest water table).

During the mid-1980s, African-American children chained themselves to the axles of waste-filled dump trucks in South Chicago, Illinois. As the decade progressed, on the West Coast, a multiracial coalition organized by people of color from South Central Los Angeles blocked the placement of an incinerator in their community. Native American tribes around the country resisted being inundated with proposals to site disposal facilities on their lands.

In the 1990s, activists of color continue to campaign, march, and protest against environmental racism. As a result of the environmental justice struggle, indigenous groups have changed the complexion and content of environmental issues in this nation. Today, conventional environmental organizations face an environmental landscape that is very different from what it was twenty years ago, for local grassroots environmental organizations have increased rapidly. Several landmark events underscore the emergence of local groups as a national force. In 1983, the federal government documented disproportionate risks by correlating race as a predictor of the location of commercial hazardous waste facilities in the South (U.S. General Accounting Office, 1983). In 1987, the United Church of Christ Commission on Racial Justice authored *Toxic Wastes and Race in the United States,* a national statistical survey of the demographics of communities where hazardous waste sites and facilities are located.

The report compared the location of these facilities and revealed that "race proved to be the most significant among variables tested in association with the location of commercial hazardous waste facilities." Race was an even better predictor of location than income (United Church of Christ, 1987).

In 1988, the Southern Environmental Assembly convened a conference of nearly 1,000 activists from across the South to Atlanta for a presidential forum on the environment in conjunction with the Super Tuesday primaries. The event began as an effort by conventional environmentalists to command the attention of the presidential candidates.

Although most candidates ignored the event, the conference was ignited by the presence and leadership of civil rights activists who addressed environmental justice issues. Rep. John Lewis of Georgia opened the conference with the declaration that "working for clean air, clean water, and a clean planet is just as important, if not more important, than anything I have ever worked on, including civil rights" (*Atlanta Journal,* 1988: 1E).

Rev. Benjamin Chavis, then executive director of the United Church of Christ Commission for Racial Justice, electrified the crowd with a keynote address on the *Toxic Wastes and Race* report. Rev. Joseph Lowery of the Southern Christian Leadership Conference gave the closing address and led a multiracial group of local activists and environmentalists on a march to the site of the GOP presidential debate hosted by the *Atlanta Journal Constitution*, to protest the lack of attention to environmental justice issues.

In 1989, Gulf Coast Tenants Organization, directed by Pat Bryant, organized a nationally publicized event, the Great Louisiana Toxics March through Cancer Alley, from Baton Rouge to New Orleans. Community-based organizations were maturing into networks, sharing information, developing common strategies, and taking joint actions against industrial pollution and the inaction of state and federal agencies.

In 1990, the University of Michigan School of Natural Resources sponsored a ground-breaking conference featuring leading researchers and scholars in the environmental justice field, activist leaders, and EPA officials. The meeting resulted in an EPA working group on environmental justice issues (Bryant and Mohai, 1990).

Another watershed event occurred in 1991, the First National People of Color Environmental Leadership Summit convened in the nation's capital. The event featured nearly 1,000 environmental justice activists from across the country, Africa, and South America, who met to develop a statement of principles and a call for national and worldwide action.

Building on the growing momentum following the Summit, two groups formed: the Indigenous Environmental Network to promote the interests of grassroots Native American activists; and the Southern Organizing Committee, which organized the Southern Community Labor Conference for Environmental Justice in New Orleans in 1992, a gathering of nearly 2,000 activists from fourteen states. During that same year, the Southwest Network for Environmental and Economic Justice convened its third regional conference representing ten states at The Annual Gathering, in Albuquerque. Community-based groups in the Midwest and Northeast also began the process of aggregating into regional networks.

While the list is not exhaustive, these events establish that local and regional environmental justice organizations have successfully organized to push environmental justice to the forefront of the nation's environmental agenda.

Expanding the Green Agenda

Since its birth almost 25 years ago on Earth Day in 1970, the environmental movement has expanded tremendously. Its evolution has been accompanied by massive growth spurts, centralization into large and financially secure national organizations, and a shift in philosophy from more radical protest and activism to acceptance as a mainstream public-interest group.

Even leading environmentalists note the shift and lament the loss in the community's ability to articulate a clear environmental vision (McClosky, 1991). Other environmentalists lament the lack of cultural diversity in a movement which has an explicit commitment to preserving biological diversity, thus pointing out the negative effect of monoculturalism upon the movement (Dowie, 1992).

These concerns are sharply focused when discussions turn to whether there is a role for environmentalists in the environmental justice movement. For the future, the environmental justice movement presents to environmentalists the reality of a broader vision and a redefined mission encompassing greater diversity for the environmental community in terms of both issues and organizational structure.

Historically, the conventional environmental movement has exhibited a commitment to biological diversity. Demonstrating this commitment by launching campaigns dedicated to preserving habitat for wildlife, environmentalists have waged precedent-setting battles for the preservation of small populations of individual species, and at times opposed billions of dollars worth of human enterprise and development.

This commitment to biological diversity is based on concepts of strength through preservation of genetic diversity and on the belief that each part of any ecosystem is a fundamental part of the health and functioning of the global ecosystem. This mandate to preserve diversity affirms that mixing and sharing in the genetic pool is crucial to the growth and improvement of both individuals within the system and to survival of the system as a whole.

Furthermore, inherent in the environmental movement's commitment to diversity is an overarching sense of fairness—a belief that all forms of life are interdependent and that all species have an inherent right to survive and prosper in the natural order. In keeping with this sense of equality between humans and wildlife, environmentalists have assumed the role of champion, protecting species that cannot defend themselves from the often deadly intrusions of human society.

Despite this fundamental commitment to biological diversity, there is very little racial or cultural diversity either in the employment spectrum of environmental groups or in their political or educational activities. Mainstream environmental activists should no longer ignore the protection of ecosystems inhabited by people of color who are disproportionately exposed to environmental hazards. Ignoring the detestable environmental conditions in communities of color leads also to ignoring the resources that people of color can contribute to the defense of the environment. In terms of both issues and the workforce, environmentalists must capitalize on the different perspectives, skills, and traditions that greater diversity would bring to their movement.

Typically, national environmental groups center on national legislation, a tactic that does not always benefit communities experiencing disproportionate exposure to toxic hazards. According to experts, any benefits to such communities are usually unintentional. To the extent that this issue has undergone any scrutiny, it is asserted that people of color receive fewer benefits from environmentalists' efforts to protect the environment than any other segment of the population (Gelobter, 1990).

Too often, people of color are disproportionately polluted, whether by toxics emitted from burned stacks, or by toxics discharged from pipes, or by toxics leaked from landfills. Far more often than other segments of society, communities of color are affected by manufacturing facilities, sewage treatment plants, incinerators, landfills, and subsistence consumption of contaminated fish and wildlife. To protect communities of color requires not only the application of the law, but a holistic worldview steeped in an environmental and social justice ethic. True environmentalists cannot fail to see the connection.

The question of how to define environmental issues is another key concern. The provision of bottled water to replace a contaminated aquifer is easily defined by most environmentalists as a concern within their realm; however, to define the development of a supermarket in the inner city in order to provide, produce, and to replace contaminated home gardens would be a stretch for many in the mainstream environmental community. Similarly, preservation of a wetland as a habitat for environmentally stressed wildlife easily meets the conventional test, while development of low-income housing to provide habitat for environmentally stressed people would not fall within the typical environmental agenda.

Combining these concerns within a broader environmental agenda would be one of the most positive outcomes of partnership between the movements. Broadening the environmental movement would signal the importance of social issues and the strength of diversity, and would allow it to draw upon different traditions, such as the animism of indigenous people and the variety of cultural perspectives and skills found in people of color communities. Broadening the movement would also increase the political power of such groups as the Hispanic Congressional Caucus and the Congressional Black Caucus, which have the best historical voting record on environmental issues in the United States Congress.

Development and implementation of inclusive environmental policies are critical to achieving the basic goals of the environmental community: preservation of planet earth's ecosystems and the natural order. These goals are compatible with the principle of equal protection for all people from environmental hazards.

Environmental justice activists are on the front line of struggles in the United States to battle pollution, waste, and environmental degradation of human health. As long as there is a place to dump or emit toxic substances, these substances will be produced. Communities of color are the first and hardest hit by this contamination, and the battle to preserve the environment will be won or lost in these neighborhoods. To paraphrase the Rev. Martin Luther King Jr., preventing pollution that harms one will ultimately protect everyone.

Clearly, fundamental changes must occur in society's attitudes, operations, and institutions. Environmentalists can be effective partners in communicating this message to the public and private sectors. But the environmental movement cannot become a genuine, credible catalyst for change until the environmental and health concerns of people of color are firmly interwoven into the green agenda.

The Future: Establishing Partnerships between the Movements

Decisions to incorporate an environmental justice agenda naturally evolve from the realization that a partnership between the movements has considerable advantages. Environmentalists and advocacy institutions that seek linkages with the environmental justice movement must first examine their internal framework and eliminate barriers to the establishment of more inclusive organizational staff and memberships. Strategic planning is essential to development of an effective environmental policy that incorporates the principles espoused by environmental justice advocates.

The tenets of equal protection from pollution impel radical rethinking by organizations accustomed to arguing in favor of solutions that shift pollution burdens to communities of color already struggling with disproportionate hazards. Pollution prevention, the watchword of environmental justice advocates, assumes new force and meaning when articulated as a strategy to ensure that *all* people are protected from environmental contamination.

In general, the strategy that environmental groups could pursue has five parts. They are:

(A) Creating programs that facilitate community defense

(B) Initiating educational efforts to assist communities of color

(C) Increasing interaction with people of color organizations and community-based groups

(D) Promoting public policy advocacy

(E) Diversifying boards, staff, and membership

(A) Create Programs That Facilitate Community Defense

A key to broadening the environmental justice agenda is recognizing both the long- and short-term demands of communities of color. In the short term, for most community activists, environmental degradation is a life and death situation. From anacephalic babies in Matamoras, Texas, to the two-thirds of the children in Buffalo, New York, who exceed the threshold for lead poisoning, to the children in the Cancer Cluster of MacFarland, California, people of color are fighting for immediate relief from widespread environmental health threats.

Environmental groups could focus their extensive technical and scientific resources on helping communities to develop solutions to immediate pollution threats identified by them. In addition, they could design initiatives to build the capacity of these communities to collect and use data and information to defend themselves.

In the long term, society must end actions that treat communities of color as if they are expendable. Both policies and programs must be developed that truly meet the needs of people victimized by overexposure to contamination, and policies and programs must be developed that facilitate the ability of these communities to control and make informed environmental decisions.

Environmental groups seeking to expand the green agenda by developing programs should incorporate three essential criteria. Programs must:

- Provide tangible and measurable benefits to specific communities of color
- Involve significant interaction with and be guided by people of color, preferably those in the affected communities
- Strengthen the ability of communities of color to defend themselves

(B) Initiate Educational Efforts to Assist Communities of Color

Environmental groups can invest in the future of this nation by expanding educational programs to increase public awareness about the effects of disproportionate exposure to pollution and the causes and effects of environmental hazards. Educational programs can facilitate grassroots advocacy and action to eliminate pollution in order to help restore the vital connection between all people and planet earth.

(C) Increase Interaction with People of Color Organizations and Community-Based Groups

One of the principal challenges to successfully addressing environmental justice concerns is limited interaction between environmentalists and people of color communities. Environmentalists must focus attention on dialogue, information exchange, and developing relationships that foster joint projects and ventures. Communication, mutual respect, and equality are key to developing these relationships.

Above all, environmentalists and environmental justice activists must observe a protocol of trust—trust must exist to develop fruitful working relationships. To develop trust requires a consistent track record. Differences in perspective and background can be bridged once trust has formed the basis for closer working relationships.

(D) Public Policy Advocacy

Public policy advocacy on the national, state, and local levels is essential to protecting those hit first and hardest by environmental contamination. Recent studies indicate that not only is government failing to fulfill its duty to provide equal protection to all citizens from environmental hazards, but that environmental inequities may be worsening.

In 1987, when the United Church of Christ Commission on Racial Justice compared demographic distribution of illegal dumpsites and federally permitted sites, it found that both were more likely to be located in communities of color. Furthermore, the study found that federally permitted facilities were even *more* likely to be sited in a racially biased manner than illegal sites. The Commission empirically established that when government made a decision, the bias was even greater than when private institutions chose the dumpsites.

In 1992, *The National Law Journal* compared a number of enforcement actions filed by the U.S. Environmental Protection Agency (EPA) in white communities and communities of color (Lavelle and Coyle, 1992: S1). Underscoring the results of the United Church of Christ study, the report found that the government responded to white communities faster, with better results, and with stiffer penalties than it did when the communities were black, Hispanic, or "other."

In response to these findings and other data gathered since the early 1970s, environmental groups must ask to what extent they influence government action on environmental issues, and to what extent government actions promote racial bias, and what role will the environmental community assume in eradicating that bias.

If the environmental community is true to its mission of protecting the environment, it will work with the environmental justice movement to ensure that government at all levels fulfills the duty to protect the environment, including equally protecting everyone's environment.

(E) Diversify Boards, Staff, and Membership

It is inconsistent for organizations whose existence is based upon a fundamental commitment to the value of diversity in the earth's ecosystems to lack diversity in their structures. Also, it is illegitimate for essentially monocultural groups to claim to represent the interests of the public, which in this country is increasingly multicultural. To survive in a multicultural society, environmentalists must openly and visibly recognize the value of cultural and racial diversity.

If environmental groups seek to meet the needs of the broader society, their boards of directors, leadership, and staff must represent that multicultural society. These changes must occur if these groups are to interact with people of color and build relationships with them to work on the issues. Diversification in environmental organizations will occur *only* where there is commitment and direction from the uppermost levels of management.

People of color must assume decision-making roles throughout these organizations, and those who are hired must be promoted to leadership positions. As witnessed during the 1991 First People of Color Environmental Leadership Summit and in various regional environmental justice conferences throughout this country before and since, the pool of talented and dedicated people of color knowledgeable about environmental issues has increased. Immediate progress can occur by hiring people of color into responsible positions.

Membership diversity is also a pivotal area of focus if the environmental agenda is meant to become inclusive. However, caution should be exercised to prevent putting the proverbial cart before the horse. Efforts to diversify membership could be deemed exploitive unless accompanied by a vigorous campaign to implement an inclusive environmental agenda, along with recruiting, hiring, and promoting people of color.

Conclusion

Linkages between environmental justice activists and environmentalists can capitalize on the vitality and morality of the social justice agenda, and on the resources, strategies, and tactics that, since the first Earth Day in 1970, have propelled environmental issues to the forefront of this nation's priorities. Partnerships between environmentalists and environmental justice activists have the potential to accelerate shifts in the public policymaking process toward incorporation of the principle of equal protection from pollution.

Advocating equal environmental protection as part of a holistic green agenda is in keeping with, and builds upon, such traditions of environmentalists as protecting wildlife and preserving the ecosystem. Expansion of the green agenda to protect human health and the environment could expedite redirection of public and private sector resources to eliminate disproportionate exposure to pollution risks, and result in implementation of government policy that effectively proscribes environmental degradation and the associated deleterious effects on human health.

6

Residential Segregation and Urban Quality of Life

Robert Bullard

Urban quality is also affected by environmental racism. Environmental racism is defined as practices or policies that disparately impact (whether intended or unintended) people of color and exclude people of color from decision-making boards and commissions. White communities benefit from environmental racism; people of color bear most of the costs. Historically, racism has been a "conspicuous part of the American sociopolitical system, and as a result, black people in particular, and ethnic and racial minority groups of color, find themselves at a disadvantage in contemporary society."

Introduction

The nation's urban areas have become forgotten places. They seem to get attention only after conditions reach crisis status or when human frustration spills into a major uprising. Nowhere is this more apparent than in America's large urban centers, where the majority of people of color are concentrated. Much of the nation's infrastructure is crumbling at the seams. The physical infrastructure includes such things as roads and bridges, housing stock, schools, job centers, public buildings, parks and recreational facilities, public transit, water supply, wastewater treatment, and waste disposal systems. Taken as a whole, this infrastructure decline has a negative effect on the well-being and quality of urban life. At present, too many of our cities and their inhabitants are at risk from infrastructure decay, environmental degradation, health threats, and economic impoverishment (Murray, 1992; Bullard, 1992).

This chapter examines the pattern of residential housing and its relationship to the nation's decaying urban infrastructure; it also examines the accompanying social, environmental, and health risks to African-Americans.

Robert Bullard is a professor of sociology at the University of California, Los Angeles. He was on the advisory committee for the First National People of Color Environmental Leadership Summit and the Clinton transition team. He was on the protocol committee for the Symposium on Health Research Needs to ensure environmental justice. Presently, he is the director of the Environmental Justice Resource Center at Clark-Atlanta University. For more than a decade, Professor Bullard has focused his research on the politics of pollution and how blacks and lower-income groups have been disproportionately impacted by environmental stressors. He is the author of Confronting Environmental Racism *and* Dumping in Dixie.

Impact of Institutional Racism

The United States continues to be segregated along racial lines. Racism and residential segregation are facts of life in urban America (Kushner, 1980; Feagin and Feagin, 1986; Bullard and Feagin, 1991). Institutionalized racism is part of the national heritage. It is defined as "those laws, customs, and practices which systematically reflect and produce inequalities in American society... whether or not the individuals maintaining those practices have racist intentions" (Jones, 1972: 131). The 1967 National Advisory Commission on Civil Disorders implicated white racism in the creation and maintenance of the black ghetto and the drift toward two "separate and unequal societies" (Kerner Commission, 1967). These conditions exist today (Hacker, 1992; Massey and Denton, 1993; Bullard, Grigsby, and Lee, forthcoming).

The legacy of institutional racism lowers the nation's gross national product by almost two percent a year, or roughly $104 billion in 1989 (Updegrade, 1989). A large share of this loss is a result of housing discrimination. The roots of discrimination are deep and have been difficult to eliminate (James, McCummings, and Tynan, 1984: 138). Housing discrimination contributes to the physical decay of inner-city neighborhoods and denies a substantial segment of the African-American community a basic source of wealth and investment through home ownership (Foust, 1987; Feldman, 1989; Glastris and Minerbrook, 1989). The number of African-American homeowners would probably be higher in the absence of discrimination by lending institutions (Darden, 1989). Only about 59 percent of the nation's middle-class African-Americans own their homes, compared with 74 percent of whites.

Urban quality is also affected by environmental racism. Environmental racism is defined as practices or policies that disparately impact (whether intended or unintended) people of color and exclude people of color from decision-making boards and commissions. White communities benefit from environmental racism; people of color bear most of the costs. Historically, racism has been a "conspicuous part of the American sociopolitical system, and as a result, black people in particular, and ethnic and racial minority groups of color, find themselves at a disadvantage in contemporary society" (Jones, 1981: 47).

The most polluted urban communities are often communities with crumbling infrastructure, deteriorating housing, inadequate public transportation, chronic unemployment, high poverty, and an overloaded health care system. The riot-torn South Central Los Angeles neighborhood typifies the results of urban neglect. It is not surprising that the "dirtiest" zip code in California, using federal EPA toxic release inventory (TRI) data, is in the mostly African-American South Central and Latino East Los Angeles neighborhoods (Kay, 1991). The "dirtiest" zip codes in California's other major cities include the mostly African-American Hunter's Point neighborhood in San Francisco and the mostly Latino neighborhoods of Barrio Logan in San Diego and Casa Blanca in Riverside.

In the heavily populated Los Angeles air basin, over 71 percent of African-Americans and 50 percent of Latinos live in areas with the most polluted air, while 34 percent of whites live in highly polluted areas (Mann, 1991). National Argonne Laboratory researchers found that African-Americans and Latino Americans are more likely than whites to live in areas with reduced air quality. In 1990, for example, 57 percent of whites, 65 percent of African-Americans, and 80 percent of Latinos lived in counties that failed to meet at least one of the EPA ambient air quality standards (Wernette and Nieves, 1992).

Not only are people of color exposed to dirtier air, they are more likely than their white counterparts to live near locally unwanted land uses, or LULUs. Communities of color are often targeted for treatment facilities, landfills, and incinerators by government and private industry. Cerrell Associates Inc. (1984) provided the California Waste Management Board with a "profile" of neighborhoods mostly likely to organize effective resistance to incinerators. The report states:

> All socioeconomic groupings tend to resent the nearby siting of major facilities, but middle and upper socioeconomic strata possess better resources to effectuate their opposition. Middle and higher socioeconomic strata neighborhoods should not fall within the one-mile and five-mile radius of the proposed site. (Cerrell Associates Inc., 1984: 43)

It is clear that low-income communities of color would best fit this profile. Historically, these same communities are vulnerable to freeway construction, industrial encroachment, and other nonresidential land uses that many people consider to be intrusive and undesirable.

Redlining and Urban Disinvestment

Studies over the past twenty-five years have clearly documented the relationship between redlining and disinvestment decisions, and neighborhood decline (Feagin, 1990a, 1990b; Jaynes and Williams, 1989). From Boston to San Diego, African-Americans still do not have the access to lending by banks and saving institutions that their white counterparts enjoy. A 1991 report by the Federal Reserve Board found that African-Americans were rejected for home loans more than twice as often as Anglos (Rosenblatt and Bates, 1991). After studying lending practices at 9,300 U.S. financial institutions and more than 6.4 million loan applications, the federal study uncovered the rejection rates for conventional home mortgages were 33.9 percent for African-Americans, 21.4 percent of Latinos, 22.4 percent for American Indians, 14.4 percent for Anglos, and 12.9 percent for Asians.

Loan denial rates for African-Americans varied widely among large urban centers (see Table 6.1). For example, a third of African-American loan applicants

Table 6.1. Mortgage Rejection Rates in 19 Large Metropolitan Areas

Metro Area	Asian	Black	Latino	Anglo
Atlanta	11.1	26.5	13.6	10.5
Baltimore	7.3	15.6	10.1	7.5
Boston	15.4	34.9	21.1	11.0
Chicago	10.4	23.6	12.1	7.3
Dallas	9.3	25.6	19.8	10.7
Detroit	9.1	23.7	14.2	9.7
Houston	13.3	33.0	25.7	12.6
Los Angeles	13.2	19.8	16.3	12.8
Miami	16.9	22.9	17.8	16.0
Minneapolis	6.4	19.9	8.0	6.1
New York	17.3	29.4	25.3	15.0
Oakland	11.6	16.5	13.3	9.6
Philadelphia	12.1	25.0	21.0	8.3
Phoenix	12.8	30.0	25.2	14.4
Pittsburgh	12.2	31.0	13.9	12.0
St. Louis	9.0	31.8	13.5	21.1
San Diego	11.2	17.8	15.1	9.8
Seattle	11.6	18.3	16.8	10.7
Washington, DC	8.7	14.4	8.9	6.3

Source: Federal Reserve Bank Board (1991).

were rejected in the Boston, Houston, St. Louis, Pittsburgh, and Phoenix metropolitan areas. The lowest loan rejection rate for African-Americans occurred in the Washington, D.C., Baltimore, Oakland, and San Diego metropolitan areas. Federal regulators continue to ignore discrimination in lending. These alarming loan rejection statistics still leave some government and industry officials in doubt as to whether the culprit is a function of discrimination. Discriminatory lending practices subsidize the physical destruction of African-American communities. These same communities must now share in paying the hundreds of billions of dollars to bail out the failed savings and loan institutions, many of which engaged in redlining African-American communities (Bullard and Feagin, 1991).

Eight out of every ten African-Americans live in neighborhoods where they are in the majority. Residential segregation decreases for most racial and ethnic groups with additional education, income, and occupational status (Denton and Massey, 1988). However, this pattern does not hold true for African-Americans. African-Americans, no matter what their educational or occupational achievement or income level, are exposed to higher crime rates, less effective educational systems, high mortality risks, more dilapidated surroundings, and greater environmental threats because of their race (Denton and Massey, 1988; Bullard and Wright, 1986; Bullard, 1990, 1993). For example, in the heavily populated South Coast air basin of the Los Angeles area, it is estimated that over 71 percent of African-Americans and 50 percent of Latinos reside in areas with the most polluted air, while only 34 percent of whites live in highly polluted areas (Ong and Blumenberg, 1990: 9; Mann, 1991: 31).

The development of spatially differentiated metropolitan areas where African-Americans are segregated from other Americans has resulted from governmental policies and from marketing practices of the housing industry and lending institutions. Millions of African-Americans are geographically isolated in economically depressed and polluted urban neighborhoods away from the expanding suburban job centers (Bullard, 1987, 1990; Bullard and Wright, 1987, 1990; Logan and Molotch, 1987).

The infrastructure conditions in urban areas result from a host of factors, including the distribution of wealth, patterns of racial and economic discrimination, redlining, housing and real estate practices, location decisions of industry, and differential enforcement of land use and environmental regulations. All communities are not created equal. Apartheid-type housing and development policies have resulted in limited mobility, reduced neighborhood options, decreased environmental choices, and diminished job opportunities for African-Americans (Bullard, Grigsby, and Lee, forthcoming).

It has been difficult for millions of African-Americans in segregated neighborhoods to say "not in my backyard" (NIMBY) because they do not have a backyard (Bullard and Wright, 1987). Nationally, only about 44 percent of African-Americans own their homes compared with over 66 percent of the nation as a whole. Homeowners are the strongest advocates of the NIMBY positions taken against locally unwanted land uses, or LULUs, such as the construction of garbage dumps, landfills, incinerators, sewer treatment plants, recycling centers, prisons, drug treatment units, and public housing projects. Generally, white communities have greater access than their African-American counterparts when it comes to influencing land use and environmental decision making.

The ability of an individual to escape a health-threatening physical environment is usually related to affluence. However, racial barriers complicate this process for many African-Americans (Denton and Massey, 1988). The imbalance between residential amenities and land uses assigned to central cities and suburbs cannot be explained by class factors alone. Blacks and whites do not have the same opportunities to "vote with their feet" and escape undesirable physical environments (Bullard, 1990).

Institutional racism continues to influence housing and mobility options available to African-Americans of all income levels and is a major factor influencing the quality of neighborhoods they have available to them. The "web of discrimination" in the housing market is a result of action and inaction of local and federal government officials, financial institutions, insurance companies, real estate marketing firms, and zoning boards. More stringent enforcement mechanisms and penalties are needed to combat all forms of discrimination.

Uneven Development and Land Use

Uneven development between central cities and suburbs, combined with the systematic avoidance of inner-city areas by many businesses, has heightened social and economic inequalities. For the past two decades, manufacturing plants have been fleeing central cities and taking jobs with them. Many have moved to Third World countries, where labor is cheap and environmental regulations are lax or nonexistent.

Industry flight from central cities has left behind a deteriorating urban infrastructure, poverty, and pollution. What kind of replacement industry can these communities attract? Economically depressed communities do not have a lot of choices available to them. Some workers have become so desperate that they are forced to choose between unemployment and a job that may result in risks to their health, their family's health, and the health of their community. This amounts to "economic blackmail" (Kazis and Grossman, 1983). Economic conditions in many African-American communities make them especially vulnerable to this practice.

Some polluting industries have been eager to exploit this vulnerability. Some have even used the assistance of elected officials to obtain special tax breaks and government operating permits. Clearly, economic development and environmental policies flow from forces of production and are often dominated and subsidized by state actors. Numerous examples abound where state actors have targeted cities and regions for infrastructure improvements and amenities such as water irrigation systems, ship channels, road and bridge projects, and mass transit systems. On the other hand, state actors have done a miserable job in protecting central city residents from the ravages of industrial pollution and nonresidential activities that have a negative impact on quality of life (Bryant and Mohai, 1992).

Racial inequality is perpetuated and reinforced by local governments in conjunction with urban-based corporations. In general, "at a certain point in community development . . . trajectories of economic growth and quality of life converge" (Gottdiener, 1988: 172). Race continues to be a potent variable in explaining urban land use, streets and highway configuration, commercial and industrial development, and industrial facility siting. Moreover, the question of "who gets what, where, and why" often pits one community against another.

Competition intensifies for residential amenities and infrastructure improvements that are not always equitably distributed. Some residential areas and their inhabitants are at a greater risk than the larger society from unregulated growth, ineffective regulation of industrial toxins, and public policy decisions authorizing industrial facilities that favor those with political and economic clout. Zoning is probably the most widely applied mechanism to regulate urban land use in the United States (Kelly, 1988; Plotkin, 1987). Zoning laws broadly define land for residential, commercial, or industrial uses, and may impose narrower land-use restrictions (e.g., minimum and maximum lot size, number of dwellings per acre, square feet and height of buildings, etc.).

Zoning ordinances, deed restrictions, and other land-use mechanisms have been widely used as a NIMBY tool, operating through exclusionary practices. Thus, exclusionary zoning has been used to "simply zone against something rather than for something" (Marshall, 1989: 312). Exclusionary zoning is "one of the most subtle forms of using government authority and power to foster and perpetuate discriminatory practices" (Marshall, 1989: 313). With or without zoning, deed restrictions, or other devices, various groups are "unequally able to protect their environmental interests" (Logan and Molotch, 1987: 158). More often than not, African-American communities get shortchanged in the neighborhood protection game.

African-Americans and the "New South"

The South has always been home to a large share of the African-American population. More than 90 percent of African-Americans lived in Southern states at the turn of the century. In 1990, over 53 percent of all African-Americans lived in the South—the same percentage as in 1980 and 1970. African-Americans comprise about one fifth of the region's population. The South has been defined in different ways by a host of journalists, social scientists, and government bureaucrats. For example, the Census Bureau has defined the South as a statistical entity comprising sixteen states and the District of Columbia. This is the definition used in this chapter. The South has the largest population of any region in the country, containing a third of the nation's population (Bullard, 1991).

The 1970s saw the South become a geographic magnet that attracted people from all over the nation. Beginning in the mid-seventies, the number of African-Americans moving into the South exceeded the number departing for other regions of the country. This trend led some to conclude that the "black exodus" had ended and a "New South" was at hand. The "Go South" theme became a potent message in African-American communities outside the region. This message continued into the 1980s, as African-Americans searched for improved economic opportunities and quality of life. The region attracted both the skilled and unskilled, the educated and uneducated, as well as low-income and middle-income African-Americans who sought to make their fortune (Bullard, 1991).

Where did these migrants settle? Most settled in the central cities at the time jobs were moving to the suburbs. The city's traditional function as an "economic launching pad" for upwardly mobile African-Americans was diminished by the disinvestment process taking place in central cities and the relocation of new industries to distant suburbs. In 1990, more than 57 percent of African-Americans lived in central cities, the highest concentration of any racial and ethnic group. On the other hand, 26.8 percent of African-Americans lived in the suburbs and 16.2 percent in rural areas.

The South was not as segregated as the Midwest and Northeast in 1990. Nevertheless, blacks and whites in Southern cities continue to live apart. The South is far from being a utopia of racially integrated housing. In 1990, Birmingham, Memphis, and Baltimore were the most segregated metropolitan areas in the region (Udansky, 1991). Birmingham is the sixth most segregated metropolitan area in the United States, and the only Southern metropolitan area in the top ten most segregated metropolitan areas in 1990 (see Table 6.2 below). The Birmingham metropolitan area had a segregation index of 77 (i.e., 77 percent of either blacks or whites would have to move from segregated neighborhoods to achieve integration). Blacks make up 27.1 percent of the five-county Birmingham metropolitan area. White flight has left the central city with a 63 percent black population and a suburban ring that is 89 percent white.

Five of the six cities that have the largest percentage of African-Americans are located in the South. In 1990, African-Americans were 75.7 percent of the population in Atlanta, 65.8 percent in Washington, D.C., 61.9 percent in New Orleans, 59.2 in Baltimore, and 54.8 percent in Memphis.

The data in Table 6.3 show the population change in the seven Southern cities that had the largest black population in 1990. Three of these cities experienced a drop in their black population during the 1980s: Washington, D.C., Atlanta, and

Table 6.2. Segregation in Southern Metropolitan Areas with Highest Percentage of Blacks (1990)

Metropolitan Area	% Black 1980	% Black 1990	Segregation Index
Memphis	39.9	40.6	75
Richmond-Petersburg	32.6	34.7	63
Norfolk	29.1	28.5	55
Birmingham	27.2	27.1	77
Washington	26.9	26.6	67
Atlanta	24.6	26.0	71
Baltimore	25.5	25.9	75
Charlotte	20.0	19.9	62
Houston	18.2	18.6	71
Miami-Fort Lauderdale	15.1	18.5	72

Source: Udansky (1991).

New Orleans. On the other hand, black Houston grew by four percent between 1980 and 1990 (from 440,257 to 457,990). Houston's black population grew by more than 39 percent during the 1970s, making it one of the fastest growing black communities in the South. Blacks made up just under 27.6 percent of the city's total population—a figure that is nearly unchanged from 1980. Still, Houston's black population is the largest African-American community in the South.

African-Americans have long struggled to get a piece of the American Dream and reap the benefits of an expanding economy. They want and expect what all Americans want and expect, an opportunity to buy houses and live in quality neighborhoods of their choice. However, institutional barriers still limit housing options available to millions of African-Americans.

Nevertheless, home ownership continues to be an integral part of the American Dream. Home-ownership rates among African-Americans have increased over the past four decades. Nationally, as stated above, 44 percent of African-Americans own their homes, but the home-ownership rate is highest in the South, where more than half (51.1 percent) of all African-Americans own their homes compared with 44.4 percent in the North Central, 39.9 percent in the West, and 31.1 percent in the Northeast regions (Udansky, 1991).

There can be little doubt that the opportunity of home ownership changed during the 1980s. However, many social, economic, and political barriers have not lowered. Ownership of property, land, and private businesses remains a central part of the dream of success, a dream that has eluded millions of African-Americans. The housing owned and occupied by African-Americans continues to be of lower value, with more deficiencies, than the homes of their white counterparts. Home-ownership options are often limited to older central city areas or suburban areas experiencing demographic transition.

Table 6.3. Population Change in Seven Southern Cities

Cities	% Black 1990	Black Population 1990	Black Population 1980	%Gain/Loss
Houston	27.6	457,990	440,257	+4.0
Baltimore	54.8	435,768	431,151	+1.1
Washington	65.8	399,604	448,229	-10.8
Memphis	54.8	334,737	307,702	+8.8
New Orleans	59.2	307,728	308,136	-0.13
Dallas	30.0	296,262	265,594	+11.5
Atlanta	67.1	264,262	282,912	-6.6

Source: U.S. Bureau of the Census (1991).

Many cities' older suburban neighborhoods now mirror the physical decay of their inner-city counterparts. Generally, homes in these older areas do not yield the same return on investment as in other parts of the city or surrounding suburbs.

Most single-family homes built in the United States during the 1980s were in the suburbs and in targeted developments outside the central city neighborhoods where African-Americans have been concentrated. Construction priorities of developers increased housing opportunities primarily for whites, higher income households, and former homeowners who had accumulated capital to finance down payments. Much of urban America, however, has not escaped the national trend of a dwindling supply of low- and moderate-income housing.

Conclusion

Residential segregation and housing discrimination have been difficult to eliminate in urban America. Institutionalized racism created the urban ghettos and accompanying housing, economic, and environmental ills that afflict their inhabitants. This is true for people of color in the Northeast, Midwest, West, and South. Southern and "Sunbelt" inner cities, for example, are well on the way to duplicating the fiscal and infrastructure problems of urban centers in other regions of the country, i.e., unemployment, dependency, limited education, crowded housing, and poverty.

This country needs a national policy that addresses these pressing urban problems. The time is long overdue for the nation to turn its attention to the problems of housing discrimination, residential segregation, neighborhood disinvestment, redlining, and environmental racism—all of which contribute to urban decline.

7

The Net Impact of Environmental
Protection on Jobs and the Economy

Roger H. Bezdek

As the world economy becomes ever more competitive, marketplace imperatives increasingly favor those companies (and nations) that are more efficient and less polluting. The world is confronted with problems caused by the cumulative effects of increasing consumption, industrialization, population growth, and ecological degradation. Regulations that promote environmentally sound, efficiency-enhancing, innovative technologies and processes represent an important advance on the road toward a 21st century production and transportation system that is far less environmentally degrading and wasteful. At present, and increasingly in the future, wealth (and jobs) will accrue to individuals, companies, industries, regions, and nations that adapt accordingly.

Introduction

The net impact of environmental protection on the economy and job market is a timely and highly controversial issue. Indeed, during the 1992 presidential campaign the net effects of environmentalism on the economy and employment in general—and loggers' jobs vs. spotted owls in particular—were major issues. The Republicans depicted the Clinton–Gore environmental positions as radical ones which would seriously damage American industry, reduce U.S. international competitiveness, and cost many thousands of jobs. Naturally, the Clinton–Gore campaign team countered that just the opposite was true: Environmental programs benefit the economy and actually create jobs. Both sides quoted their own studies, experts, and anecdotal examples to prove their contentions.

Wherein lies the truth? This is an important issue and, because of the following, will likely become more so in the near future:

- First, the Clinton–Gore ticket won and generated a new wave of environmental activism.

Roger H. Bezdek is president of Management Information Services Inc., an analytical research and management consulting firm in Washington, D.C., specializing in economic, energy, human resource, and environmental issues. He has 25 years experience in consulting and management in the energy, environmental, economic forecasting, and labor market analysis fields, serving in private industry, academia, and the federal government.

- Second, the Clinton administration has made economic growth and job creation top priorities. Policymakers of all points of view agree that there is a strong relationship between environmentalism and jobs—it is just the sign of the correlation coefficient that is under debate.

- Third, the economic and jobs impact of the environmental legislation enacted over the past three decades—such as the Clean Air Act Amendments of 1990—will continue to be felt well into the next century, even in the event that no new environmental laws are passed.

- Finally, and most important, irrespective of political factors, since the late 1960s spending to protect the environment has been growing three times faster than gross domestic product (GDP), and by 1992 had reached $170 billion—2.8 percent of GDP (Management Information Services Inc., 1992c). Further, while the rate of growth of environmental protection (EP) spending is decreasing, Management Information Services Inc. (MISI) forecasts that by the year 2000, EP spending will total nearly $250 billion (1992 dollars), accounting for 3.1 percent of GDP, and will exceed the nation's total spending on national defense (Management Information Services Inc., 1992c). The net impact of environmental policies and legislation on the economy and job market will thus inevitably be of increasing concern.

What is the net impact of environmental protection on jobs and the economy? To answer this question, we first examine the available evidence: theoretical, anecdotal, econometric/simulation, and empirical/statistical. We then estimate the comprehensive economic and employment impacts on the United States of environmental protection spending, forecasting these effects through the year 2005.

Theoretical Considerations

The conventional standard argument that environmental policies have negative economic and job impacts can be summarized as follows:[1] Businesses invest capital and create jobs to produce goods and services for a profit. Each firm seeks to minimize capital and operating expenses while maximizing sales and profits. As more environmental restrictions on production are enacted, the costs of production increase. This increases the cost of the product and, depending on the product's price elasticity, reduces its sales. Reduced sales decrease employment. When regional or international considerations are taken into account, it is argued that economic activities, pollution, and jobs are exported to those regions and nations ("pollution havens") with relatively lax environmental standards (Walter, 1982, and Walter and Ugelow, 1979). Thus environmental regulations and standards

impose nonproductive expenses on the economy, thus reducing economic growth
and eliminating jobs.

However, while seemingly convincing in its simplicity, this argument is, at best,
incomplete. For one thing, simply because the environmental costs of production
are external to the firm does not mean that they do not exist.[2] Further, the
conventional analysis ignores the benefits that may be produced by environmental
programs and policies. More broadly, some researchers even argue that the
traditional economic analysis is flawed and is incapable of dealing with long-term
environmental degradation and resource scarcity issues.[3]

Anecdotal Evidence

Anecdotal evidence on the relationship between the environment, the economy,
and jobs abounds. Critics of environmental regulation can cite many examples of
the negative impact of environmentalism on employment. For example:

- Protection of the northern spotted owl in the Pacific Northwest has
  purportedly cost anywhere from 20,000 to 140,000 jobs—hence the
  bumper sticker "Save a Logger, Kill an Owl" (Cooper, 1992: 411–412).

- Phillips Petroleum Company announced 1,350 layoffs in April 1992 and
  blamed environmental regulations (*New York Times*, April 4, 1992).

- The Chemical Council of New Jersey claimed in August 1992 that
  environmental regulations cost the state 12,000 jobs in the chemical
  industry over the past ten years (Van Leer, 1992).

- Local sugar growers in Florida claim that measures to protect the
  Everglades will cost 15,000 jobs (Cooper, 1992: 411–412).

- The American Petroleum Institute blames environmental restrictions for
  the loss of 400,000 jobs during the 1980s (Hong and Yang, 1992).

- The Motor Vehicle Manufacturers Association claims that increasing
  fuel economy standards will cost 300,000 jobs (Linden, 1992).

- The 1992 closing of a polluting oil refinery in Wyoming cost 200 jobs
  (Cooper, 1992: 411–412).

- An analyst has estimated that every job "protected" by clean air legislation costs more than a million dollars per year (Portney, 1982).[4]

- Several years ago the Canadian paper and pulp industry and its labor
  unions successfully opposed federal regulations mandating production
  using "environmentally benign" processes, thus preserving existing industrial plants and thousands of jobs (Management Information Services
  Inc., 1992a).

Environmentalists respond with their own anecdotal evidence purporting to show that environmentalism is good for the economy and creates jobs:

- Recycling created 14,000 jobs in California in 1991 (Shirley, 1992: 5).

- Recent energy conservation programs have created 600 jobs in British Columbia (Jaccard and Sims, 1991).

- EPA estimates that the 1990 Clean Air Act Amendments will create 60,000 new jobs (ICF Resources Inc. and Smith Barney, Harris Upham & Co., 1992).

- Diversification into environmental business is credited with saving the Fluor Corporation from extinction—and thousands of its workers from unemployment; environmental work accounted for more than half of the firm's new 1992 revenues of $8 billion (Schine, 1992).

- A disproportionate share of the jobs forecast by BLS to be the fastest-growing during the 1990s are environment-related (Basta, 1991; Lord et al., 1992; Silvestri and Lukasiewicz, 1991).

- In the United States, many of the sectors subject to the most stringent environmental regulations—including chemicals, plastics, synthetics, fabrics, and paints—have become the most efficient and have actually improved their international competitiveness (Porter, 1990: 728–729; 1991).

- The formerly Communist nations of Eastern Europe promoted economic development while ignoring environmental concerns, and produced both environmental catastrophe and economic failure.

- The European Economic Community recently banned the imports of pulp and paper products not produced in an "environmentally benign" manner, thus devastating the Canadian pulp and paper industry and costing thousands of jobs (Management Information Services Inc., 1992a).

Of course, anecdotal information can be used to prove most anything. It will always be possible to find at least a few jobs lost due to an environment-related plant closing or law. Similarly, one can always find jobs created in environmental and cleanup programs.

Econometric Simulations

Numerous studies have been undertaken over the past two decades by economists attempting to estimate the economic and employment effects of environment-related programs. Generally, these analyses utilize large-scale econometric/input–output models to determine the impacts of a particular environmental program or set of regulations, or to estimate the likely economic and employment situation in the absence of these programs.

At MISI we have conducted many such analyses, for example:

- We simulated the impact on the economy and labor market of 1985 capital investments in pollution abatement and control and found that these created 170,000 jobs (Management Information Services Inc., 1986a; Bezdek, Wendling, and Jones, 1989).

- We estimated the impacts on the state of Ohio of acid deposition control legislation and found that the state would gain 6,000 more jobs than it would lose (Cook and Rosenberg, 1986).

- We simulated the impact of the major acid rain control bills being considered in the U.S. Congress and found that 100,000 net jobs would be created in the country (Management Information Services Inc., 1987; Wendling and Bezdek, 1989).

- We estimated the direct and indirect impact on the job market of solid and hazardous waste control programs, estimating that the former resulted in 500,000 jobs and the latter in 170,000 jobs throughout the economy (Management Information Services Inc., 1992b).

In 1990 Dale Jorgensen and Peter Wilcoxen (J-W) estimated the impact on the U.S. economy of environmental regulations by simulating the growth of the economy between 1974 and 1985 with and without these regulations (Jorgensen and Wilcoxen, 1990). Without attempting to estimate any benefits, they concluded that the effect of these regulations was that the economy grew about 0.2 percent per year more slowly than it would have in the absence of the regulations. As a consequence, they estimated that GNP in the early 1990s was about 2.5 percent less than it would otherwise have been.

In 1992 J-W extended their analysis by assessing the impacts of the Clean Air Act Amendments of 1990 (Jorgensen and Wilcoxen, 1992). Using the same methodology, they concluded that the net impact of the amendments would be to further reduce the rate of growth of GNP as they are phased in over the next two decades. As a result, GNP in 2005 will, they estimate, be about three percent lower than it otherwise would.

J-W made no estimate of employment impacts. However, assuming that there is a roughly linear relationship between GNP losses and job losses, we can extrapolate from the J-W results of a 2.5 percent loss in GNP and estimate that as of 1992 approximately three million fewer jobs existed in the United States due to the environmental regulations enacted over the past quarter-century.

One way of deriving an overall "net job impact estimate" would be the following: The J-W results imply that EP (environmental protection) legislation has cost, in 1992, approximately three million jobs. As discussed below, MISI estimates that in 1992 EP, as broadly defined, created approximately four million jobs. Does this imply that in 1992 the "net" jobs resulting from EP totaled about one million? Not necessarily, because the two studies are dissimilar. It does, however, imply that the net economic and jobs impact may be different from what the J-W findings imply.

Several points must be noted here. First, the J-W work represents the state-of-the art econometric/input–output modeling approach and is technically correct. Second, it possesses the industry detail of most input–output (I-O) models and, significantly, estimates the costs to different industries of environmental regulations. Third, it graphically emphasizes that at least in the short run, there is no free lunch, and protecting the environment will cost money and consume resources that could be otherwise used for myriad productive purposes. Finally, it emphasizes that while early EP measures may be "cheap," further environmental gains are becoming increasingly expensive.

Nevertheless, the J-W work is subject to criticism:

- As the authors have noted, they make no attempt to assess the benefits of EP to either consumers or producers (Jorgensen and Wilcoxen, 1990: 314).

- Such models do not account for the emergence of new industries or export opportunities that may eventually result from EP compliance activities—see the discussion below.

- It may be questioned how realistic it is to model the economy on the assumption that no EP legislation had been enacted over the past quarter-century.

Significantly, other researchers using similar econometric input–output models have come to different conclusions.

- In 1979 the Council on Economic Priorities simulated the impacts of environmentally benign energy sources and concluded that they would result in net economic and job benefits (Council on Economic Priorities, 1979). In that same year similar findings were reported by Grossman and Daneker (1979).

- In 1991 Tennis, Goodman, and Clarke found that investments in environmental and conservation programs would have substantial net economic and employment benefits for the state of New York (Tennis, Goodman, and Clarke, 1991).

- In 1992 Clark et al. found that environment-motivated, demand-side management programs would create more jobs in Maine than the alternatives (Clarke et al., 1992).

- In 1992 Geller, DeCicco, and Laitner found that a national strategy of investment in environmentally benign energy sources, conservation, and energy efficiency would create one million net new jobs in the United States within about ten years (Geller, DeCicco, and Laitner, 1992).

Other studies reported over the past decade came to varying conclusions.[5] In sum, the results of the simulation approach are inconclusive.

Empirical Studies of the Issue

Since theoretical, anecdotal, and simulation approaches yield indeterminate findings, the next logical step is to assess what is actually happening in the real world, both in the United States and abroad. Does the empirical evidence available indicate a negative or positive relationship between EP and economic/job growth?

It can be hypothesized that:

- Within a nation those regions with the most stringent EP regulations should show less economic and job growth than those with more lax EP rules.
- Internationally, those nations with the least stringent environmental laws should profit at the expense of others.

The most comprehensive recent study of the impact of environmental legislation on interstate rates of economic performance was conducted by Stephen Meyer (Meyer, 1992). Meyer tested the hypothesis that pursuit of environmental quality hinders economic growth and job creation. He ranked the 50 states on the basis of the stringency of their environmental laws and then compared the environmental rankings with measures of economic growth and job creation between 1973 and 1989.

His findings are striking. Not only did he find no evidence to support a negative relationship between environmental regulation and economic growth, his results showed just the opposite. That is, he found that the states with the most ambitious environmental programs had the highest levels of economic growth and job creation over the period. While his study does not necessarily prove that environmentalism causes economic growth or job creation, it does repudiate the hypothesis that environmentalism reduces economic growth and job creation.

Additional insight is provided by the U.S. Bureau of Labor Statistics, which found that during 1988 employers attributed only 0.1 percent of all layoffs to environment-related causes (Lee, 1990). While this finding is not conclusive, if anything near 99.9 percent of the jobs lost in the United States are the result of factors other than EP, one cannot identify environmentalism as a significant factor in job loss.

What of the "pollution haven–industrial flight" hypothesis? This states that industries will tend to relocate to those nations with the least stringent environmental policies to minimize compliance costs (Walter, 1982; Walter and Ugelow, 1979). Once again, the empirical evidence unambiguously refutes that assertion:

- Jeffrey Leonard, in a case study of trade and investment flows, found little evidence that pollution control measures had exerted any systematic effect on international trade (Leonard, 1988).

- James Tobey, in an econometric study of international trade patterns in "pollution-intensive" goods, could not identify any negative effects of stringent domestic environmental policies (Tobey, 1990).

- Michael Porter, after a seminal study of the comparative advantage of nations, reports that environmental protection does not hamper economic competitiveness. Rather, he found the opposite: Those nations with the most stringent environmental laws also had the highest rates of economic growth and job creation (Porter, 1990: 728–729, 1991).

- Maureen Cropper and Wallace Oates, in the most extensive recent review of the literature, report that "in short, domestic environmental policies, at least to this point in time [June 1992], do not appear to have had significant effects on patterns of international trade" (Cropper and Oates, 1992: 699).

Assessment of the Available Evidence

Several conclusions emerge from this brief review. First, anecdotal examples of the positive and negative impacts of environmental protection can be cited to prove almost anything. Second, econometric/I-O simulation models have been developed which show both the positive and negative effects of environmental legislation and related programs. Thus, while they are important in identifying the detailed effects of EP legislation and in emphasizing that environmental protection is not a "free" good, their findings are inconclusive. Third, and most significant, it is noteworthy that recent major empirical studies unanimously reject the hypothesis that there is a negative relationship between environmental protection and economic growth/job creation. In fact, where statistically significant relationships are found, they are invariably positive, i.e., the states within the United States and the nations of the world with the more stringent environmental regulations show the best economic performance.

Why is this so? Why is the conventional wisdom apparently so wrong? Why are these somewhat counterintuitive effects not accurately accounted for in the standard economic analyses and state-of-the-art econometric simulation models? There appear to be several explanations for the positive relationship between environmental protection and increases in jobs and economic activity.

First, EP is what economists refer to as a "superior good"—one for which the demand increases as income increases. As societies' incomes and wealth grow, as they have in recent decades, their citizens demand higher levels of environmental quality and more stringent control and abatement of pollution and waste products.

Second, EP is a universal need, an area of growing expenditure in all of the major national economies and an important, rapidly expanding export industry. Without competitive technology, the United States (or any other nation) not only loses a major growth industry, but will also find more and more of its own environmental spending being devoted to imports (Porter, 1991).

Third, strict environmental codes may actually foster competitiveness. Environmental standards encourage companies to re-engineer their technology, which results in many cases in processes that not only pollute less but also lower costs and improve quality. Production methods will be modified to decrease use of scarce or toxic resources and recycle wasted by-products. Strict environmental standards can also induce companies' innovation in producing less polluting, more resource-efficient products that are highly valued internationally (Porter, 1991).

Fourth, environmental regulations do not necessarily diminish the wealth of a nation, rather, they largely transfer wealth from polluters to pollution controllers and abaters and to less polluting firms. Lax environmental standards, rather than increasing jobs and profits, just temporarily insulate inefficient, wasteful, polluting firms from the need to innovate and invest in new equipment—while penalizing those firms that undertake such measures (Silverstein, 1992a, 1992b).

Fifth, the point becomes obvious when stated bluntly: Assume that *no* environmental, energy-efficiency, resource conservation, automobile mileage, or related standards and legislation had been enacted in the United States over the past 25 years. Is it really credible to argue that the quality of the products and manufacturing processes of the late 1960s could sustain a prosperous, growing industrial and job base during the 1990s—much less into the 21st century? Where would the market be for such environmentally degrading, energy-inefficient, resource-wasting goods and processes? The answer is clear: There would be few markets and few jobs. Policies that encourage lax environmental standards and energy inefficiency are no more "pro-business/pro-job" than the disastrous policies of the Soviet bloc of the past 40 years was "pro-industry" (Silverstein, 1992b).

Finally, and most basically, as the world economy becomes ever more competitive, marketplace imperatives increasingly favor those companies (and nations) that are more efficient and less polluting. The world is confronted with problems caused by the cumulative effects of increasing consumption, industrialization, population growth, and ecological degradation. Regulations that promote environmentally sound, efficiency-enhancing, innovative technologies and processes represent an important advance on the road toward a 21st century production and transportation system that is far less environmentally degrading and wasteful. At present, and increasingly in the future, wealth (and jobs) will accrue to individuals, companies, industries, regions, and nations that adapt accordingly (Silverstein, 1992b; Wirth, 1992).

Employment Created by Environmental Protection

It thus appears that the concept of "net" job creation by EP is nebulous. At the least, we have determined that in the short run the jobs created and lost from EP may be a wash—although the weight of evidence is that even in the short run environmentalism may create more jobs than it eliminates. However, in the long run industries, regions, and nations must compete for EP-related growth and jobs—there is really little choice in the matter. Indeed, any short run job gains that may result from a lessening of environmental standards will be overwhelmed by the negative consequences in the long run. This represents a classic case of being able to do well by doing good, and serves to refute the notion that economics is inevitably a "dismal science."

What Is the Environmental Protection Industry?

Before we can determine the overall EP economic and job effects, we must define the EP "industry." Various estimates (1992 dollars) of the size of the industry in the early 1990s have been made.[6]

- The U.S. Commerce Department (Census Bureau and Bureau of Economic Analysis) estimates the size of the industry as $105–$110 billion (Rutledge and Leonard, 1991).

- The U.S. EPA estimates the size of the industry as $120–$125 billion (U.S. Environmental Protection Agency, 1990).

- Farkas Berkowitz estimates the size of the industry as $60–$65 billion (*Environmental Business Journal*, 1992).

- Environmental Economics Inc. estimates the size of the industry as $125–$135 billion (Silverstein, 1992a, 1992b).

- EnviroQuest estimates the size of the industry as $120–$145 billion (*Environmental Business Journal*, 1991, 1992).

- MISI estimates that in 1992 the size of the industry was approximately $170 billion (Management Information Services Inc., 1992c).

One major point that is obvious from the above data is that there is a wide variation in the estimates of the current size of the industry. There are a number of reasons for this divergence: the universe of companies and activities included, whether environmental costs or EP revenues are being estimated, whether estimates are being made from the "buy" side or "sell" side, the definition of "environmental protection" used, the base year of the dollar estimates, etc. An in-depth discussion of these conceptual and definitional differences is outside the scope of this chapter. The second salient point is that the MISI estimate is the largest. The reason for this is discussed below.

The U.S. Environmental Protection Industry in 1992

Table 7.1 gives the MISI estimates of the 1992 EP industry in the United States. The two components of the EP industry are seen to be Pollution Abatement and Control (PABCO)—$139 billion, and Other Environment-Related Expenditures—$31 billion.

The PABCO components are directly related to the control and remediation of the major media types of environmental degradation—air, water, solid waste, radi-

Table 7.1. Environmental Protection Expenditures in the U.S. Economy, 1992 (millions of 1992 dollars)

Environmental Protection Expenditures, Total	$169,814
Pollution Abatement and Control (PABCO), Total	138,979
Air Pollution Control	37,448
Radiation Pollution Control	603
Water Pollution Control	57,904
Land Pollution Control	37,975
Chemical Pollution Control	2,438
Multimedia Pollution Control	2,611
Other Environment-Related Expenditures, Total	30,835
Environmental Research, Design & Development	4,918
Environment-Related Energy	2,834
Misc. Federal Environment-Related Expenditures[a]	5,360
Misc. State and Local Environment-Related Expenditures[a]	10,680
Utilities' Environment-Related Expenditures[a]	$7,043

Source: Management Information Services Inc., 1992c.

[a]Exclusive of environmental and PABCO expenditures included elsewhere.

ation, etc. The estimates here are generally comparable to those derived from federal, state, and local government data sources referring to analogous activities. Other Environment-Related Expenditures include spending on programs closely associated with environmental concerns and objectives, such as global warming research, clean energy technologies, utility conservation, demand-side management, and similar programs; and federal, state, and local government environmental expenditures not included elsewhere.[7] Some of these categories are included in the estimates of the EP industry made by other organizations, and some are not.

The MISI estimates of the EP industry are the most comprehensive available and, we believe, give the most accurate accounting of the resources currently devoted to environmental protection in the United States.

Economic and Job Impacts of 1992 EP Spending

Since the late 1960s protection of the environment and abatement and control of pollution have grown rapidly to become a major sales-generating, profit-making, job-creating industry. Expenditures in the United States for PABCO and related environmental protection programs have grown (in constant 1992 dollars) from $27.7 billion per year in 1970 to $169.8 billion per year by 1992—increasing much faster than GDP (gross domestic product) over the same period:

Year	Environmental Protection Spending (1992 dollars)
1970	$27.7 billion
1975	$54.7 billion
1980	$90.3 billion
1985	$109.6 billion
1992	$169.8 billion (see Table 7.1)

Many companies, whether they realize it or not, owe their profits—and in some cases their existence—to EP spending. Many workers, whether they realize it or not, would be unemployed were it not for these expenditures. As shown in Table 7.2, in 1992 environmental protection (EP) spending created nearly four million jobs (1.9 million directly, 2.1 million indirectly) distributed widely throughout the economy. So much for the contention that protecting the environment destroys industries and costs jobs.

Further, while MISI forecasts that the rate of growth in expenditures for environmental protection will decline during the 1990s, these expenditures will continue to increase at about twice the rate of GDP. By the late 1990s EP expenditures will likely equal and then exceed the U.S. Department of Defense

Table 7.2. Environmental Protection-Related Jobs Created in the U.S. Economy, 1992, by Major Economic Sector (thousands of jobs)

Total, All Sectors	3,958
Manufacturing, Total	1,305
Textile and Apparel	33
Chemical & Petroleum Products	129
Fabricated Metal Products	71
Machinery	190
Transportation Equipment	100
Other Manufacturing	782
Agriculture, Forestry & Fisheries	135
Mining	38
Construction	189
Transportation, Communications & Utilities	498
Wholesale and Retail Trade	503
Finance, Insurance, and Real Estate	197
Services	585
Government (Federal, State, Local)	508

Source: Management Information Services Inc., 1992c.

budget—both EP spending and the DOD budget will total $200–$220 billion (1992 dollars) and will constitute about three percent of GNP.

The question may be asked, aren't investments in environmental protection "nonproductive?" Wouldn't spending lots of money on anything—for example, building pyramids in the desert—stimulate industry and create jobs?

These investments are not at all like building useless pyramids. Rather, they produce a healthier, safer, cleaner, and more livable environment. Environmental protection is an exemplary public good, and according to the Harris pollsters this issue has consistently enjoyed wider and stronger public support than virtually any other issue over the past quarter century.[8] Investments in plant and equipment which produce this strongly desired public good are as productive as those that produce automobiles, television sets, golf balls, or defense systems that we are willing to pay for directly in the prices of products or indirectly through the government.

Over the past quarter century protecting the environment has been a major U.S. priority. The legislation enacted has significantly improved the nation's environment and has set in motion ongoing programs that will have significant effects on the nation's environment, economy, and job market well into the next century. Protection of the environment and remediation of environmental problems will continue to be one of the most rapidly growing and profitable industries in the United States. Astute business executives, labor leaders, and policymakers must be aware of this.

Don't environmental standards penalize certain states and regions at the expense of others? Sometimes, yes. This point has been so overused, however, that almost any state or region suffering economic hardship places some of the blame on unreasonable environmental laws. Further, it was found that the overall relationship between state environmental policies and economic/job growth is positive, not negative.

For example, according to MISI estimates, Resource Conservation and Recovery Act–related spending for solid and hazardous waste management and control created 670,000 jobs in 1992. It is significant that many of these employment benefits will flow directly to states such as Pennsylvania, Michigan, Illinois, and California that presently see only costs and disadvantages from such legislation. It must be recognized that funds expended on pollution abatement and control programs are not wasted. Investments in environmental protection contribute as much to the well-being of the nation as money spent on other goods competing for scarce private and public funds.

More generally, Figure 7.1 and Table 7.3 show the distribution among the states of the $170 billion in EP expenditures and the four million jobs created. It is seen that all regions and states benefit substantially.

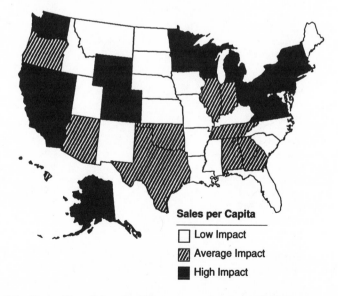

Figure 7.1. States Benefiting the Most, per capita, from 1992 Environmental Protection Spending. (Source: Management Information Services Inc., 1992c)

Table 7.3. Job and Sales Created in Each State in 1992 by
Environmental Protection Expenditures

State	Jobs (thousands)	Sales (billions)
Alabama	70	$ 2.9
Alaska	9	0.4
Arizona	51	2.0
Arkansas	33	1.2
California	484	20.5
Colorado	73	3.0
Connecticut	74	3.0
Delaware	11	0.4
District of Columbia	11	0.4
Florida	163	7.0
Georgia	96	3.6
Hawaii	16	0.6
Idaho	16	0.6
Illinois	141	7.6
Indiana	91	3.7
Iowa	43	1.8
Kansas	33	1.3
Kentucky	47	2.0
Louisiana	56	2.6
Maine	16	0.7
Maryland	74	2.5
Massachusetts	123	5.1
Michigan	188	7.9
Minnesota	79	3.2
Mississippi	33	1.3
Missouri	78	2.9
Montana	10	0.4
Nebraska	25	1.0
Nevada	16	0.6
New Hampshire	19	0.8
New Jersey	140	6.2
New Mexico	19	0.8
New York	306	13.7
North Carolina	105	3.7
North Dakota	9	0.4
Ohio	148	9.0
Oklahoma	48	2.0
Oregon	48	2.0
Pennsylvania	137	9.5
Rhode Island	16	0.7
South Carolina	48	1.8
South Dakota	11	0.3
Tennessee	83	3.3
Texas	270	10.5
Utah	25	1.0
Vermont	10	0.4
Virginia	123	5.3
Washington	78	3.2
West Virginia	42	1.6
Wisconsin	79	3.3
Wyoming	30	1.3
Total	3,958	$169.8

Source: Management Information Services Inc., 1992c. Additional detail available upon request.

The Emergence of the U.S. Environmental Protection Industry

Spending to protect the environment has been one of the most rapidly and consistently growing "recession proof" industries in the economy for the past 20 years. Real EP spending (1992 dollars) increased from $28 billion in 1970 to $170 billion in 1992. This represents a six-fold increase in expenditures in 20 years—a sustained real average annual rate of growth of nearly 9 percent per year over the period. This compares with an average annual rate of growth of GDP that averaged between 2 and 3 percent during the 1970s and 1980s. That is, since the late 1960s, spending for pollution abatement and control has been increasing at a rate nearly four times as large as GDP.

As might be expected, this rate of growth has not been consistent. In the early 1970s, EP expenditures were increasing nearly 15 percent per year, whereas by the late 1980s they were increasing at about 7 percent annually. This is to be expected as the industry grew and matured—but even the most recent growth rates of 4 percent are more than twice the growth rate of GDP. In 1970, EP spending accounted for 0.9 percent of GDP, while by 1992 the United States was devoting about 2.8 percent of GDP to pollution control and abatement and related environmental programs.

More interesting, perhaps, is the "recession-proof" nature of this industry:

- In the late 1970s the U.S. economy was reeling from inflationary shocks, record interest rates, energy crises, and anemic economic growth; but between 1975 and 1980 EP expenditures grew more than 60 percent, from $55 billion to $90 billion.

- In the early 1980s the United States experienced the most severe economic recession in half a century, with many industries experiencing depression-level problems; but between 1980 and 1985 EP spending increased by $20 billion—22 percent.

The Current (1992) Size and Structure of the Industry

If "EP" were a corporation, it would rank far higher than the top of the Fortune 500:

- MISI estimates that in 1992 EP expenditures totaled $170 billion.

- In 1991 General Motors, the largest U.S. industrial corporation, had sales of $124 billion; the number two U.S. industrial corporation, Exxon, had sales of $103 billion; while the third-ranked corporation, Ford Motor Co., had sales of $89 billion (*Fortune*, April 20, 1992).

Clearly, providing the goods and services required for environmental protection has become a major U.S. industry with significant effects on the economy and labor market. In 1992 MISI estimates that EP expenditures of $170 billion will have generated:

- $355 billion in total industry sales
- $14 billion in corporate profits
- 4 million jobs
- $63 billion in federal, state, and local government tax revenues

As was shown in Table 7.2, EP spending in 1992 created about 4 million jobs, including 1.3 million jobs in manufacturing. This represents about 3 percent of total 1992 employment, and about 4 percent of total 1992 manufacturing employment.

Table 7.4 illustrates the distribution by major occupation group of these jobs, and Table 7.5 shows the numbers of detailed engineering jobs created by EP spending.

Table 7.4. Environmental Protection-Related Jobs Created in the U.S. Economy, 1992, by Major Occupational Group

Major Occupational Category	Jobs (thousands)
Managerial and Professional Specialty Occupations	
Executive, administrative, and managerial occupations	464
Professional specialty occupations	330
Technical, Sales, and Administrative Support Occupations	
Technicians and related support occupations	109
Sales occupations	576
Administrative support occupations, including clerical	601
Service Occupations	
Protective service occupations	27
Service occupations, except protective	370
Farming, Forestry, and Fishing Occupations	
Farm operators and managers	27
Other agricultural and related occupations	41
Forestry and logging occupations	(*)
Fishers, hunters, and trappers	*
Precision Production, Craft, and Repair Occupation	
Mechanics and repairers	204
Construction trades	288
Extractive occupations	(11)
Precisions production occupations	200
Total	3,958

Source: Management Information Services Inc., 1992c. Additional detail available upon request.
Note: "*" is fewer than 500 jobs

Table 7.5. Engineering Jobs Created by 1992 Environmental Protection Spending

Total, All Engineers	124,794
Aeronautical/Aerospace	4,009
Chemical	13,996
Civil	14,560
Electrical	27,812
Industrial	18,511
Mechanical	15,782
Metallurgical	1,421
Mining	2,094
Petroleum	2,888
Sales	2,415
Engineers, n.e.c.	21,306

Source: Management Information Services Inc., 1992c.

Prospects for the Future

Table 7.6 and Figure 7.2 indicate that MISI forecasts EP to continue to be a rapidly growing, "recession proof" industry well into the next century, offering unique entrepreneurial, profit, and job opportunities throughout the economy for all types of businesses and workers MISI forecasts that real expenditures (1992 dollars) will increase from $170 billion in 1992 to:

- $198 billion in 1995
- $246 billion in 2000
- $292 billion in 2005

Through 2005 spending on PABCO will continue to increase substantially faster than the rate of growth of GDP, although the rate of growth will decline from 7 percent in the late 1990s to about 3 to 4 percent annually by the early years of the next century. Thus, EP expenditures as a percentage of GDP will continue to gradually increase, reaching 2.9 percent of GDP in 1995, 3.1 percent in the year 2000, and 3.2 percent by 2005. The growing significance of the magnitude of EP expenditures is not fully appreciated:

- By the late 1990s—within five years—EP spending will equal and then exceed the nation's spending on national defense.

As illustrated in Table 7.2, environmental protection expenditures generate an increasing number of jobs throughout all sectors of the economy. MISI forecasts

Table 7.6. Environmental Protection Expenditures and Jobs
in the U.S. Economy, 1992–2005

	Expenditures (millions of 1992 dollars)	Jobs (thousands)
1992	$169,814	3,958
1995	$198,033	4,352
2000	$246,351	4,944
2005	$292,482	5,385

Source: Management Information Services Inc., 1992c.

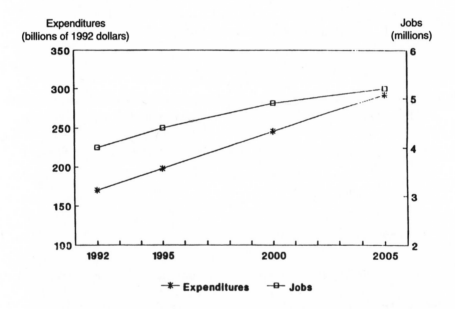

Figure 7.2. Growth of Environmental Protection Spending and Jobs, 1992–2005.

that the employment created directly and indirectly by EP spending will increase from 4 million jobs in 1992 to:

- 4.4 million jobs in 1995
- 4.9 million jobs in 2000
- 5.2 million jobs in 2005

Implications for Environmental Equity

The following salient points emerge with respect to the implications of EP expenditures for environmental equity:

- Joblessness disproportionately affects the poor, minorities, and the disadvantaged, and therefore the 4 million jobs resulting from 1992 EP spending is crucial.

- Economic growth is the most effective anti-poverty, employment-opportunity program, and the net impact of environmentalism is to enhance prospects for long-term sustainable economic and job growth.

- There is nothing magic about the EP industry or the jobs that result from it: The lucrative, attractive jobs will largely flow to persons who are neither poor nor minorities—the latter will be disproportionately concentrated in the less desirable, relatively low paying, more dangerous jobs such as the physical cleanup of Superfund sites, asbestos removal, hazardous waste handling, toxic waste disposal, etc.

- Even if a major effort is made to alleviate the environmental degradation in low-income and minority-populated areas, the persons residing there will likely get little of the secondary benefits of the income and jobs created—unless the current "business as usual" scenario changes.

- Due to the tight fiscal situation at all levels of government, pressures will mount to compete environmental programs against equity-type programs on a zero sum basis; e.g., construction of low-income housing vs. construction of waste treatment facilities, spending for air pollution control vs. spending for prenatal care, and so forth. Given the universal appeal of environmentalism, the EP programs will likely win this competition.

- The environmental movement remains largely elitist and upper- and middle-class oriented, and the concerns addressed generally reflect this orientation. With rare exceptions, the relationship between environmentalism and jobs for minorities, the disadvantaged, and poor people is not even an afterthought.

Basically, a major implication emerging here is that the nascent environmental equity movement has yet to adequately address the positive effects of environmentalism on jobs, incomes, technological change, and economic growth and how these can be integrated with the objectives of the movement.[9] This oversight needs to be remedied expeditiously.

Notes

1. For a more in-depth discussion see Cropper and Oates (1992: 678–697).

2. A seminal discussion of external cost is given in Coase (1960).

3. Over the past two decades a number of analysts have attempted to create a nonconventional economic analysis to account for energy and resources scarcities, longer time horizons, intergenerational equity, and environmental concerns. See, for example, Lovins (1977), Lovins and Lovins (1982), Borman and Keller (1990), Gordon and Suzuki (1990), Clark (1975), and Renner (1992).

4. Here we express his data in 1992 dollars.

5. See, for example, Shirley (1992), Dower and Zimmerman (1992), Zimmerman (1992), Alliance to Save Energy et al. (1991), and Geller et al. (1987). Contrary results are presented in Manne and Richels (1991; 1992) and Bradley, Watts, and Williams (1991).

6. For purposes of comparison we have converted the different estimates of EP spending to constant 1992 collars using GDP deflators.

7. These federal, state, and local government expenditures do not include these governments' spending on parks, recreation, or natural resource functions.

8. This is one reason why spending on environmental protection programs will likely increase rapidly throughout the 1990s.

9. For example, the entire 70-page March/April 1992 issue of the *EPA Journal* was devoted to environmental equity; the issues discussed in this chapter were addressed in only one three-page article in the issue.

8

Toward a New Industrial Policy

Cynthia Hamilton

The profit motive which drives business cannot adequately factor in the value of family, community, love of the land, rootedness, culture, or hope. The emphasis on "alternative" approaches means we urgently need a "new bottom line" in discussions about the economy—one that measures success in terms of people and human values rather than dollars and return on investments. Even locally controlled enterprises can miserably fail the people working in them unless they are infused with genuine democracy . . . (Bookser-Feister and Wise, 1986: 2-3).

Plant closings, recession, and the end of the Cold War have left a landscape dotted with the residue of America's earlier climb to industrial and technological superiority. But the costs of this triumph have been great and include the ecological destruction and human inequality we currently experience. Globally the consequences include global warming, desertification, and environmental refugees fleeing from land no longer usable. Do we need a new industrial policy to respond to current conditions or are we facing a demand for entirely new approaches to growth and development which might include a critique of industrialization as we have known it?

A critique of industrialization will allow for the development of a new definition of problems and solutions; the critique should lead us to a new vision of the future, one in which we do not automatically assume that more and bigger, faster and automated, is better. It is time that we assess the costs of industrialization, time to recognize that the most advanced stage of industrialization has been the most toxic, resulting from the petroleum, chemical, petro-chemical, electronics, and aerospace industries, as well as urbanization. The post–World War II economies of the East and West alike ushered in the nuclear age, resulting in Chernobyl, Three Mile Island, Times Beach, Love Canal, and Bhopal.

Cynthia Hamilton is a political scientist, social activist, and the author of several articles on social justice and civil rights. Dr. Hamilton has been teaching for twenty years, and is now the director of African and African-American Studies at the University of Rhode Island.

This is not meant to imply that industrial development has no positive social value or that its benefits have not been great. But the costs may include our common future.

Critique of Industrialization

Socialist and capitalist economies alike have operated on a similar fallacy: Earth's resources are inexhaustible. But today there is growing official recognition that more economic growth is not sustainable, that industrial society based on excessive resource consumption and on nonrenewable resources can no longer be sustained. Even the authors of the theory of unlimited industrial growth and development have begun to modify their positions. In 1968 scientists, educators, industrialists, and others representing over ten countries gathered for the Club of Rome's Project on the Predicament of Mankind. Their purpose was to discuss "the present and future predicament of man." Their report, *The Limits to Growth*, identified four important points regarding the effects of man's activities on the natural environment:

1. The few kinds of pollution that have been measured over time seem to be increasing exponentially.
2. We have almost no knowledge about what the upper limits of these pollution growth curves may be.
3. The presence of natural delays in ecological processes increases the probability of underestimating the control measures necessary, and therefore of inadvertently reaching those upper limits.
4. Many pollutants are globally distributed; their harmful effects appear long distances from their points of generation. (Meadows, 1972: 23–24)

This information and other details coming from the United Nations (which would sponsor a Conference on Human Environment in 1972) were the basis for the alarm expressed by U Thant, then Secretary General of the United Nations. He remarked at the time:

> I do not wish to seem over-dramatic, but I can only conclude from the information that is available to me as Secretary General that the members of the United Nations have perhaps ten years left in which to subordinate their ancient quarrels and launch a global partnership to curb the arms race, to improve the human environment, to defuse the population explosion, and to supply the required momentum to development efforts. [If not], I very much fear that the problems I have mentioned will have reached such staggering proportions that they will be beyond our capacity to control. (Meadows et al., 1972: 17)

Walter W. Rostow, one of the architects of the unlimited growth model, wrote in his book *Getting from Here to There* (1978) that by the year 2000 we must create new energy resources based on renewable sources and we must recycle and control pollution. Such are the warnings of the proponents of unlimited growth, who hypocritically now call on the Third World to be partners in the crisis although the growth proceeded without them.

Growth policies were the embodiment of the West's insatiable appetite for natural resources and the basis for colonial land-use practices that led to today's crisis. Decisions to maximize profit encourage governments to use their best land for export crops and commodities, often resulting in basic food shortages or high-priced imports. Many of the crises that have been called "natural occurrences" may now be recognized as man-made: hunger, desertification, famine (Rostow, 1978).

While it may be conceptually incorrect to assume the earth's resources are inexhaustible, the opposite is not automatically true; the world's problem is not one of scarcity or overpopulation. According to the Institute for Food and Development Policy:

> It is not, then, the growing population that threatens to destroy the environment either here or abroad, but other forces: land monopolizers that export nonfood and luxury crops, forcing the rural majority to abuse marginal lands; colonial patterns of cash cropping that are reinforced by elites today; and a system that promotes the utilization of food-producing resources simply according to profit-seeking criteria. (Lappe and Collins, 1978: 7)

Unlimited industrial production not only consumes resources but produces dangerous by-products. The United States produces between 250 and 400 million metric tons of toxic waste per year; each individual is said to produce one ton of domestic waste per year. The Environmental Protection Agency (EPA) says that 6,000 industrial plants in the United States are producing dangerous chemicals, most if not all are in working-class residential districts with high percentages of people of color. EPA has also identified 74,000 dumpsites in the country, 32,000 worse than Love Canal (only seven or eight a year are cleaned up by Superfund).

Industrial production has of course exacerbated the problem of waste. As the controversy over dumping grows, along with knowledge of potential consequences, protest increases in the United States; less developed countries are expected to bear the burden of toxic dumping, which some label the "new imperialism." Africa has become a prime dumping ground for toxic waste, industrial and pharmaceutical residues, and even deadly radioactive material, and has received shipments from Norway, France, Italy, Belgium, Luxembourg, Netherlands, Germany, Canada, and the United States. South America and Central America, as well as the Caribbean, have had U.S. states and the federal government as clients. As organized resistance raises consciousness, governments simply move the problem. At the same time, banks are anxious to acquire equity in Third World debtor countries and have initiated "debt for nature swaps" (in which debts are reduced in exchange for unspoiled land). Like communities of color at home, the Third World is offered economic incentives in exchange for the unknown future of hazardous waste.

Our legal and political system protects those who destroy our future; in the name of private property, corporations are allowed to pollute the air, water, and soil we all share. In the name of progress and development, they consume vital resources and transform harmless, often safe elements into toxic by-products and waste. There are deadly social by-products to this century's adherence to unlimited growth: structural inflation, structural unemployment, depletion of resources, and destruction of the environment are now constants, not externalities. In the words of Herbert Marcuse, "Intensified progress seems to be bound up with intensified unfreedom" (Marcuse, 1961: 4).

> Concentration camps, mass exterminations, world wars, and atom
> bombs are no "relapse into barbarism," but the unrepressed implemen-
> tation of the achievements of modern science, technology, and domina-
> tion." (Marcuse, 1961: 4)

Philosophical and policy alternatives must rise against this backdrop. We need a reconceptualization of the problem of growth; a cultural revolution which would include a decentralization of empowerment, allowing for new forms of political participation before totalitarian measures are imposed to control the crisis of resource scarcity. The political premises of liberalism and conservatism are largely responsible for today's crisis. The elements of Western liberalism and conserva-tism—that is, notions of individualism, private property, and the free market—provide the philosophical structure for the model of industrial democracy that dominates modern thought and society. The industrial revolution also gave rise to Marxism, which ironically chronicled the inequities and irrationalities of capital-ism while accepting industrial development and the domination of nature by man with machines as a requirement for the evolution of communism. Applied Marxism has taken a place alongside liberalism and conservatism in its defense of industrial growth and development. Even liberal policies that emphasize fairness, opportunity for all, and state regulation of outcomes are predicated on the promise of growth.

The greatest defense of corporations most active in the destruction of the environment is the liberal/conservative tenet of private property. The fact is we have a legal, cultural, and economic system that has promoted the good of one over that of many. The corporations' victorious achievement of legal "personhood" has therefore allowed them to place their narrow profit concerns above those of community. Our only hope is to break categorically with thought that excludes community, nature, and virtue (Robertson, 1983).

To halt this self-destructive march of industrial growth and development, citizen action is necessary. But it must be guided by a critical approach to community development and industrial production. It must be action that can transcend isolated individual crises and confront the national consequences of corporate industrial behavior. So far, environmental activists and thinkers have been slow to develop a theory of political action or community development because of their focus on instrumentalities: rules, bureaucracy, and administration (in the tradition of liberal and conservative thought). What is needed is an economic democracy that accepts people making decisions about work and the work environment, the arena with the greatest impact on our daily lives. In the area of policy, the macroeconomic approach should be replaced by decentralized, local, and regional approaches to development. In particular we must recognize that cities have become the center of injustice as a result of current development models, and therefore alternatives should embrace multiple needs at this level. According to the World Commission on Environment and Development (WCED), "The future will be predominantly urban, and the most immediate environmental concerns of most people will be urban ones" (WCED, 1987: 225).

The connection between the urban crisis and the environmental crisis was further developed at commission hearings in 1986, where it was stated:

> Large cities by definition are centralized, man-made environments that depend mainly on food, water, energy, and other goods from outside. Smaller cities, by contrast, can be the heart of community-based development and provide services to the surrounding countryside.

> Given the importance of cities, special efforts and safeguards are needed to ensure that the resources they demand are produced sustainably and that urban dwellers participate in decisions affecting their lives. Residential areas are likely to be more habitable if they are governed as individual neighborhoods with direct local participation. To the extent that energy and other needs can be met on a local basis, both the city and surrounding areas will be better off. (WCED, 1987: 243)

New planning must be undertaken with the assistance of multiple disciplines and neighborhood empowerment. In the area of technological alternatives, we must focus our attention on renewable resource methods (like solar energy and recycling) over nuclear energy.

Economic democracy must recognize class interests in Western and developing societies. Alternatives require us to acknowledge the political intentions and consequences of growth and development strategies, e.g., those which have destroyed urban working-class communities. This approach necessitates that we reject an assessment of development as simple technological advance and thereby ethically neutral.

Philosophically a new social contract is necessary between citizens and the state, as well as between citizens and their representatives. The dominating presence of transnationals in communities requires this. These corporations have used special interest processes to influence political officials and thereby government decisions. The consequence is that present political leadership is completely unresponsive to communities. Before accountability can be assured, new leadership and new forms of participation will be necessary, e.g., if we reform existing models that would mean making the composition of city councils more inclusive, creating smaller districts, reinstituting district-wide elections. Multiple decision-making units (like neighborhood councils) are needed to regulate development and to ensure citizen input on growth decisions. Centralized units of political decision making, as well as centralized planning methods, must be replaced by decentralized units. This is the essence of what Henderson means by "thinking globally and acting locally" (Henderson, 1981: 355).

If we are to develop a more complete definition of social justice and democracy, we must transcend the limitations of private property, we must recognize environmental rights as human rights, and we must embrace the idea of community activism in the name of the common good. Liberal and conservative political philosophies have served only to justify industrial development and thereby individual rights.

Community Economic Development

The approach to growth and development in the United States demonstrates a lack of concern for communities. In fact workers and communities are among the victims rather than beneficiaries of this process. This is particularly true for black and Hispanic communities, and should force us to reconsider values and priorities.

The principles of sustainability and democracy, and the consideration of scale, should guide the development of an alternative approach, one that focuses on community economic development, on use rather than exchange, and on the creation of employment rather than consumption. Community economic development strategies, up to this point, have been focused externally; much like development strategies in the developing world, the emphasis is on production for global (or national rather than local) markets for consumption at high prices. Driven by the profit motive of existing manufacturing, even government policy has emphasized "tax breaks" over job creation—e.g., enterprise zones and community representation—and thereby has marginalized community concerns (for wages, employment, and safe, clean neighborhoods).

What we need is development strategies that place community needs first. This means we must begin by producing for community needs first. The emphasis must be on the reinvestment in the community to preserve neighborhoods, family, culture, and hope.

Producing for community needs does not mean that items may not be useful to, and therefore sold on, a larger scale. Some examples may include the manufacture of environmentally benign, prefabricated housing materials that could be purchased by individuals and schools in low-income communities, but also be sold on national and international markets, and thereby generate a greater number of jobs.

In its study, "Reconstructing Los Angeles from the Bottom Up," the Labor/ Community Strategy Center offers additional suggestions for community-based manufacturing for national and international markets. For example, "low emissivity coating, which doubles the thermal retention of windows (where about 25% of the heat from homes is lost)" (Labor/Community Strategy Center, 1993: 23).

The emphasis on community economic development does not mean that large national and multinational corporations are "off the hook." Mechanisms must be created to make and keep them socially responsible. The first step for many will be developing new products and new production processes; retrofitting existing industries to meet stricter environmental standards; and producing with a minimum of waste and toxic by-products.

Government must assert a more aggressive regulatory role. This means reversing a decade of deregulation based on "free market" ideology. Government must not be allowed to relinquish its role as employer. This is particularly important for people of color, who have found more and better employment in the public rather than the private sector.

Conclusion

> In general, industries and industrial operations should be encouraged that are more efficient in terms of resource use, that generate less pollution and waste, that are based on the use of renewable resources, and that minimize irreversible adverse impacts on human health and the environment. . . .(WCED, 1987: 213)

> New technologies in communications, information, and process control allow the establishment of small-scale, decentralized, widely dispersed industries, thus reducing levels of pollution and other impacts on the local environment. (WCED, 1987: 215)

A new industrial policy must begin with a new vision, one that internalizes the costs of industrialization as we have known it and embraces the standards of sustainability: use of renewable sources of energy and raw materials. Products and the processes used in manufacturing " must not generate chemicals that poison the air, water, or earth—or damage public health" (Labor/Community Strategy Center, 1993: 10).

A new industrial policy must have a micro focus that would not ignore global and national concerns and needs. No longer is it acceptable to sacrifice workers, communities, and their social health for profit.

Government must retain and assert a regulatory role that would help to keep industry socially responsible, and also ensure that basic social needs such as education and health care are met. In the past decade social needs have been sacrificed to private profit. We have seen low-income neighborhoods and housing disappear, replaced by any development that increases the value of property and moves poor people farther away from the city's new and transforming corporate center. We have seen low-income housing eliminated while the number of homeless increased; we have seen factories move, close down, and in some cases be bulldozed while hundreds of thousands of workers are dismissed without warning; we have seen wages decrease as the economy moves from heavy manufacturing to service. New production is necessary for job creation and must be directed by consideration for use value rather than merely exchange. We must begin to see some reconsideration of scale as we move from centralized authority to a more decentralized and participatory model. Planning must replace the ideological cry for market-driven solutions. Planning will allow regional integration and solutions, and facilitate the ties between local and global solutions.

This new approach should bring us closer to a much needed, revised social contract, one in which government and citizen are equal partners, one in which corporations no longer have complete control of natural, political, or other resources.

9

Environmental Equity and Economic Policy: Expanding the Agenda of Reform

Robert M. Wolcott, William Drayton, and Jamal Kadri

[We propose] the imposition of a general energy or fuels tax, as well as the elimination of a diverse set of existing federal subsidies that serve to increase the utilization of non-labor inputs in the production process. The objective of these elements is to remove distortional subsidies which discriminate against human capital, to reduce externalities associated with excessive energy and materials use, to generate substantial new federal revenues, and to reduce the regressiveness of federal tax and resource management policy.

Introduction

The environmental equity movement has registered substantial gains in the brief course of its ascent to the center stage of environmental policy. It has shattered the myth of dichotomy between social justice and environmental risk management. It has set forth an institutional, analytic, and political agenda. It has firmly, yet affirmatively, engaged the nation's political and administrative leadership, and it has demonstrated its ability to marshal the resources of an immense array of organizations and communities to advance an agenda of enlightened reform.

Robert M. Wolcott is currently director of the Water and Agriculture Policy Division at the U.S. Environmental Protection Agency. He initiated and chaired the EPA Environmental Equity Workgroup and coauthored the EPA's June 1992 report, Environmental Equity: Reducing Risk for All Communities.

William Drayton is president and founder of Ashoka: Innovators for the Public, a foundation dedicated to supporting innovative, public-interest-oriented entrepreneurship in the developing world. He previously served as assistant administrator for policy, resources, and management at EPA from 1977 to 1981. Prior to that he was professor of law at Stanford University.

Jamal Kadri is currently a policy analyst with EPA's Water and Agriculture Policy Division. Mr. Kadri was previously a water quality specialist with Save the Bay in Providence, Rhode Island, and has worked for the Oregon Legislative Assembly, the Northwest Power Planning Council, and Greenpeace.

The dominant focus of the movement to date has been upon the policies and programs of regulatory agencies. A particular emphasis has been placed upon the siting of hazardous waste treatment and disposal facilities and the cleanup of contaminated sites. Emphasis has also been placed upon issues of chemical residues in fish, farm worker safety, toxic air and water discharges, and lead exposures. Focus upon this set of issues is likely to yield increased attention to these concerns by state and federal environmental regulatory agencies, as well as local authorities and private firms. EPA regional and headquarters program offices have developed environmental justice plans; an environmental justice office has been established within EPA headquarters; and environmental justice has been identified as a central theme of Administrator Carol Browner.

The prospect of further advancements is excellent. As EPA and its delegated states develop and begin to deliver on their equity commitments, we can expect greater regulatory attention to highly exposed populations, more research on multiple/synergistic pollutant exposure, greater environmental education resources for minority communities, and more cohesion between environmental managers and social justice advocates. The effects of such reform will include reduced toxic exposures, improved community health, and an enhanced quality of life for minority and low-income populations.

As the movement surveys and assesses its accomplishments it must also constantly strive to expand and diversify. It must consider and test additional avenues of reform, focusing on those with the greatest likelihood of substantial and long-lasting gains measurable in both economic and environmental terms. One such prospect is federal tax policy related to labor supply and earnings, energy use, materials consumption, and physical capital utilization. In addition, federal expenditure policy regarding services that support the supply of human capital, such as education, day care, and health care, are critically relevant. We do not mean to imply that such attention could or should substitute for the current focus; instead we argue that such attention would complement and reinforce the pursuits under way.

At first glance the convergence between federal tax and expenditure policies and environmental risks to minority and low-income communities is modest to nonexistent. The federal government is unable to effectively tax lead in blood or lead in soils or paint. Contaminated waste sites are clear and present in the here and now, not ephemeral imaginings of tax policy analysts. Pesticide exposures need to be strictly limited, not subjectively juggled by the facile hands of Treasury Department tax policy experts.

Despite these cautions and caveats, it does not follow that economic policy—and tax policy in particular—ought not function as a critical supplement to the established equity agenda. Price and tax signals that increase the cost of the most polluting factors of production, as well as environmentally inferior consumer goods, will support pollution prevention and bring about long-run systems change.

Further, these benefits can be magnified and reinforced when policy shifts result in an increase in employment, real wages, and distributional equity.

Context

In any modern economy, the factors of labor, capital, energy, and materials are combined to produce goods and services in response to expressed demands by consumers. The relative prices and productivity of each factor determine the specific combination of such factors that producers employ to produce goods and services. In like manner, income and the relative prices and utility of consumer goods determine what level and type of goods and services consumers purchase. Such are the elements of microeconomics to which most of us have been exposed. The level and mix of productive factors employed by producers, and the amount and composition of goods consumers demand, have a major effect on the level and distribution of environmental damages, and ultimately on the equity with which such damages are borne by our society. The relative prices and availability of such goods and factors are likely in fact to have a far greater effect on aggregate environmental damages and the distribution of these damages than on the immediate decisions of local, state, and federal regulatory authorities. As a result, tax policy pertaining to labor supply, energy consumption, resource use and extraction, and pollution itself is fertile ground for the environmental justice movement.

In the remainder of this chapter we will describe a federal tax and expenditure policy agenda that we encourage the equity community to consider. We argue that, at a minimum, this agenda is a "no regrets" package, i.e., it would at least be directionally correct at minimal cost and, more likely, constitute a massive leap forward in reducing exposures and risk for all persons. It is, in fact, the commitment to egalitarianism in risk reduction that has yielded the emphasis upon "justice," as distinct from "equity," wherein the latter is asserted by some to represent an approach to reallocating baseline risks, while "justice" connotes a dedication to a progressive yet inexorable reduction in exposures for all communities. This broad spectrum approach, absent semantic nuance, is critical to the long-run success of the movement. Success will require a broad political and economic base, drawing on members of all classes, races, regions, and religions.

We will first briefly present our proposed program of reform and then proceed to evaluate each element in turn.

The program consists of six interrelated elements:

- removal of all existing federal taxes directly placed on labor earnings, principally FICA and FUTA. Social security, unemployment, and workers compensation programs would be funded from general revenues in the future on a five-year phase-in basis

- partial recoupment of revenue losses associated with the above phase-out with a broad-based energy tax or fuels tax

- establishment of federally supported programs to enable higher levels of labor force participation, particularly among minority and low-income populations. These would include, but not be limited to, day care/child development centers, targeted individualized education/tutoring and home health care services

- adoption of a broad spectrum of fees and taxes related to pollution-based externalities. These would address toxic discharges to the environment and include, among many others, fees on motor vehicle, building, and appliance sales based on their energy efficiency

- elimination of a wide array of federal tax expenditures and related subsidies that artificially inflate the price of human capital in relation to physical capital, energy, and materials; these could include investment tax credits, accelerated depreciation of capital, depletion allowances, and sale and lease policies on federally owned resources

- institution of a federal cost share program to establish community environmental management districts (CEMDs).

The premise of this proposed program is that federal tax and expenditure policies have substantially distorted the price of labor in relation to other factors of production. The effect of this distortion is a national economic production base that is substantially more energy and materials intensive than it needs to be, as well as less progressive in terms of the distribution of returns to those supplying these factors.

The secondary effects of these primary economic impacts include:

- higher unemployment
- reduced job base
- lower real wages
- increased aggregate environmental damage
- higher poverty rates
- greater inequality of income and wealth
- greater depletion rates of finite natural resources
- greater class and general social dissonance
- foregone growth potential owing to undervitalized human capital
- increased energy dependence on foreign nations

Elimination of Payroll Taxes

The establishment of the Social Security system by the Roosevelt administration in 1936 was a grand stroke of social policy that elevated nearly a third of the nation's elderly from poverty to economic dignity and independence. It will forever stand as the showcase social program of the New Deal.

An unfortunate legacy of this accomplishment is a highly regressive and distortional tax borne solely by those supplying their human labor to our modern 1990s economy. Although originally set at less than 2 percent, the payroll tax that generates the revenues to support the fiscal needs of our elderly now exacts 15.7 percent of the relevant national earnings base and is slated to rise to nearly 18 percent. This rate is split evenly between employee and employer on a flat tax basis capped at annual earnings of up to $58,000. While envisioned and characterized as an insurance vehicle, the system has evolved as a broad-scale income maintenance program for the aged, in many cases bearing little relationship to an individually or even generationally funded mechanism. The maintenance of the pretext that Social Security is a form of insurance is particularly desirable from a political perspective for maintaining the integrity of the disbursement system, yet the regressive tax baggage is very costly in terms of distributional equity and environmental residuals.

The FICA and FUTA taxes, but especially FICA, are highly regressive. We must consider alternative revenue options for maintaining if not enhancing the Social Security system. Payroll taxes artificially raise the price of labor vis á vis other productive factors, and they extract a noteworthy fraction of workers' gross earnings. Such general welfare ought to be the object of general revenue allocation, not a single factor tithe. FICA and FUTA collectively yielded just over $340 billion in 1992, more than one third of gross federal receipts. The effect of these taxes has been to tilt an already moderately regressive federal tax structure and render it further regressive. In addition it has raised the price of labor (up to the $58,000 per annum ceiling) by 4 to 7 percent, depending on what one assumes regarding the actual after-tax worker/employer split of the employer share of the tax. Assuming standard elasticities of supply and demand for labor, this burden exerts a dampening effect of up to four million jobs and a commensurate, i.e., 2 to 4 percent, restraint on real wage levels, as distinct from a general revenue financing of this amalgam of social security programs.

The significance of these effects for those concerned with environmental equity is obvious. Reduced employment opportunities, particularly for entry level jobs, which are most impacted by the FICA/FUTA cost margin, result in poverty and alienation, and thus to political and institutional powerlessness. Persons and communities with little wealth are less able to force accountability of regulatory agencies and private firms, and less able to inform and lead the process. Poverty and its blood brother, racism, yield the result described in the all too familiar adage: waste flows to the lowest common social denominator.

An additional perverse effect of labor-borne taxes is the distortional inflation of labor prices in relation to physical capital, energy, and materials. In aggregate production functions, labor serves as a relative substitute for energy and materials and as a complement to physical capital. The effect of an arbitrary price increase of labor is to shift to a more energy- and material-intensive form of production (and thereby consumption). The effect of this shift is a relatively greater reliance upon energy inputs. This is noteworthy because excess energy consumption yields a large fraction of the nation's total residual flow and ultimately environmental damage. Further, the increment in energy use associated with FICA-inflated labor prices is both substantial and, like many other pollutant forms, disproportionately imposed upon low-income/minority communities. Examples include power plant emissions and related waste, coal mining and hauling near Native American communities, particulate emissions from motor vehicles, and petrochemical-related emissions in the multiple "cancer alleys" of the United States.

Getting the Price Right for Energy and Resources

Two related elements of our proposal are intended to directly reinforce the effect of removing payroll taxes. They are the imposition of a general energy or fuels tax, as well as the elimination of a diverse set of existing federal subsidies that serve to increase the utilization of nonlabor inputs in the production process. The objective of these elements is to remove distortional subsidies that discriminate against human capital, to reduce externalities associated with excessive energy and materials use, to generate substantial new federal revenues, and to reduce the regressiveness of federal tax and resource management policy. The net increase in revenues would be limited due to concerns about dampening near-term growth in the economy, although they must be sufficient to fund several key programs that would unshackle many persons to participate in the labor force in response to the relative factor-price-induced increase in labor demand.

There has been extensive discussion and debate of late regarding the merits and feasibility of various forms of energy taxation. President Clinton offered a modest, broad-based option in the form of a BTU tax. Predictable foes reacted and the proposal was ditched. An alternative option, a fuels tax at an even lower level, has surfaced. Passage of even this modest tax appears problematic.

Minority and low-income communities have been enticed to publicly oppose energy taxes because of the nominally regressive nature of excise taxes generally, and because of the extreme dependence of some communities on high relative amounts of energy use for basic subsistence. As a result the political leadership of minority/low-income communities has generally abstained and selectively opposed these measures. We believe this is a serious mistake. For all the reasons we note above, energy price increases, and attendant energy conservation, in tandem with a payroll tax phase down, would be beneficial to these communities. Health and ecological costs and risks would decline, real wages would increase, employment (particularly at the low- to moderate-skill level) would increase, and economic growth would expand. These beneficial effects, particularly in the mid to long run, would vastly exceed the near-term real-income effects of the energy price rise. In addition, the administration's proposal offsets these effects in the near term through adjustments to the earned income credit. Thus, if fully implemented, this package, or others akin to it, would be win/wins for minority and low-income communities.

In addition to raising the price of energy, immense gains could be realized by eliminating subsidies to energy, and to nonrenewable resource extraction and use. These subsidies have been thoroughly assessed elsewhere (see *Reducing the Deficit: Spending and Revenue Options*, Congressional Budget Office, February, 1993). They are estimated to cost the federal treasury in excess of $50 billion annually and to distort factor prices leading to the same type of misallocation in the economic base cited above. The subsidies include those related to water prices and allocations, minerals, timber and mineral sale-and-lease policies, minerals-depletion allowances, and commodity-transport policies, e.g. coal-slung pipelines in the Southwest.

Our proposal offers the added political benefit of constituting a tax shift, not a tax increase. The proposal is not intended to reduce the deficit. But by not dampening growth, it could increase the efficiency of the economy by reducing highly distortional taxes and replacing those revenues with efficient taxes.

Liberating Millions to Earn a Living

A high demand for a moderate educational attainment will free more people to participate in the expanding service sector. These service sectors include day care, individualized education (i.e., tutoring), and home health care. Increased availability of high-quality, affordable day care would free many persons to obtain full- or part-time employment, and thereby income and political power. Affordable individualized education would rapidly and efficiently prepare many low- to moderate-skill persons to secure employment and to serve as more valuable and independent members of their community.

In the face of high health care costs and the limited ability of many to secure health care insurance, many persons who must provided care for the infirm and elderly are prevented from active, income-generating employment. The efficient expansion of the home health care sector, available through means-tested prices, would liberate many to obtain income and experience. Further, the sector itself is fertile ground for employment across a broad spectrum of skills and experience.

Each of these sectors, in fact, offers multiple skill level employment opportunities while addressing blockages in the labor supply pipeline. Each affords opportunities for minority and low-income communities to become more aware of, and better able to respond to, environmental and public health risks. Home health care networks could be invaluable for monitoring health status and trends, and sharing perspectives across communities. Day-care centers could serve this same function, as well as provide detection and education, regarding exposure avoidance and treatment. Individualized education/tutoring services for basic skills, while less directly relevant to community environmental risk, could better prepare people to respond more intelligently to real or potential exposure while primarily preparing them to participate more effectively and independently in the economy and society.

A final element of our proposal is more directly linked to environmental equity concerns. It reflects the belief by many that local and community-based environmental institutions can play a progressive, efficient, and innovative role in the environmental risk management infrastructure. Akin to community development corporations of the 1960s and 1970s, CEMDs could be highly responsive, cost effective, and trusted institutions. They could focus on community health assessment, exposure monitoring and mapping, environmental education, and outreach, including comparative risk assessment and risk response surveys; effluent and discharge monitoring related to permit compliance; conflict resolution; brokerage of pollution prevention initiatives; and a wide array of other community environmental support services.

In the face of severe federal budget constraints, a repeat of 1960s disbursement levels and approach is unlikely, and even unwise in many cases. Instead of high fixed cost centers, the districts would be lean, cost-shared units with large contributions by volunteers and modest compensation of community-based youth and elderly. Further, many resources could be leveraged through local government, universities, YMCAs, hospitals, schools, churches, and private firms. The objectives and focus would vary from community to community, but in general the goal would be to empower communities through organization, information, education, and representation. The key to success would be explicit and enforceable accountability for objective results measured in terms of toxicity, exposure levels, fish tissue concentrations, and water quality; namely, the full range of results-based measures that reflect the quality of a community's environmental life.

In terms of funding CEMDs, we envision a federal grant program with state pass-through (the principal delivery mechanism for federal environmental programs), possibly under the environmental justice provisions of the evolving EPA/DEP cabinet legislation. The funding would be cost-share based, however, with significant fractions coming from states, local governments, foundations, and community resources, possibly of an in-kind nature. A series of pilot projects prior to full implementation would be logical, possibly in communities that have already demonstrated the will and ability to marshal resources and deliver results.

Implications

The results of adopting this agenda are very difficult to project precisely. It appears unequivocally that the effects would be at least directionally correct in terms of employment, real wages, tax system progressivity, energy and materials consumption, environmental damage, social dissonance, and community empowerment. These effects would vary greatly by region and community and over time. Based on our preliminary assessment, one can expect employment levels to increase by anywhere from two to ten million person years, depending on a wide variety of assumptions regarding level and rate of adoption, supply and demand elasticities, technical substitutability of productive factors, and economic growth rates and levels. This latter is key because constraints on economic growth induced by the misguided application of elements of this package could undermine the entire endeavor. A key is maintaining high relative levels of savings and capital formation/investment, particularly in sectors that are environmentally benign or even beneficial.

As noted at the outset, the environmental equity movement has focused its attention elsewhere in its formative period. Its attention to regulatory policy and facility siting has been predictable and logical. As the movement matures, expands, and evolves, however, it should consider a broad spectrum of complementary and potentially reinforcing agendas. Mutual pursuit of such agendas would expand the political base of the movement, add strength and resilience through sheer diversity, and thereby provide a more powerful base for combatting the forces that necessitated the formation of the movement in the first place— racism and economic injustice.

10

Minorities and Toxic Fish Consumption: Implications for Point Discharge Policy in Michigan

Patrick West, J. Mark Fly, Robert Marans,
Frances Larkin, and Dorrie Rosenblatt

If we are to achieve fish consumption standards more protective of minorities on par with the states of Minnesota and New York, we'll have to fight vigorously here in Michigan and in other states. Nothing comes easy in the realm of environmental justice.

The 1991–92 Michigan Sport Anglers Fish Consumption Study: Introduction and Policy Context

The primary purpose of this study was to test the fish consumption assumptions in Michigan's Rule 1057, which regulates "point discharge" (e.g., from a factory waste pipe) of toxic chemicals into Michigan surface waters, including the Michigan Great Lakes and Michigan rivers that empty into the Michigan Great

Patrick West is an associate professor of natural resources/environmental sociology at the University of Michigan School of Natural Resources and the Samuel T. Dana Professor of Outdoor Recreation. His specific research foci include natural resources and Native Americans, and urban outdoor recreation and minorities.

J. Mark Fly is an assistant professor of outdoor recreation at the University of Wisconsin, Madison. Dr. Fly has research interests in outdoor recreation and reverse migration and in toxic fish consumption and fish consumption advisories in relation to minorities and the elderly.

Robert Marans is a professor in the Urban Planning Program and a research scientist at the Institute for Social Research at the University of Michigan. His research interests include Great Lakes issues, outdoor recreation and quality of life, minorities and urban recreation, and toxic fish consumption related to minorities and the elderly.

Frances Larkin is a professor of public health at the University of Michigan School of Public Health. Her general research interests are in dietary assessment methodology related to nutrition and food consumption.

Dorrie Rosenblatt is an assistant professor of internal medicine in the University of Michigan School of Medicine and an assistant research scientist in the University of Michigan's Institute of Gerontology.

Lakes. The research project covered a full year and included both sport fish consumption and total fish consumption.

Fish consumption patterns are an important component used in setting water quality standards in Michigan under the state's Rule 1057. While the whole formula of Rule 1057 is very complex, the fish consumption component is fairly easy to comprehend. The greater the fish consumption that is assumed in Rule 1057, the fewer toxic chemicals are permitted to be discharged into Michigan surface waters. If the fish consumption assumption is too low (i.e., the assumption is lower than actual consumption by Michigan sport fishermen), then high fish consumers may be exposed to excessive amounts of chemicals and their health may be at greater risk. Thus it is important to conduct careful studies to determine the levels of fish consumption of both average fish consumers and those who consume over the mean.

The current fish consumption assumption used in Rule 1057 is 6.5 grams per person per day. Many people have questioned the validity of this figure. Studies in surrounding states and in Canadian provinces were showing sport fish consumption 15–20 grams/person/day; with commercial fish added in, the total ranged from 25 to 30 grams/person/day. Our initial study in Michigan of just half the year (excluding the main summer fishing season) indicated total consumption to be 16.1 grams/person/day for the off season alone (adjusted for nonresponse bias). A full year-round study was badly needed for Michigan and was the main purpose and objective of this study.

Study results are in the same range as other recent studies in the region and indicate that the 6.5 grams/person/day assumption is much lower than it is for sport anglers in Michigan. Total average fish consumption for licensed anglers is 24.4 grams/person/day, while sport fish consumption alone is 14.5 grams/person/day (both figures adjusted for nonresponse bias). The question is also raised as to whether the average fish consumption is the most appropriate figure to use. Roughly speaking, if it is accurate, it protects about half the sport fishermen, but those that consume over the average are left vulnerable. This is why Minnesota and New York use what is called the "80th or 95th percentile figures" in their water quality standards. This means that about 80% of the fishermen are under the standard set, thus protecting all but the highest fish consumers. In its standards Minnesota uses about 30 grams/person/day as the 80th percentile standard. Our data for Michigan show that the 80th percentile for sport-caught fish in Michigan is 30 grams/person/day, and for total fish consumption it is 40.8 grams/person/day. The importance of protecting those persons who eat more than the average is obvious, but the argument is further bolstered when it is recognized that lower-income anglers and minorities are key subgroups that eat more fish on average than other subgroups in the population. The methodology of the current study, including basic mean and 80th percentile figures and the results related to minorities, are presented below followed by policy recommendations.

Data and Method

Sampling Design

A "stratified random sample" was drawn from fish license records from the DNR fisheries division by the University of Michigan's Institute for Social Research (ISR). The sample was drawn from a data tape of the passbook file of Michigan licensed anglers. The main bases for stratifying the sample were type of license and geographic residence as indicated by zip codes. A total of 7,000 licensed anglers were selected in the initial sample. Full details of the sampling rationale and procedure are shown in Appendix C of the final report to the Great Lakes Protection Fund (West et al., 1993).

Recall Accuracy and Cohort Structure of the Sample

Very accurate recall of fish consumption is essential for use in setting standards. Year-long recall ("What did you eat this last year") is woefully inaccurate. Short-term recall periods must therefore be used. In our previous study it was determined that a seven-day recall would be optimal (West et al., 1989a, pp. 15–20 and Appendix F to that report). We found that this worked well both in pretests and in the full study, and so we adopted this procedure for our second study in Michigan. Because a seven-day recall period does not give full year coverage, the sample had to be staggered in cohorts to get full year coverage. There were 25 cohorts derived from a random division of the full sample by computer at ISR. The cohort sampling plan is shown in Appendix D of West et al. (1993). This structure meant we needed to gather data over a full year, sending out new cohort waves every two weeks. However, this was necessary to have both short-term recall and full year coverage to capture fluctuations in fish eating over a full year cycle.

The Mail Survey Design

Given budget limitations a mail survey was necessary to get a large enough sample both for dividing into cohorts and for statistical analysis. A mail survey design also has the advantage of being able to give key visual aids to respondents to help them fill out the survey. A standard mail survey design was used following the Dillman method. This consisted of an initial survey with a cover letter, a second-wave post card, third-wave survey, and fourth-wave post card. We could not afford the fifth-wave call back we had used in the first survey because we had to put limited resources into gaining a year-round cohort sample. We faced this dilemma because our initial budget of $100,000 was reduced to $50,000. We compensated for this by simplifying the survey in several places to make it easier for the respondents to fill out and return the survey.

The survey itself was a modification of our original TSCC survey (West et al., 1989a; 1992). We pretested the survey changes, but did not need to do so as extensively as the first survey, which had been heavily pretested. As a result of the pretest some changes were made to improve the survey design.

Visual Aids and the Measurement of Meal Portion Size

In addition to using a seven-day recall period with staggered mailings over a year period, we enclosed two visual aids in the survey mailings to assist respondents in detailed recall. First we enclosed a high-quality map of Michigan showing all bordering Great Lakes, all rivers, and any other key features necessary to assist respondents in recalling any geographic detail that is asked for in the survey (for instance, which Department of Natural Resources zone the sport fish had been caught in). The map was professionally drawn and included major fishing rivers and streams, key river mouth lakes, and DNR region zones. The map also helped remind respondents to include only sport fish caught in Michigan waters. It was the same map we used in the prior study. It was validated there and we adopted it in this study without changes.

The second enclosure we used to help stimulate more accurate recall were two pictures of "about ½-pound " (8-oz) fish meals on a normal-sized plate (one a steak, the other a filet). People were able to respond more accurately in terms of visual size than in terms of weight or proportion of length of fish to weight. The pictures of portion sizes were seen by the respondent in relation to an average size plate, silverware, napkin, and other food items for visual reference. The pictures we used were comparable to the 8-oz fish meal pictures used and validated by Humphrey (1976, 1983) in his diary studies that compared picture reference recall with actual weight measurements of fish meal portions. We thus judged the use of his method to be as scientifically sound a recall method as could be expected of respondents.

The questionnaire booklet also contained photos of common fish species, along with a longer species list that increased visual interest and helped in recall of species-specific information. All visual enclosures are enclosed in West et al. (1993) as the respondents received them in the survey booklet (inside back cover of that report).

Measuring Fish Meal Portion Size

Respondents were asked in the survey to identify the portion size they ate at each fish meal. The enclosure pictures discussed above were of "about ½-pound" (8-oz) fish meals of different types (steak and filet). Respondents were asked to indicate whether the portion consumed at each fish meal was "more," "less," or "about the same" as that in the pictures. Asking for any finer level of detailed portion sizes estimates would not have yielded more valid data than this because people could not really make any finer distinctions than this and represent valid responses [see also Humphrey (1976; 1983), who used the same method]. For calculating average grams of fish eating, these categories had to be converted into ounce (and then gram) estimates. We estimated that for those indicating they ate more than 8 oz, this would average 10 oz (only 2 oz more than the picture size of 8 oz). If they said "Less" we assumed the average to be 3 oz less (or 5 oz). Note that while there are probably fish eaters who consume, for instance, 3 oz, these are balanced on average by those who eat 6–7-oz meals or over 10 oz. Again this methodology was derived from prior diary studies of fish consumption by Great Lakes sport fishermen in Michigan developed, pretested, and utilized in two highly regarded diary studies by Dr. Hal Humphrey of the Michigan Department of Public Health. Our choice of the 8-oz reference point in the pictures (similar to Dr. Humphrey's) was based on the prior testing of this method by Dr. Humphrey and a mutual desire to make our studies comparable for synthesis of findings.

Mail Survey Return Rate

The details of the factors included in the calculation of the return rate are discussed in Appendix F of West et al. (1993). The mail survey return rate was 46.8%. The return rate for this second study is comparable to the return rate in our initial study for TSCC, which was 47.3% (West et al., 1989a: 14). In that study we carried out a phone call-back study of nonreturn bias (West et al., 1989b). It showed that nonrespondents tended to eat less fish, but only slightly less in relation to averages found in both studies. A downward adjustment of 2.2 grams/person/day was used in the TSCC study for means only. Because the samples are similar, the surveys are similar, and the response rates are similar, we will use this same adjustment factor in this study. However, this adjustment can be applied mainly to average statistics, as the nonresponse rate study did not test for differences in nonresponse by different socio-economic groups (due to lack of funding) or for variance calculations such as the 80th percentile. However, the study demonstrates that, on average, nonresponse bias is minimal in comparison with the average fish consumption rates by sport fishermen for sport fish and total fish consumption shown below.

Data Weighting

As in our previous study (West et al. 1989a, Appendix H), we decided that the most important dimension on which to weight data was time period over the year. While we tried for an even flow of responses over the year, empirically there were variations. First, because February 1991 response rate was somewhat low due to start up of the survey, we included responses from February 1992 that were still coming in to increase the N size for weighting February. We then weighted the data for every two-week period in the year to make them roughly equal. The detailed procedures and results of this are shown in Appendix G of West et al. (1993).

Table 10.1. Mean and Variance for GPD

Fish Category	Mean GPD	Adjusted for Nonresponse (GPD)	Standard Deviation	80th Percentile (GPD)
Sport Fish Only	16.7	14.5	35.36	30
Total Fish (sport and commercial)	26.5	24.3	41.74	40.8

Results

Basic Results Relevant to Fish Consumption Assumptions in Rule 1057

Table 10.1 shows the basic means test of the relevance of the current 6.5 grams/person/day (hereafter GPD) assumption in Rule 1057 for sport fishermen. Both sport fish mean GPD's and total GPD (including sport fish and commercial fish) are shown. Commercial fish alone (including restaurant and market fish) are not shown, as this figure is the simple difference between total and sport fish. In Table 10.1, two measures of variance are shown—the standard deviation and the 80th percentile. The sport-fish-only mean GPD (adjusted for nonresponse bias) is between two and three times the current 6.5 GPD assumption in Rule 1057. Note that only the mean GPD can be adjusted for nonresponse bias; 80th percentile figures cannot be adjusted from data in the nonresponse survey (West et al., 1989b).

The 80th percentile figures in Table 10.1 can be interpreted to represent that about 80% of the respondents ate below this figure, while roughly 20% ate above this amount. The detailed tables from which these 80% figures were derived are shown in Tables 8 and 9 of West et al. (1993).

Race/Ethnicity: Bivariate Results

From our previous studies (West, 1992a, West et al., 1989a; West et al., 1992) we hypothesized that in this year-round study race/ethnicity would be a significant factor. In particular we hypothesized that minorities would have higher fish consumption rates than white anglers. Tables 10.2 and 10.3 show these relationships for sport fish and total fish consumption, respectively. The race/ethnicity variable was not broken down into individual minority groups due to low subsample sizes for some groups. But the two main minority groups were black anglers and non-reservation Native American anglers.

Table 10.2 shows that our hypothesis is confirmed for sport fish consumption. Minorities consume quite a bit more sport fish (23.2 GPD) than do whites, who consume near the average for the full sample. These differences are statistically significant. Minorities are the single highest consumers of sport fish in the bivariate analysis (West et al., 1993). A similar pattern is seen for fish consumption total, including sport and commercial fish (Table 10.3). Again the differences are statistically significant. Minorities are the only group to show a significantly higher than average total fish consumption (West et al., 1993).

In sum, it can be seen that minorities have the single greatest consumption rate above the mean of all bivariate relationships examined. As previously stated, one important reason for concern for those above the mean is that certain subgroups, such as minorities, may consume at higher than average levels. This was of critical importance to the Michigan Water Resources Commission in their response to the first negotiated agreement on fish consumption assumptions in Rule 1057. (See Appendix B, West et al., 1993.)

Table 10.2. Race/Ethnicity by GPD for Sport Fish Consumption

Race/Ethnicity	N	Mean GPD	Standard Deviation	95%	Confidence Interval
Minority	160	23.2	63.2	13.4	33.1
White	2289	16.3	32.6	14.9	17.6
Total	2450	16.7	35.4	15.3	18.1

F= 5.7, d.f.= 1, P < .05.

Table 10.3. Race/Ethnicity by GPD for Total Fish Consumption

Race/Ethnicity	N	Mean GPD	Standard Deviation	95%	Confidence Interval
Minority	160	35.9	68.6	25.3	46.7
White	2289	25.9	39.1	24.3	27.5
Total	2450	26.6	41.8	24.9	28.2

F= 8.7, d.f.= 1, P < .05.

Multivariate Results: Race/Ethnicity and Income

In the bivariate relationships between race/ethnicity and GPD, and income and GPD, significant relationships were found. Minorities and lower-income groups both had higher than average consumption of sport fish (for income results see West et al., 1993). The multivariate relationship between race/ethnicity and income by GPD for sport fish is shown in Table 10.4. There is both a strong combined and interaction effect between race/ethnicity and income. Both main effects F tests and statistical interaction are statistically significant. This implies that minority status and income interact to create the high fish consumption rate for the minority/low-income cell. The key combination is lower-income minorities. (Note: this is relatively lower income, not absolute low income, because the income cutoff point was $25,000.) Lower-income minorities had a sport fish consumption rate of 43.1 GPD. This is many times higher than the 6.5 GPD figure that has been used in standard setting in Michigan, and even exceeds the 80th percentile figure for sport fish established in this study.

The comparable table for the joint relationship between race/income and GPD for total fish consumption is shown in Table 10.5. Again both main effects and statistical interaction are statistically significant. And again the combination of minority status and low income has the highest fish consumption rate—57.9 GPD, which is the highest fish consumption figure established in this study.

Policy Recommendations for Rule 1057 in Michigan

The current fish consumption assumption in Rule 1057 that regulates point discharge of toxic pollutants into Michigan surface waters is 6.5 GPD. The findings presented above demonstrate that for the subpopulation of Michigan sport anglers, fish consumption is higher than the 6.5 figure currently in use. In this section we develop and evaluate policy options and scientific findings associated

Table 10.4. Race/Ethnicity and Income by GPD for Sport Fish Consumption

	Income	
	$24,999 or Less	$25,000 or More
Minorities	43.1 (GPD)	11.1 (GPD)
	(60)[a]	(84)
White	18.6 (GPD)	16.21 (GPD)

Main Effects: F = 6.7, d.f. = 2, P < .001
Interaction: F = 21.65, d.f. = 2, P < .001
[a]Numbers in parentheses are cell subsample sizes (*N*).

Table 10.5. Race/Ethnicity and Income by GPD for Total Fish Consumption

	Income	
	$24,999 or Less	$25,000 or More
Minorities	57.9 (GPD)	22.9 (GPD)
	(60)[a]	(84)
White	18.6 (GPD)	16.21 (GPD)
	(600)	(1451)

Main Effects: F = 4.5, d.f. = 2, P < .001
Interaction: F = 23.5, d.f. = 2, P < .001
[a]Numbers in parentheses are cell subsample sizes (*N*).

with each policy option. We also make recommendations with respect to these policy options to the state of Michigan and separately to its citizens.

From the existing policy context and the findings of this study, seven policy options were developed:

- *Policy Option 1:* Assume the average unit of consumption should be based on the population of the state of Michigan as a whole (not just sport anglers). Assume this level to be 6.5 GPD, as no state studies have been conducted on the full population. This is the no-change option.

- *Policy Option 2:* Set fish consumption assumption in Rule 1057 at average sport fish consumption level by Michigan sport fishermen, adjusted for nonresponse bias (14.5 GPD).

- *Policy Option 3:* Set fish consumption assumption in Rule 1057 at average total fish consumption level by Michigan sport fishermen, adjusted for nonresponse bias (24.3 GPD).

- *Policy Option 4:* Set fish consumption assumption in Rule 1057 at 80th percentile for Michigan sport fish only (30 GPD).

- *Policy Option 5:* Set fish consumption assumption in Rule 1057 at 80th percentile of total fish consumption by Michigan sport fishermen (40.8 GPD).

- *Policy Option 6:* Set fish consumption assumption in Rule 1057 to protect the highest consuming sport fish subgroup (lower-income minorities) and other high-consuming subgroups above the mean. This policy option would set fish consumption levels in Rule 1057 at 43.1 GPD.

- *Policy Option 7:* Set fish consumption assumption in Rule 1057 to protect the highest total fish consuming subgroup (lower-income minorities) and other fish consumers above the total mean consumption level. This policy option would set fish consumption levels in Rule 1057 at 57.9 GPD.

We will first analyze and make a policy recommendation with respect to Policy Option 1, the no-change option. It is clear to us and to many others that the current 6.5 GPD figure in Rule 1057 should be revised to be more protective of sport anglers, who are likely to consume more fish than the average Michigan resident. This is not just our opinion. At the time Rule 1057 was being negotiated, the Michigan Water Resources Commission expressed strong concern for subgroups such as sport fishermen who may consume more than the average state resident. The specific wording of the Water Resources Commission's concern is as follows from their Resolution of November 15, 1984:

> Now therefore be it resolved that the Commission strongly supports the need to undertake a study to determine the fish consumption patterns of Michigan residents *with specific attention to sub-groups particularly susceptible to risks arising from the consumption of fish.*

The full text of the Water Commission's resolution is presented in Appendix B of West et al. (1993). Clearly, the general subpopulation of sport fishermen is a major subgroup that may consume more than the average state resident does and therefore possibly be at greater risk. Secondly, virtually every state and province surrounding Michigan that has sponsored studies of fish consumption has focused on the higher-risk group of sport fishermen, rather than general population surveys (see Appendix H of West et al., 1993, which reprints Olson's summary of Midwest region fish consumption surveys). All of these studies focus on sport fishing subgroups of the general state or province populations. These studies converge on an average of around 20 grams/person/day for sport fishermen samples. Third, a recent national conference held by the United States Environmental Protection Agency (USEPA) drew together researchers from all over the country doing work on fish consumption methodologies. Virtually all focused on sport fishermen subpopulations or on subsistence fishing communities rather than on the general population. The results of this conference were synthesized in a USEPA report (U.S. Environmental Protection Agency, 1992). It would seem both the scientific and policy communities are now clearly focused on higher-risk subgroups of the population, including especially sport fishermen. New York, Wisconsin, and Minnesota have set fish consumption assumptions in their counterparts to Michigan's Rule 1057 at levels that will better protect at least the average sport fishermen (Olson, reprinted as Appendix H of West et al., 1993; Pam Shubat, personal communication, Minnesota Dept. of Public Health). Our disagreement with Policy Option 1 is thus based on far more than our own view of this issue. Not only is the health of the average sport fisherman at stake in considering this policy option, but indeed the health of the multimillion-dollar sport fishing industry in the state of Michigan. Based on our own perspectives and that of many others, we thus make the following policy recommendation:

> *Recommendation 1:*   Based on the above analysis and our own values, we recommend to the state and the people of Michigan that they abandon Policy Option 1, which has been state policy since the inception of Rule 1057. The assumption of 6.5 GPD should likewise be abandoned and be replaced by fish consumption levels that better protect sport fishermen and hence also the sport fishing industry in Michigan.

It follows that if the state adopts recommendation *1*, it should adopt *at least* minimal safeguards for the protection of the average sport angler. We view this as a minimal step the state should take, although it is not our most strongly recommended option.

> *Recommendation 2:*   At the very least the state should adopt Policy Option 2, in which an average sport fish consumption for sport anglers (adjusted for nonresponse bias) of 14.5 GPD is adopted for use in Rule 1057.

However, this minimal change in policy does not account for those who consume more than the mean or for the cumulative effects of total fish consumption. We will first consider the issue of total fish consumption as a policy option (Options 3, 5, and 7 above).

In meetings with state officials, we have asserted that the use of total fish consumption should at least be seriously considered. The state has argued strongly that fish consumption should be considered for Michigan waters only. The rationale for our disagreement with this stance is fourfold:

1. Even if the basis for the standard is fish from Michigan waters only, a sizable (but unknown) amount of commercial fish (both market and restaurant) come from Michigan surface waters, including especially the Great Lakes and species like whitefish and lake trout. Consumption of commercial fish from Michigan surface waters should be included in Michigan water-quality standards.

2. Commercial fish that come from outside the state of Michigan are also part of the total risk of fish consumption, for they too come from waters that may be contaminated with toxic chemicals, increasingly including ocean waters. There is very little monitoring and testing of commercial fish entering Michigan. Therefore, we feel that total fish consumption, including commercial fish from all sources, should be included in fish consumption assumptions in state water-quality standards. Such a standard would more adequately represent the total cumulative risk to the sport angler in Michigan.

3. The 6.5 GPD figure that has been used all these years, and that many in the MDNR still defend, derives from measures of seafood consumption that by definition derive from non–Michigan waters (see footnote 2, Chapter 1, of West et al., 1993). We do not understand how the DNR can take this stand and simultaneously deny the importance of commercial fish (and hence total fish) consumption as relevant to Rule 1057.

4. The U.S. EPA, basing itself on our TSCC study that used total fish consumption, adopted our use of the total fish consumption assumptions in its recommendations for fish consumption studies (U.S. Environmental Protection Agency, 1992) and in its new "Great Lakes Initiative," in which it recommends this approach to the states bordering the Great Lakes, including Michigan.

In view of these considerations we would recommend the inclusion of commercial fish, and hence the use of cumulative total fish consumption measures in fish consumption assumptions in Rule 1057. But the resistance to this notion in the MDNR is intense, and given the anti-regulatory climate in Michigan, this recommendation may be politically infeasible at the present time. We hope that some time in the future the logic of using total fish consumption data will become more understood and accepted by policymakers in the state. We have provided the relevant total consumption scientific data that would be needed to establish and implement such policies. Other studies in the region have done the same (see Olson, Appendix H of West et al., 1993). However, for the time being we expect the regulatory debate to revolve around policy options involving just sport fish consumption.

Whether average sport fish consumption or fish consumption above the mean should be the regulatory criterion is the final issue that must be addressed. Both alternatives stay within MDNR's preference for dealing only with sport fish caught from Michigan surface waters. Using only average fish consumption protects those who consume at or below the mean, but it does not necessarily protect the roughly half of the angling public that consumes above the mean. There is thus a very clear-cut rationale for considering options that protect those above the mean if the objective of state point discharge water-quality standards is to protect most of the sport fish consuming public, and hence also the health of the sport fishing industry in Michigan. We have presented scientific findings about levels of sport fish consumption above the mean in two ways: (1) by considering subgroups such as low-income groups or minority groups that consume more than the average to a statistically significant degree, and (2) by calculation of an 80th percentile figure. This 80th percentile figure indicates the approximate point at which 80% of anglers consume at or below this figure and roughly 20% above it. Either method, if adopted, would be more protective of those consuming above the mean.

The highest consuming subgroup of anglers is lower-income minorities with an average sport fish consumption of 43.1 GPD (Policy Option 6 above). In addition to protecting this most vulnerable group, using the total-above-mean-consumption standards, such standards would protect all other high fish consuming groups as well. While this and Option 7 represent our most ideal policy scenarios, we are realists. It would simply be politically unrealistic to hope that the state would adopt levels this high in its water-quality standards at this time. However, we feel strongly that those above the mean should be protected adequately in the regulation of point discharge of toxic chemicals regulated by Rule 1057. We therefore conclude as a more pragmatic alternative that the state should adopt Option 4, which is the 80th percentile figure for sport fish consumption. This figure will adequately protect most sport anglers above the mean, including most of both minority and non-minority anglers above the mean (total minority average sport fish consumption is 24.3 GPD). We have calculated this figure to be about 30 GPD, which is similar to standards currently in use by two other Great Lakes states— Minnesota and New York. Thus our final and most strongly recommended option is as follows:

> *Recommendation 3:*   The state of Michigan should adopt Policy Option 4, the 80th percentile figure for sport fish consumption (30 GPD) for use as its revised fish consumption assumption in Rule 1057.

We urge the MDNR to adopt this policy and encourage the environmental and civil rights communities and the people of Michigan to support this policy recommendation. The state may say that it has final authority in this matter and choose to ignore this recommendation. The state should remember, though, that it is simply the representative of the people of Michigan. We urge the state in this spirit to reopen the issue of fish consumption levels in Rule 1057, to renegotiate these levels in light of the data and findings of this report, and to weigh our recommendations with participation by all affected parties. It is our hope that out of this process the state of Michigan will adopt recommendation 3 (Option 4) and move to more adequately protect those (including the highest consuming sub-group—minorities) who consume above the average sport fish consumption levels.

It is also recommended that policies be established by EPA to sponsor fish consumption studies of subsistence consumption of on-reservation Native Americans in Michigan and elsewhere. Less is known about these groups because they do not require state fishing licenses and therefore have not been included in the mounting number of sport angler fish consumption studies (West, 1992b). This imbalance needs to be redressed so that point discharge policies sensitive to their consumption needs can be more fully established.

It is quite possible that the minimum recommendation of using average fish consumption (about 15 GPD) will be adopted by the state if for no other reason than that the EPA's Great Lakes Initiative may impose this standard on Great Lakes states, including Michigan. Moving to 30 GPD, while less than we would wish, will be strongly resisted by the state of Michigan. It will take a concerted effort to gain this level of protection for minorities and others who consume over the mean toxic-contaminated fish—an effort involving civil rights and environmental groups exerting political pressure on the state. It will not be enough to simply make this policy recommendation based in part on the findings of this study. If we are to achieve fish consumption standards more protective of minorities, and on par with the states of Minnesota and New York, we'll have to fight vigorously here in Michigan and in other states. Nothing comes easy in the realm of environmental justice. It never has and, alas, it never will.

11

Indigenous Nations: Summary of Sovereignty and Its Implications for Environmental Protection

Tom B. K. Goldtooth

In 1975, 100 percent of all federally produced uranium and four of the ten largest coal strip mines in the United States came from Indigenous lands. The Arctic National Wildlife Refuge, slated numerous times to be opened for drilling, is inhabited by Indigenous people. Eleven of fourteen county, state, and tribal governments under review for storing nuclear waste in Monitored Retrievable Storage (MRS) facilities are Indigenous communities. The single largest hydroelectric project on this continent is on Indigenous lands on James Bay, Canada. America's energy policy, which is the cornerstone of its industrial policy, is based upon Indigenous resources, and we are paying a heavy price.

Introduction

The United States is aboriginal Indigenous land. According to the oral history of many Indigenous people, the Creator of this world and the universe put the American Indian (Indigenous people) here on this continent as the caretakers of this land. To many of our tribal groups, this land of North America, including the whole Western Hemisphere, is called Turtle Island. This Turtle Island is only one portion of the whole earth, what Indigenous people call Earth Mother.

Indigenous people throughout the United States are facing environmental issues that impact all humanity thus requiring a different national perspective in our relationship to the earth. Indigenous people have been fighting for 500 years to preserve the future for our generations to come. Our resistance to the degradation of forests, prairies, rivers, deserts, mountains, arctic areas, wetlands, and lakes, and to the assaults on the survival of our people, is also the hope for all humanity in the protection of this earth.

Tom B. K. Goldtooth is an Indigenous traditional ecologist, director of the Red Lake Anishinaabeg Nation Tribal, Environmental Protection Agency, and a National Council officer, affiliated with the Indigenous Environmental Network, an alliance of Indigenous grassroots groups that are a part of the people of color environmental justice movement.

In recent years the environmental community has become more aware of Indigenous thinking as a possible way to deal with the environmental crisis we are facing. The non–Indigenous community does not always wish to admit they suppress and often trivialize the Indigenous struggle for recognition of our treaty rights and sovereignty. The Indigenous people have always worked to protect the earth, for the right to have a sustainable lifestyle, to protect their religious right to gather medicinal plants, and to have access to sacred sites and holy places. Only recently has sovereignty, as it relates to the environment, become a global discussion point (Earth Summit: UNCED, 1992).

During the First National People of Color Environmental Leadership Summit in Washington, D.C., 60 Indigenous grassroots people participated in drafting a seventeen-point *Principles of Environmental Justice*. Principle 11 states: "Environmental justice must recognize a special legal and natural relationship of Native People to the U.S. government through treaties, agreements, compacts, and covenants affirming sovereignty and self-determination" (*Principles of Environmental Justice*, 1991). In the words of an Anishinibe Ojibwe (Chippewa) treaty rights educator, "Treaties may provide us with a last line of defense against serious environmental problems facing society" (Bresette, 1992). Recognition of Indigenous treaties strengthens the sovereignty of its people.

The following is only a brief summary and is not meant to portray all the definitions, implications, and issues pertaining to the complex question of sovereignty as it relates to environmental management within Indigenous tribal nations of the United States.

Treaties

A treaty is a binding legal agreement between two or more sovereign nations. Treaties are the "supreme law of the land" (*U.S. Constitution*, Article VI), meaning that they are superior to state laws and constitutions and rank with laws passed by Congress. The United States entered into treaties with Indigenous tribal nations to end wars and to acquire access to Indigenous lands. The tribes used these treaties to retain rights such as the sovereign right of self-government, jurisdictional rights over designated Indigenous lands, and the right to fish, hunt, and gather within their lands and waters. The U.S. government's entry into treaty agreements stands as evidence that Indigenous nations were sovereign independent nations (*U.S. Constitution*, Article I).

Over 400 treaties have been signed between the United States and Indigenous nations (Institute for the Development of Indian Law, 1973). In the opinion of this author there is no doubt that the United States formally recognized the full sovereign national status and character of North American Indigenous governments. This was undoubtedly due in large part to the fact that Indigenous nations had held the balance of military power in many respects in various regions of the young American republic (Jennison and Tebbel, 1960). Indigenous nations, many of which had already been formally recognized through treaties as legitimate sovereignties by various European kingdoms, were in a better position to recognize the legitimacy of the United States than the other way around (Schaaf, 1990). Including the over 400 treaties with the United States, 800 treaties overall had been entered into with other colonial governments of Spain, Holland, France, and England during earlier centuries (Cohen, 1972: 46).

According to the U.S. legal theorist Felix Cohen, the concept of treaty making between European powers and Indigenous nations was based upon three basic assumptions:

1. That both parties to the treaty are sovereign powers.

2. That the Indian (Indigenous nation) has a transferable title of some sort to the land in question; and

3. That the acquisition of Indian lands could not safely be left to individual colonists, but must be controlled by government monopoly. (Cohen, 1971: 47)

In 1905, the Supreme Court made clear in *United States v. Winans* that Indigenous treaties were not a grant of rights from the United States to the tribes, but rather a grant from the tribes to the United States. Thus, all sovereign powers of tribes are retained unless expressly granted away by the tribe in a treaty or taken away from the tribe by a federal statute.

Sovereignty

Sovereignty is difficult to define. It cannot be seen or physically felt, but has a power that exhibits a feeling or attitude of a people. As a result, what can be seen is the exercise of sovereign powers. Sovereignty is the supreme power from which all specific political powers are derived (Kickingbird et al., 1977). Kickingbird defines sovereignty as the inherent power that causes people to band together to form a nation and govern themselves.

Webster's New Twentieth Century Dictionary of the English Language (1957), a document of Western European concepts, defines sovereignty as "supreme and independent power or authority in government as possessed or claimed by a state or community." To be sovereign is assumed to have supreme rank and is linked to European notions of a king, queen, or other monarch.

The Great Lakes Indian Fish and Wildlife Commission, a tribal natural resource group in the Great Lakes area, refers to sovereignty as a "right of self-government and self-determination, or the ability of people to make decisions for themselves." The United States and other colonial powers dealt with Indigenous nations as sovereign governments. The tribes were recognized as sovereign nations and the United States government dealt with tribes on a nation-to-nation basis.

The most basic power of a sovereign people is the power to select their own form of government. Government is the system or machinery through which a political unit or nation exercises its sovereignty (Kickingbird, 1977). Traditionally, Indigenous nations of Turtle Island were entirely autonomous and self-regulating, having developed highly complex and sophisticated governmental systems before the invasion of the European nations (Schusky, 1970). Certain governmental structures and principles of the Haudenosaunee (Iroquois) Confederacy, consisting of the Onondaga, Mohawk, Cayuga, Oneida, and Tuscarora nations, were so advanced that they were used as a model for the U.S. Constitution (Grinde, 1977).

The inherent right of tribal sovereignty was first recognized by the United States Supreme Court in the 1832 case of *Worcester v. Georgia* (1832: 519), which stated ". . . the very fact of repeated treaties with them recognizes [the Indians' right to self-government] and the settled doctrine of the law of nations is that weaker power does not surrender its independence—its right to self-government—by associating with a stronger, and taking its protection," and further declared that Indian nations "had always been considered as distinct, independent political communities, retaining their original natural rights."

However, the "plenary power doctrine" asserted by the United States claimed legislative right to limit the sovereignty of Indigenous nations. The U.S. policy of colonizing the Indigenous people and the implementation of various Constitutional and legislative policies have created a federal government position that Indigenous nations today are quasi-sovereign or domestic dependent nations. In these legislative policies, there was a baseless notion that self-sufficient Indigenous nations were somehow "dependent" upon the United States, thus forming the idea that the federal government thereby inherited a "trust responsibility" to Indigenous tribes. This led to actual control over remaining Indigenous lands (Churchill, 1992). This "trust doctrine," one of the most important principles in Indian law, was first developed by the Supreme Court in two early decisions, *Cherokee Nation v. Georgia* (1831) and *Worcester v. Georgia* (1832). "Trust" obligation continues to today. In 1977, a Senate commission expressed this obligation as follows:

> The purpose behind the "trust" doctrine is and always has been to ensure the survival and welfare of Indian tribes and people. This includes an obligation to provide those services required to protect and enhance Indian lands, resources, and self-government, and also includes those economic and social programs which are necessary to raise the standard of living and social well-being of the Indian people to a level comparable to the non-Indian society. (American Indian Policy Review Commission, 1977)

Before colonization, Indigenous nations possessed complete sovereignty. Many Indigenous people today argue that Indigenous sovereignty remains in force and regard all federal laws limiting tribal sovereignty as illegal. During 200 years of

U.S. implementation of the "trust doctrine," more aboriginal land has been taken from the Indigenous people, either by force or by paper, but in no case with Indigenous consent.

Recently, Indigenous people involved with environmental justice and treaty rights implemented Principle 10 of the *Principles of Environmental Justice* (1991) mentioned above. Principle 10 states, "Environmental justice considers governmental acts of environmental injustice a violation of international law, the Universal Declaration on Human Rights, and the United Nations Convention on Genocide." A historic International Tribunal of Indigenous People and Oppressed Nations (1992) was convened on the eve of the 500th anniversary of the Columbus invasion. In the spirit of seeking recognition of sovereignty, some Indigenous groups have appealed to the United Nations. The purpose of the tribunal was to examine the long history of international criminal activity perpetrated by the U.S. government against the Indigenous people and other people of color living in North America since 1787. Some of the *Significant Bill of Particulars*, drafted during the International Tribunal of Indigenous People and Oppressed Nations relevant to this topic, are listed below:

> Bill of Particulars 7: The Defendant (U.S.) has denied and violated the international legal right of Native American People to self-determination as recognized by the 1945 United Nations Charter, the 1966 International Covenant on Civil and Political Rights, the 1966 International Covenant on Economic, Social, and Cultural Rights, fundamental principles of customary international law, and *jus cogens*.
>
> Bill of Particulars 8: The Defendant has violated the seminal United Nations Declaration of the Granting of Independence to Colonial Countries and Territories of 1960 with respect to Native American Peoples and Territories. Pursuant thereto, the Defendant has an absolute international legal obligation to decolonize Native American Territories immediately and to transfer all powers it currently exercises there to the Native American Peoples.
>
> Bill of Particulars 10: The Defendant has deliberately and systematically permitted, aided and abetted, solicited and conspired to commit the dumping, transportation, and location of nuclear, toxic, medical, and otherwise hazardous waste materials on Native American Territories in North America and has thus created a clear and present danger to the lives, health, safety, and physical and mental well-being of Native American People in gross violation of Article 3 and Article 2(c) of the 1948 Genocide Convention, *inter alia*: "Deliberately inflicting on the group conditions of life calculated to bring about its physical destruction in whole or in part."

Even accepting the federal government's limited interpretation, sovereignty still leaves substantial powers. These powers include the authority to define membership, structure, and operation of tribal government; regulate domestic relations; settle disputes; tax; regulate business; regulate property use; administer justice; enforce laws; and manage resources (Kickingbird, 1977). It is within these powers that Indigenous governments are examining environmental inequity issues and disparate environmental protection by the federal government.

Indigenous Lands: Summary of Disproportionate Environmental Impacts

While disproportionate environmental impacts should be investigated for all groups at-risk, Indigenous people have a unique cultural and legal claim in U.S. history and cannot be treated as simply one among many ethnic or socioeconomic groups. Despite the massive disruptions and dislocations of the past five centuries, Indigenous nations remain a people tied to the land (Wenzel, 1992). Many Indigenous people have a land-based subsistence economy. Only recently has the need for developing appropriate and equitable models of comparative risk analysis been recognized.

Land has always been the issue of the original "boat people" (Europeans). The entire political system of the United States is based upon economics and ownership of the land. Those who control the land are those who control the resources. Approximately two-thirds of uranium resources, one-third of western U.S. low-sulphur coal, and 20 percent of known U.S. reserves of oil and natural gas, pristine water, and stands of unexploited old growth timber lie within U.S. Indigenous territories (LaDuke, 1992). The multinational corporations have been extracting these resources from Indigenous lands for years and want to increase and expand extraction and production leases.

In 1975, 100 percent of all federally produced uranium and four of the 10 largest coal strip mines in the United States came from Indigenous lands. The Arctic National Wildlife Refuge, slated numerous times to be opened for drilling, is inhabited by Indigenous people. Eleven of fourteen county, state, and tribal governments under review for storing nuclear waste in Monitored Retrievable Storage (MRS) facilities are Indigenous communities. The single largest hydro-electric project on this continent is on Indigenous lands on James Bay, Canada. America's energy policy, which is the cornerstone of its industrial policy, is based upon Indigenous resources, and we are paying a heavy price (LaDuke, 1992).

No comprehensive survey has been conducted of environmental conditions on Indigenous lands as a whole. Various limited surveys, however, suggest that Indigenous lands experience a broad range of problems, including surface and groundwater contamination, improper disposal of municipal solid waste, waste-water sewage disposal problems, drinking water violations, human health risks stemming from uranium tailings and other hazardous wastes, and unsafe levels of air pollution (Americans for Indian Opportunity, 1986).

Forty-one percent of reservation-based Indigenous people live below the poverty level, more than triple that of 12 percent for the general population (Bureau of Indian Affairs, 1986). Poverty is also reflected in living conditions, such as substandard housing, the majority beyond repair, and limited access to clean water and sanitation (Snipp, 1989).

Because of the poverty status in many Indigenous communities, economic blackmail is increasingly practiced by private waste companies which approach Indigenous governments with lucrative offers of huge profits to permit the siting of toxic mega-landfill and incinerator facilities on Indigenous lands.

Updated figures indicate that over 200 Indigenous communities have been approached by the waste disposal industry. Waste industry officials, knowing of the lack of Indigenous environmental infrastructure, are targeting vulnerable Indigenous communities to construct waste disposal facilities. These facilities would deal with wastestream materials ranging from toxic sludge, hazardous waste, medical and "low" level radioactive waste, solid waste, asbestos, nuclear waste, and just about anything the "not-in-my-backyards" don't want (Angel, 1992). In addition to the economic vulnerability of tribal governments, other factors waste companies consider in approaching Indigenous communities are the limited (if any) public input or review process in Indigenous communities and the very minimal permit process required through the Bureau of Indian Affairs.

Religious rights and protection of sacred sites under assault from destruction are historical issues, but they are also emerging as issues to be discussed by Congress. When we speak of Indigenous religious freedom, we are talking of protecting a belief system that is interwoven with many other issues, including issues that are currently identified as environmental—land rights, sovereignty, human rights, treaty rights, natural rights, etc. In 1988 the U.S. Supreme Court, in *Lying v. Northwest Indian Cemetery Protection Association* (1988), ruled that the freedom of religion clause in the First Amendment of the U.S. Constitution does not restrict the government's management of lands—even if certain governmental actions would infringe upon or destroy an Indigenous religion. Other examples of threats to the protection of religious freedom are:

1. Red Butte, Arizona. U.S. Forest Service plans a uranium mine in a religious area of the Havasupai Indians.

2. Badger Two Medicine, Montana. U.S. Forest Service plans to have oil and gas development in the religious area of the Blackfeet Indians.

3. Snoqualmie Falls, Washington. A waterfall that is a vision quest site and center of creation for nearby tribes is scheduled to be restricted by hydropower development.

4. Crazy Mountain, Montana. U.S. Forest Service plans oil, gas, timber, and other developments in a Crow Indian vision questing and religious area.

5. Big Horn Mountain, Wyoming. U.S. Forest Service plans timber and tourism development near the Medicine Wheel, a sacred site of the Northern Plains tribes.

6. Mount Hood, Oregon. U.S. Forest Service plans a large timber sale near Spirit Falls at Enola Hills on the slopes of Mt. Hood, which is an ancient vision questing and religious site for the Columbia River tribes.

7. Hawaii Volcanoes National Park, Hawaii. Geothermal development at sacred site. The volcano is Pele, sacred goddess.

8. Pipestone, Minnesota. Sacred pipestone being commercially exploited under federal permits (Native American Rights Fund, 1992).

As a part of its historic trust responsibility, the U.S. federal government has the obligation to enact enforceable federal policies that would protect the cultural integrity of Indigenous communities and the free exercise of Indigenous religions. Denial of Indigenous religious rights is an infringement of Indigenous sovereignty.

Whether it is in regard to the siting of waste disposal facilities on Indigenous lands or the protection against environmental degradation from other sources, the need for Indigenous nations to develop their own environmental tribal laws, codes, and regulations is of the utmost importance. In the opinion of the author, the right of Indigenous nations to determine and define environmental strategies is a fundamental right of sovereignty. Developing environmental initiatives would strengthen the ability of the community to make environmentally sound decisions concerning the management of Indigenous natural resources.

There is a need to look at federal environmental laws, their implication to Indigenous nations, the role of the Environmental Protection Agency (EPA), and jurisdictional claims.

Federal and State Jurisdiction, Sovereignty, Environmental Laws, and Indigenous Nations and Lands

This is a brief analysis of jurisdictional and sovereignty issues related to federal and state environmental authority and regulation. Pollution control is primarily a regulatory activity. Which government has regulatory powers over Indigenous territories has been a source of conflict between the federal, state, and Indigenous governments.

Federal Authority

Due to the ramifications of the "domestic dependent nation" status and the "trust doctrine" (*Cherokee Nation v. Georgia*, 1831 and *Lone Wolf v. Hitchcock*, 1903), Congress exercises its full plenary power to legislate and regulate within Indigenous territories. This federal regulatory power stems from two basic sources: (1) Congress's asserted right of plenary power over Indigenous nations allows it to enact legislation specifically affecting Indigenous nations, lands, and people; and (2) general federal legislation, on the other hand, usually is held applicable to Natives through a judicially created doctrine that Indigenous people ordinarily should not be immune from federal laws of general applicability (Royster and Fausett, 1989). Federal environmental laws will generally be interpreted to apply to Indigenous nations and people (*Blue Legs v. United States Bureau of Indian Affairs*, 1989). The *Blue Legs* case determined that the Pine Ridge Lakota government could be held liable under the Resource Conservation and Recovery Act (RCRA) for illegal disposal of municipal solid waste in a reservation open dump site.

State Authority

State jurisdiction over Indigenous lands is preempted if it interferes or is incompatible with federal and tribal interests reflected in federal law (Gover, 1992), unless the state interests at stake are sufficient to justify the assertion of state authority (*California v. Cabazon Band of Mission Indians*, 1987).

Federal courts have prohibited the application of state environmental laws to Indigenous lands (*Washington Department of Ecology v. United States EPA*, 1985). In this case, the state of Washington was not allowed to include Indigenous lands in its state permit program.

Tribe Authority

Despite various U.S. colonial governmental policies that have usurped aboriginal Indigenous sovereignty, Indigenous governments have the unquestioned power to enforce tribal laws, including environmental laws, against their own tribal members. However, the right to regulate non–Indigenous persons on Indigenous lands is limited (*Montana v. United States*, 1981). Tribes could regulate the conduct of non–Indigenous people even on fee lands when "that conduct threatens or has some direct effect on the political integrity, the economic security, or the health or welfare of the tribe" (*Montana v. United States*, 1981). There is a growing demand by Indigenous governmental leaders and Indigenous grassroots environmentalists that full tribal regulatory and enforcement authority over non–Indigenous persons residing within Indigenous territories, or nonresidential persons dumping within Indigenous territories, is necessary. Indigenous environmental laws, regulations, and enforcement capabilities are sovereign rights.

EPA Role and Policy

Like other federal agencies, the EPA has a statutory obligation to act as a trustee in its relationship with Indigenous tribal governments. It wasn't until 1984 that the EPA issued a Policy for the Administration of Environmental Programs on Indian Reservations (Environmental Protection Agency, 1984). In summary, the policy establishes a commitment to work directly with tribal governments on a one-to-one basis rather than through governmental units. The stated intention is to assist tribes in assuming regulatory and program management responsibilities for Indian lands; to encourage cooperation between tribal, state, and local governments; to resolve environmental problems of mutual concern; and further, to ensure that EPA will make grants to Indian tribes for environmental management similar to those currently available to states.

The intended EPA policy, as written, was to be very supportive of the development of Indigenous environmental management programs, but it has never been thoroughly implemented. In 1993, most Indigenous governments are over 22 years behind the states in environmental infrastructure development. EPA has consistently failed to fund tribes on an equitable basis, compared with the states. EPA has a statutory responsibility to allocate financial resources that will provide an equitable allocation between tribal governments and states.

Federal Environmental Laws

Many major federal environmental laws allow EPA to treat Indigenous nations as states and to delegate primary enforcement responsibility to the tribal nations. The following federal environmental laws have been amended.

1. Clean Water Act, 33 U.S.C. Sec. 1251-1387 (1988);
2. Safe Drinking Water Act, 42 U.S.C. Sec. 300f-300j-26 (1988);
3. Comprehensive Environmental Responses Compensation and Liability Act (CERCLA) or (Superfund), 42 U.S.C. Sec. 9601-9675 (1988);
4. Clean Air Act Amendments, 104 Stat. 2464 (1990);
5. Surface Mining Control and Reclamation Act of 1977 (SMCRA), 30 U.S.C. Sec. 1235(k) (1988).

The Resource Conservation Recovery Act (RCRA), 42 U.S.C. Sec. 6901-6991i (1988), has not been amended to allow specifically for tribal primacy. However, two federal courts have determined that RCRA applies to Indigenous lands and could be enforced against Indigenous tribes. In *Washington Department of Ecology v. United States EPA* (1985) the Ninth Circuit held that RCRA applied to Indian reservations. In *Blue Legs v. United States Bureau of Indian Affairs* (1989) the court held that RCRA applied to open dumps on the reservation and imposed liability on the Oglala Lakota tribe for RCRA violations. The court found that the tribe was subject to suit because it had the "responsibility to regulate, operate, and maintain" the dumps on the reservation stemming from the inherent sovereignty Indigenous tribes possess.

Implications for the Future

Protecting and preserving Indigenous territories are challenges facing the Clinton administration. Indigenous tribal laws and court systems must be prepared to meet the challenge because the federal government has not fulfilled its "trust" responsibility to Indigenous tribes on environmental issues.

In Wisconsin, Indigenous tribes are exercising their treaty rights to hunt, fish, and gather in an area that is a hotbed of metallic minerals and uranium mining ventures by multinational corporations. State, county, and federal governments continue to maintain a pro-development mentality. Indigenous treaties are becoming the last line of defense against serious environmental problems. Treaties guarantee Anishinibe Ojibwe access to off-reservation fish, game, and wild rice— precisely the natural resources that would be endangered by mining pollution. The Mole Lake Anishinibe Ojibwe tribe has already sued the Exxon Corporation to protect Ojibwe rice beds from the company's proposed copper mine (Chicago–Indian Treaty Rights Committee Newsletter, 1991). If treaties are weakened, non-Indigenous people would be robbed of a legal tool to protect off-reservation waterways, prairies, wetlands, mountains, deserts, arctic areas, and other ecosytems. Protection of Indigenous treaties strengthens their sovereignty. Despite the federal government's limited interpretation of their sovereignty, Indigenous sovereignty still leaves substantial tribal powers to regulate and enforce tribal authority to protect Indigenous territories. It is within these inherent powers that Indigenous governments are examining environmental inequity issues, environmental injustice, and inequitable environmental protection by the federal government.

12

Toward a Democratic Community
of Communities:
Creating a New Future
with Agriculture and Rural America

David Ostendorf and Dixon Terry

While the number of farms has been declining steadily since the 1930s, there were by the end of the 1980s fewer owners of U.S. farmland than at any other time in this century (USDA/ERS, 1991). The skewed concentration of control over the land itself has resulted in an ownership pattern that rivals that of any oligarchy: today nearly half of all the nation's farmland is held by about four percent of all farmland owners, and over 40 percent of the 833 millions acres of private farmland in 1989 was held by owners or organizations who did not themselves farm the land. (USDA/ERS, 1991)

The future of American agriculture is grim. Virtually every economic indicator points to the continuing loss of family farms and the consolidation of control over food production, processing, and distribution by a shrinking number of powerful corporate interests. By the turn of the century it is indeed likely that 50,000

David Ostendorf is an ordained minister of the United Church of Christ and director of the Center for New Community. He was the former director of PrairieFire Rural Action, a rural organization based in Des Moines, Iowa. Since 1974 he has organized throughout the rural Midwest and Plains states and has written extensively about the nation's heartland. He now directs a faith-based rural-urban initiative to revitalize congregations, communities, and democracy.

The late Dixon Terry was founder and chair of the Iowa Farm Unity Coalition. He was also co-chair of the National League of Rural Voters, director of the League of Rural Voters, and president of the National Family Farm Coalition. He was the founder or president or board member of many farm organizations, including PrairieFire Rural Action.

superfarms will account for 75 percent of all agricultural production in the United States (Office of Technology Assessment, 1986: 16). Data released by the Census Bureau in late 1994 indicated that the number of farms in the United States has now fallen to fewer than two million for the first time since before the Civil War.

Neither major political party is willing to address farm and food issues in any manner that would challenge the influence of corporate agribusiness, and even progressives on other major economic structure issues fail to analyze the key role of food production and the food manufacturing and distribution sector in the increasingly stratified U.S. economy.

We were duly warned about this future, but did not take heed. Land distribution was at the core of Jeffersonian principles of democracy, even though the axis of those principles swung through the slavery-based plantation economy of the South and the expropriation of land from indigenous people in the bloody westward expansion. Having warned of the danger of concentration of control over land, the European newcomers embraced the ruthless reality of that control to their own advantage.

Over the next two centuries, other warnings were sounded. Generations of progressive populists spanning the hundred years through the late twentieth century made significant headway, but the tide of corporate dominance and control of capital has been increasingly insurmountable. Still, the struggle has been waged and it must go on into the twenty-first century.

Dixon Terry was one of a new generation of progressive populists emerging from the harsh and deadly 1980s, when the Reagan-precipitated farm crisis was often daily fare on the nation's media menu. Born and raised in Iowa, active in the antiwar movement at Iowa State University, gifted with a keen analytical mind and an ability to bring people together, Dixon was at the center of the rural political movement that emerged from the heartland during those years. He was instrumental in forming and leading the Iowa Farm Unity Coalition, the League of Rural Voters, the National Family Farm Coalition, and PrairieFire Rural Action.

In late May of 1989, Dixon was struck and killed by lightning while baling hay on his farm. Only thirty-nine at his death, he left an extraordinary legacy of hope rooted in his own leadership and vision, and in his ability to strengthen and engage others in the political struggle in rural America.

The following speech, given by Dixon at the Save Our Soil Conference in Amsterdam in 1987, is a fine-tuned historical analysis of twentieth century U.S. agricultural policy into the middle of the Reagan–Bush era. It provides the framework for this chapter on agriculture and food policy, which concludes with an expansion and broadening of the analysis since 1987.

Soil and Water Conservation in the Age of Global Food Price Wars

Dixon Terry

Agriculture in the 1930s

This is not the first time our nation has faced a far-reaching crisis that threatened our soil and water resources. Just like the current environmental crisis in the countryside, the agricultural economic depression of the 1920s, which rolled into the cities in the 1930s, was simultaneous with a national environmental crisis.

Some modern writers often mistakenly describe the agricultural depression in the United States as being caused by the Dust Bowl era of drought, blinding sandstorms, and parched earth. In fact, the opposite was closer to the truth. Falling farm prices in the 1920s and 1930s led first to the abandonment of standard conservation practices like terracing. As the crisis worsened, farmers were forced to intensify production in hopes of making up for lower prices with greater volume. Crop rotations had to be abandoned, heavier equipment was introduced, and the centuries-old practice of allowing fields to lie fallow gave way to years of intensive cropping.

Throughout the depression decade of the 1920s, farmers brought more and more land into production to make up for low commodity prices. Total acres under cultivation in the United States reached a peak in 1931. The peak was not reached again until the early 1980s, after a period of unstable farm prices and high inflation in the 1970s led to another massive expansion in acreage. The forcing of marginal lands into production is another similarity between the Great Depression and the current one in U.S. agriculture.

Even with cost-cutting and more intensive production, many farmers could not survive the Great Depression. Literally millions of acres were abandoned—left to dry up and blow away. In some instances farms weren't abandoned, they were foreclosed on by insurance companies and other lenders who farmed these repossessed properties with an eye toward short-term, immediate returns—not the long-term protection of the land.

The battle waged by farmers of the era to restore profitability to family-farm agriculture was closely tied with the forging of a national policy to repair and restore the soil and water resources. The founding of our National Soil Conservation Service in 1936 was simultaneous with the introduction of national farm programs that restored profitability to farmers.

The farm commodity programs provided two crucial elements in the national campaign to protect our soil. First of all, the program provided a price support mechanism that kept prices at or above the cost of production, giving farmers the money they needed to buy back their land and to make the conservation investments needed. You can walk the fields of rural America and physically see the explosion of conservation investment that this era provided.

But just as important, the farm programs included strong supply-management provisions to halt the year after year of surplus production that was destroying America's soils, and which allowed farmers to de-intensify their production by restricting the amount of certain commodities that farmers could produce or sell.

These three factors—fair prices to farmers, supply management, and specific soil conservation programs funded by the government—laid the foundations for the economic recovery of farmers and the environmental recovery of the countryside. But it only lasted for 20 years.

The Expansionist Mentality

Although these farm programs were the key to survival for farmers and provided the basis for restoring our soil and water, two very powerful forces opposed these programs.

The first were the grain- and other commodity-exporting corporations that opposed the price-support programs. They wanted to pay farmers the lowest price possible to maximize their profits—even if it meant that farmers would have no money left over to maintain their soil conservation efforts.

At the same time, the agrichemical firms that sold pesticides, fertilizer, and hybrid seed opposed the supply-management programs. They believed that if farmers were controlling their production, the companies would sell fewer chemicals—which was true.

From 1953 to the early 1970s, our nation went through a very traumatic and chaotic period of agricultural policy. As farm prices were forced downward, farmers produced larger and larger crops to try to maintain their cash flow. Productivity gains were huge from improved varieties and greatly increased use of fertilizers and chemicals. Without effective supply management, huge surpluses accumulated.

Many times, as I was growing up, we would end up with so much corn that it would have to be stored on the ground, outside, all winter long. It got so bad that a huge land set-aside program—the Soil Bank—was introduced in the 1960s. The government paid farmers to idle 28 million acres of land in the program, at a considerable cost to taxpayers. But in spite of this larger conservation investment, all of this land and more—including steep slopes, wetlands, sandy prairie, vital windbreaks, and grassy areas—was pressed back into intensive production in the 1970s.

In the decade of the 1970s, federal policy shifted sharply away from a supply-management and conservation orientation to one of all-out production. An unusual confluence of world trade and weather factors in 1973 led to a brief upsurge in farm commodity prices that has never been repeated. Yet the memory of those high prices fueled a rapid mobilization among farmers for all-out production for the world market.

The agribusiness infrastructure nurtured this mentality of fence-row-to-fence-row production. The corporations, in their advertising, idolized the big farmer who expanded his farm, his production, and his investment. Banks and other lenders encouraged this investment for all-out production. Agricultural college advisors, farm media personalities, and government agencies all encouraged intensification of production and expansion of farm size.

I was working as a hired hand on my parents' dairy farm in the mid-1970s, and my wife and I were trying to borrow money to buy our own farm. But our goal of starting a traditional, moderate-sized Iowa farm went against the grain of the expansion-minded lenders. We had great difficulty in finding financing because our plans were too modest—we weren't thinking big enough.

This expansionist mentality served the deeper policy goals of the corporate input suppliers and the grain trade whose forces had come to dominate federal farm policy. But all-out production for an expanded export market proved, as it always has, to be in contradiction with price stability for farmers, who still maintained important political power. So a new farm program mechanism was developed in the 1970s—the target price system.

The Target Price System

Under this system, grain farmers were paid a direct subsidy from taxpayers on each bushel produced to make up for market prices that were set below the cost of production by low government price floors. These government payments provided grain farmers minimal income protection, but allowed the export conglomerates to pursue their world market expansion with commodities they bought at less than the cost of production.

This allowed our corporations to go into the world market and displace other exporters and local farmers from markets around the world. The U.S. share of the world market rose from 40 percent in the early 1970s to nearly 70 percent by the 1980s.

But this approach proved to be expensive in more ways than one. The Vietnam War and basic changes in the economy made federal budget deficits a growing concern. The high cost of subsidizing cheap, raw farm products for the corporations required the "target prices," which were met with subsidies, to be set too low to cover the needs of the average farmer.

Despite its aura as a "boom" decade, the 1970s saw only a very brief period of high returns for farmers. During most of the decade, farmers produced at a loss and were only kept in business by two factors that went hand in hand—increasing debt on inflating land values and intensifying production.

Although farmers lost money on their crops, they were able to borrow more and more against their land, both to cover losses and intensify operations in hope of boosting production enough to recover from the falling prices. In slightly over a decade, farm debt rose from $30 billion to $230 billion. Massive land inflation and the willingness of lenders to lend money on the inflated value gave a false sense of optimism to this world-market-oriented policy.

I was working for my father in the mid-1970s on the farm where I had grown up. This was in the heart of some of the most level and productive farmland in the United States. My wife and I wanted to buy our own farm, but general inflation and the expansionist mentality had already caused land prices in that price region to more than double.

So we moved to southern Iowa, where the land was more hilly, less productive, and less expensive—but well-suited to dairy farming. The dairy industry was different from the rest of agriculture then in that milk price supports were still relatively high. The return on dairying was good in the 1970s.

We finally found financing for our 160-acre, 20-cow farm through the government lending agency, the Farmers Home Administration, but only with a lot of arguing. Most lenders considered our farm plan to be too conservative, although it was quite typical of Iowa dairy farms up until that period.

With high milk prices and low feed grain prices, the 1970s saw much expansion of dairy production in hilly southern Iowa. Large barns housing hundreds of cows were built around the region. Many of those barns sit empty today. Their bankrupt owners were victims of the cheap grain policy that encouraged over-production of milk. The burdensome dairy surpluses that led the Reagan administration to drastically cut milk prices were directly attributable to a glut of cheap feed.

The livestock industry as a whole has suffered severely in the United States from cheap feed grains. As farmers have expanded in livestock to increase their return on low-priced grains over the last 15 years, hog, cattle, and dairy have all suffered price declines. The result has been many more family livestock farms busted, and more hills put to the plow that were once grazed by cattle.

By moving from the prime land of north-central Iowa, where farms had reached a price of nearly $2,000 per acre by 1977, to southern Iowa, we were able to buy our farm for $900 per acre. With milk prices high at the time, we were off to an encouraging start. We borrowed another $200 per acre to invest in pond terraces and other conservation improvements.

But for agriculture as a whole, the massively escalating debt and the policy of maximum production had precipitated a growing environmental crisis in the countryside.

Bankers and other lenders took greater control over farming. Dictating more and more production practices—almost always pushing more intensification: more acres, more machinery, more chemicals.

Farmers were forced more and more into tenant farming arrangements or into renting land. The break with the historic ownership link meant a sharp change in consciousness, as farmers no longer had hopes of buying the land or passing it on to their children, which was a strong incentive to preserve the land. Simple survival became the top priority.

Environmental Concerns

Perhaps the greatest environmental concern was the rapid growth of huge superfarms—some owned by wealthy individuals or families and some by big corporations. Huge irrigation systems bled dry underground aquifers, massive doses of chemicals and artificial fertilizers poisoned the water and killed the essential living organisms in the earth, and ever-larger pieces of equipment compacted the soil to the point that special deep-tillage implements requiring enormous power were developed to loosen it up.

The increasingly obvious environmental costs of the expansionist policy led to the development of "conservation tillage" techniques. Using various new tillage implements and management techniques, conservation tillage results in increased plant residues on the soil surface to inhibit erosion. Although the rate of adaptation of these techniques by farmers has been high and real soil savings have occurred, the end results have been mixed.

In many cases, conservation tillage has led to increased use of herbicides and insecticides, contributing to the growing groundwater pollution in the United States. And with the advent of "no-till" planters, we're seeing hilly pasture ground that hasn't been tilled for decades going into row crop. After the sod is killed by herbicides the first year, these hillsides are left exposed to extreme water erosion.

Increasing erosion and pollution problems indicate that conservation tillage alone cannot address the environmental degradation caused by a policy of all-out production at any cost.

Although the 1970s were a time of widespread false optimism, many farmers in the United States were not fooled about the long-term viability—either economically or ecologically speaking—of the system.

Farm Movements

Two movements of farmers were launched in the 1970s in direct response to a growing sense of crisis. The first was the growth in organic, natural, and biological farming that accompanied the explosion of the health food industry in the United States in the early 1970s. The second was the farm strike, led by the American Agriculture Movement, that grew out of the growing crisis in 1977 and 1978. This movement demanded an end to the low prices and high-subsidy policies of the federal government. We were fighting to hang on to our land.

I participated in both movements. I returned to the farm from college in 1973 with a keen sense of environmental concern, which was outraged by the growing trends in agriculture. To any objective observer, the increasing monoculture, massive use of chemicals and fertilizers, high concentrations of specialized livestock facilities, and general pressure to produce had created a system that was quite unsustainable. Yet "official" sources of information—the Extension Service, the colleges, the corporations—recognized no alternatives.

Farmers themselves—experimenting on their own, using age-old techniques of crop rotation and fertility-building, trying new ideas and sharing them with like-minded farmers—had to build the biological farming movement of the 1970s in opposition to the conventional wisdom. I learned from my father and from experience that organic farmers know how to farm in a sustainable manner.

Since buying our own farm 10 years ago, we've used no herbicides or insecticides and very little commercial fertilizer. We practice a full rotation of crops that leaves a limited amount of ground exposed to erosion. We've built up our soil with the fertility of cow manure and crop residues.

The results have been positive—reduced erosion, average crop yields, excellent herd health and milk production, and some cost saving. This kind of result is common and has led to a continuing slow growth in the United States of sustainable farming practices.

However, it was clear from the beginning that the cost savings from biological agriculture would not be enough to make up for low prices. Many farmers in the 1970s became uneasy about the dependence of agriculture on increasing debt. A sense of impending disaster sparked a remarkable grassroots phenomenon called the American Agriculture Movement in 1977.

Farmers across the country rose up in protest, driving their tractors in "tractorcades" to demand higher prices. Although nurtured in many instances by the traditional progressive farm organizations, the American Agriculture Movement as a whole was diffuse and spontaneous. Eventually, 40,000 farmers converged on Washington, D.C., demanding parity for agriculture and warning of dire consequences for the system if they didn't get it. Unfortunately, the warning went unheeded. President Carter, the Congress, and the American people had all been fooled by the false optimism of our market-oriented approach.

In the early 1980s our whole system began to collapse. Land prices began to fall, making it impossible to borrow enough new money to cover years and years of low prices.

Liquidations of farm families reached levels higher than in the 1930s. Suicides, family breakups, alcoholism, and mental depression became a worsening reality in rural America. And soil erosion and groundwater contamination, as in the 1930s, continued to accelerate.

The level of production intensity has never been as high, as farmers try to squeeze every last bushel out of the land to survive.

With record numbers of foreclosures and bankruptcies, hundreds of thousands of acres of land are falling into the hands of speculators, lenders, and insurance companies. A good example of the crisis this is creating was documented by the Land Stewardship Project in Minnesota.

Ed Hauck was an award-winning conservation farmer in Wabaska County, Minnesota. He bought a badly eroded farm in 1958 and restored it to model condition with terraces, strip cropping, waterways, and contour farming. By 1984, Hauck had cut soil erosion to less than three tons per acre per year.

But that year Hauck lost his farm in foreclosure to John Hancock Life Insurance Company of Boston. The insurance company rented the land to a farmer who plowed up the whole farm, fence row to fence row. To maximize "efficiency," 27 years worth of conservation work on terraces, waterways, and contours was destroyed—work that has been supported with thousands of dollars of taxpayers' money. The predicted soil loss is now 35–40 tons per acre.

This situation is all too common as the foreclosures have continued unabated and the value of insurance companies' landholdings more than doubled in states like Iowa just from the end of 1985 to 1986. Insurance companies now own 4.1 million acres in the United States valued at $2.3 billion. When insurance companies, lenders, speculators, and other absentee landowners take over the land, the record shows that conservation suffers.

An Alternative Farm Bill

This backdrop of economic and environmental crisis confronted farmers and farm organizations as we began formulating an alternative to the Reagan farm policy as early as 1981. In the face of the power and wealth of the corporate-dominated American Farm Bureau Federation, the weaker progressive farm organizations such as the American Agricultural Movement and the National Farmers Union joined forces in new coalitions with grassroots organizations that sprang up nationwide in response to the crisis.

These coalitions gradually developed a common program and principles through many meetings involving farmers from all over the country over an extended period of time. The movement to save family farming eventually took shape as the farm coalitions reached out to the churches, labor unions, and other progressive constituencies for support.

Operating much like a loose-knit political campaign, the farm movement has developed a tremendous capacity to educate the public through the media, local organizing, and lobbying for legislation through phone calls, letters, and visits to Washington. Family farmers, in the midst of their worst crisis in 50 years, at least have a stronger-organized voice than they have had for many years.

In 1985 we drafted an alternative farm bill, including cost-of-production farm prices, supply management to reduce the intensity of production, and a 50-million-acre conservation reserve to take fragile land out of production permanently.

At first we had good support from environmental groups. But President Reagan and his allies in Congress had a good strategy. They agreed to include the conservation reserve in their proposal to cut prices—and by so doing were able to split many environmental groups from the farm movement.

In addition, 47 liberal urban Democrats sided with Reagan, believing that lower farm prices would be better for the hungry nations around the world, thinking that those nations could buy more food to feed their hungry people if it was cheaper. Clearly they had not thought about the devastating effect that cheap U.S. grain exports have had on food self-sufficiency in the Third World.

With the defection of some environmentalists and liberal Democrats to the Reagan camp, the administration was able to put together enough votes to pass the 1985 Farm Bill. The bill gave us significant new conservation measures but cut farm prices dramatically, accelerating the family-farm foreclosures and consolidation of land into the hands of wealthy investors, insurance companies, and lenders. The conservation measures, hailed by the environmental community as a great victory, are proving of more dubious benefit.

The Fragile Land

Conservation compliance, "sodbuster" and "swamp-buster" provisions were intended to force conservation practices on highly erodible land currently tilled and to prevent new ground in this category from coming under the plow. But efforts to enforce compliance with these provisions have run right up against the economic realities created by the bill. The economic pressure to produce is so great that the government has been forced to weaken the rules of compliance and enforcement to the point that many conservationists think their impact will be minimal.

The Conservation Reserve Program, which pays farmers to idle land for 10 years, has also failed to live up to expectations. Although it's good to see many steep hillsides back in grass again, loose eligibility criteria have allowed much land that could have been farmed with good conservation practices into reserve. As a result, the CRP may have to be greatly expanded at a much greater cost to bring in the most highly erodible ground.

And the nagging question always remains: after 10 years and billions of dollars in government payments, what will then happen to this fragile land? Like the Soil Bank of the 1960s, it could be forced right back into use by a policy of maximum production.

The 1985 Farm Bill has taken much land out of production through the CRP, the set-aside, and the paid diversion. But because it lacks the marketing controls that our farm bill alternative would have incorporated, the 1985 bill has actually encouraged more intensive farming of the remaining land under production. Increasing chemical pollution and continuing soil erosion are the results.

Some have suggested that lower prices have forced farmers to cut back on chemical usage, but nothing could be further from the truth. My neighbors are using more fertilizers and pesticides than ever, squeezing out every bushel per acre they can to make up for low prices and a big set-aside.

The contamination of groundwater by nitrate fertilizers alone has made many of the wells in my part of the country unsafe for drinking. With an increasing concentration of long-lasting carcinogenic pesticides in the groundwater, agricultural pollution has become a hotly discussed national issue.

The 1985 Farm Bill has accelerated the elimination of livestock from much of the countryside. It provided a program to buy out whole dairy herds from family farmers even as new 2,000-cow facilities were being built. The bill also encourages increased concentration in hog and fat cattle production, with associated problems of manure disposal. Elimination of cattle herds has left many farmers with little choice but to plow up hillsides. Predicted lower prices for dairy, hog, and beef cattle will continue this trend.

On my own farm, I have been forced to expand from 20 to 40 cows to try to keep up with the Reagan price cuts in milk. And I've rented an additional 80 acres. This is consistent with the trend toward fewer farmers but increased production. Like the majority of American farmers, I face an uncertain future with high debt and drastically reduced land values.

Beyond U.S. Borders

But the environmental impact of the U.S. Farm Bill doesn't stop at our borders. Due to our overwhelming dominance in the world market, our policies very much affect the whole world—and our politicians know it.

Especially in relation to Third World countries—both the emerging food exporters like Brazil and Argentina and the hungry importing nations—the Reagan administration policy has been intentional—and deadly.

Republican farm policy spokesman Senator Rudy Boschwitz outlined the goal of discouraging Third World exporters in a letter to *Time* magazine describing Republican intentions. "If we do not lower our farm prices to discourage these countries now," he wrote, "our worldwide competitive position will continue to slide and be much more difficult to regain. This discouragement should be one of the foremost goals of our agricultural policy" (Boschwitz, 1985: 6).

Although their goal was to put these Third World countries out of business, a moral outrage in and of itself, the actual result has been the opposite and equally disturbing.

Faced with enormous overseas debts that must be paid with hard currency earned through exports, these countries are unable to simply go out of business. Perhaps they could but our U.S. banks would be the first and greatest victims.

Most of these countries have responded to the U.S.'s lowering of world prices by simply expanding their acreage and their production—in hope of boosting export sales enough to recover in volume what they lost with the low prices—just like the farmers have done in the United States.

President Alfonsin, in an interview with U.S. columnist Jack Anderson, made this point clear. He laid out the need for Argentina to expand exports to keep up its earnings.

Brazil is opening hundreds of millions of new acres, much of it extremely fragile, in order to expand exports enough to keep up cash flow.

It's ironic that we are destroying rain forests in Central America to produce cattle which are then shipped to the United States, putting U.S. livestock producers out of business. When the U.S. producers are forced to abandon cattle production, their fragile pastures and hillsides often are converted to row crops, such as soybeans, which have a devastating effect through soil erosion and increasing run-off of agricultural chemicals.

Although some countries have been able to make up part of their losses, most have not been able to make up enough. Falling export earnings have translated into more external debt, less money to import fuels or medicines, and a lot less money available to care for environmental concerns.

Perhaps worse, it has accelerated the trend towards the industrialization of the Third World—with all the accompanying pollution and poisons and increased competition with industries in the north—as the prices for commodities on the world market fall further and further.

Slashing the Price of Rice

The impact of the U.S. decision to slash the price of rice is yet another example of the impact of U.S. price-cutting policies on the Third World. The 1985 Farm Bill included a special provision for rice and cotton, called marketing loans, to provide an additional export subsidy above the regular deficiency payments. It gave the United States the ability to lower world prices from around $8 per hundredweight (CWT) to less than $4 per CWT.

According to the *Washington Post*, the United States will spend up to $17 for each CWT of new rice exports, currently worth only $4 per CWT.

One of the main targets of the U.S. action was Thailand, one of the world's major rice exporters, where rice exports bring in 15 percent of much-needed foreign exchange. Rice farming is also the sole source of income for many of the four million Thai farmers. U.S. action to cut world rice prices in half last year threw their economy into a crisis, prompting demonstrations against the U.S. Farm Bill at the U.S. embassy in Bangkok.

But no matter how far the United States may lower world rice prices, Thailand's huge external debt to both U.S. and European banks makes it impossible for them to cut back on their exports. Instead of reducing production, as hoped by the United

States, the Thais have simply lowered their prices to remain competitive with the U.S. price and increased their production to maintain the cash flow needed to meet their debt obligations. They opened up huge new regions of the country to rice production for export.

Although this U.S. policy has created a serious economic and political crisis for Thailand, by far the most serious impacts have been on the rice producers in the poorest countries in West Africa. Local farmers in that region, struggling to build up their productive capacity in order to feed their own nations, are being squeezed out of business by heavily subsidized U.S. rice, priced nearly $80 per ton below the local costs of production and roughly $140 per ton below the U.S. cost of production.

Not only has this damaged efforts of these nations to build food self-reliance, it has forced them to divert scarce foreign exchange earnings to pay for imported rice, resulting in a cutback of other imports like fuel, medicines, and capital goods for long-term development.

In addition to trying to put the Third World exports out of business, the Reagan administration also has clearly targeted the hungry food-importing nations as well. Reagan's agriculture secretary during the 1985 Farm Bill debate, John Block, spelled out their strategy. It was one of discouraging food self-sufficiency among certain developing countries. He stated that the postmodern trade practices may mean that countries like the United States are the best source of inexpensive food for some developing countries.

Forcing Out Local Producers

This strategy has been reinforced by cutting U.S. prices so far below the cost of production that we force out of business local producers around the world. This is an environmental catastrophe. One example is the damage being done to rain forests by farmers from around the forests' edges who are not able to survive on their land due to the low prices. Many are forced to begin "poaching" the rain forest—slashing and planting one section of forest for a year or two, and then moving on to slash and cultivate a new piece. This poaching is thought to be responsible for a significant percentage of rain forest destruction.

And we cannot hope to stop this practice if farmers and peasants cannot get a decent price for their crops grown on the land already cleared.

There has been a huge drop in U.S. beet and cane sugar consumption as a result of the 1985 Farm Bill. By using massive deficiency payment subsidies to force down the price of corn, the 1985 Farm Bill has made it possible to produce high fructose corn syrup (HFCS) at a much lower cost of production than for beet or cane sugar. In the United States, this has triggered a massive shift from sugar to HFCS by the carbonated beverage industry and other food processors. Last year the average person in the United States consumed more corn sweeteners than sugar. The U.S. decision to cut world prices in the 1985 Farm Bill had a dramatic impact on the entire world. The sugar workers on the Philippine sugar island of Negros are an example.

One immediate effect of the shift to HFCS has been a huge reduction in U.S. sugar import quotas. The Philippines has suffered a 60 percent cut in its U.S. market share quota. There are now nearly a quarter of a million people slowly starving to death on the island of Negros, thrown out of work because of the loss of the U.S. sweetener market to heavily subsidized corn.

The next round of price cuts proposed by the Reagan administration will make corn so cheap that it may be economically feasible to convert corn sweeteners into a crystallized form, which would totally ruin the world sugar trade. Already the United States is predicting an end to its sugar imports by 1990. The question is whether cheap, heavily subsidized corn will allow the United States to become a major exporter of sweeteners in direct and devastating competition with sugar producers of the Third World.

This has put Third World producers in a terrible squeeze, and will undoubtedly lead to a push by sugar producers to get Europe to import even more of their production to make up for some of the lost U.S. markets and increased competition from U.S.-produced HFCS.

Reducing the production quota for the European Community's sugar producers is one proposal for dealing with this problem, but it would unfortunately have very little impact on either world prices or oversupply.

The Challenge

Reagan's victory has meant that we must work harder, improve our arguments, and build new coalitions.

This is exactly what we did in 1986. Farm activists teamed up with peace groups, civil rights organizations, environmentalists, labor, church, and many others in the elections. In 10 farm states, coalitions mounted serious challenges to incumbent Republican senators who had been die-hard supporters of Reagan. Even before Irangate broke, we were able to mount successful challenges to Reagan's policies, throwing out of office six incumbents and giving Democrats control over the Senate and House of Representatives.

In three of those states, North Dakota, South Dakota, and Colorado, farmer votes for progressive Democrats were 2-to-1, providing a margin of victory in these races.

With these victories, the stage has been set for a new national campaign to reverse Reagan's policies—and for an exciting presidential election in 1988. The Republican contenders are lining up solidly behind Reagan's policies as defenders of the 1985 Farm Bill.

But all of the leading Democratic contenders advocate a sharp break with Reagan's policies, with higher market prices and effective supply management. Most are either sponsors or endorsers of the farm movement's alternative legislation—the Family Farm Act—such as Rep. Richard Gephardt, Rev. Jesse Jackson, Sen. Paul Simon, and Rep. Pat Schroeder.

The strong possibility of a Democratic victory in 1988 has significant implication for the world situation.

The agribusiness corporations that have profited greatly from the current administration have themselves concluded that they are likely to be out of control after 1988, and they are moving to make as many gains as possible before 1988.

The Reagan Initiative

Perhaps most significant from an environmental point of view is the Reagan administration's recently launched offensive to restructure the world's food system through the General Agreement on Tariffs and Trade (GATT) negotiations.

Reagan made a proposal to force changes in the world food trading rules that would extend to the whole world the disastrous policies that have ruined rural America. He has proposed four main demands. First, to cut farm prices worldwide. Second, to stop countries from protecting their borders from cheap food exports. Third, to stop export subsidies. And fourth, to make the rest of the world accept U.S. standards for allowable additives, hormones, and impurities in food.

If Reagan gets his way, the disaster, both economic and environmental, that we face in the United States will become global. We now must move beyond our national borders to form a global campaign to stop the Reagan initiative. Probably Europe is the most crucial place to begin expanding this campaign. We must stop the Reagan administration and the grain corporations from pushing commodity prices down even further. Perhaps even more important, we must defend the right of all countries—Third World, Europe, the United States, and others—to protect their borders from imports.

Third World countries must be able to protect their local farmers from being wiped out by cheap, subsidized exports. At the same time, we must be able to control imports in northern countries if we are going to have effective supply management programs to protect our soils and to prevent surplus.

Reagan's third demand, an end to export subsidies, is a positive goal, although it should be pointed out that the Reagan administration has spent more money on export subsidies, both direct and indirect, than all past administrations combined, and a great deal more than Europe. We must demand an end to export subsidies, but we should not confuse this with Reagan's overall free market push.

A Global Campaign

We need a global campaign to ensure that farmers and peasants regain control of the land—and we need a global campaign to ensure that the land is being farmed in an environmentally sustainable way.

This is becoming more and more crucial as we approach the twenty-first century, where the bioindustrial revolution will mean that the entire economy will be based on the transformation of the products we grow on our farms into the fuel, fiber, medicine, and manufactured goods that our whole society will need.

This can be a bright future if our economy is transformed from one based on rapidly depleting, nonrenewable, and highly polluting petroleum and coal to one based on renewable resources such as plants and trees, which can, if we choose, be grown and transformed in an environmentally safe way.

But this could turn into a dark future if corporations take control of the land and the means of producing and transforming this food we grow.

We're already seeing the threat of a few corporations controlling the seeds and germplasm—and they are trying to take control of life itself by gaining the right to patent new animals, as they have recently done in the United States.

We need a global campaign to make sure that family farmers and peasants can control the land, and that the values of sustainability, safety, and quality guide this new biotechnological future. There are many examples for us to follow in the global effort—the Nestle boycott, the cola campaign, and the worldwide efforts of the Pesticide Action Network.

But whatever direction we take, we must maintain the interlinked concepts of who controls the land and how the land is treated. We must be sure that our struggles for land reform are broadened to include what is grown on the land and how it is grown. And our struggle for sustainable agriculture must include the economics to ensure widespread, diversified, family-farm control. Only together can we win both struggles. Separated, we will lose it all.

The Long, Hard Road Since 1987

David Ostendorf

Since 1987, intensified economic stratification and increased corporate dominance have been the hallmarks of U.S. agriculture. The result is a two-tier structure of agriculture, with less than 2 percent of all farms already reaping some 40 percent of total farm sales (USDA/ERS, 1993a). In the six-year period through 1992, moreover, the number of large farms (those defined by gross sales in excess of $100,000) increased by almost 43,000 (14.8 percent), while medium-size farms continued their decline. Between 1991 and 1992 alone, over 31,000 medium-size farms went out of existence (Anthan, 1993). Today, nearly three-quarters of all farm households operate what the USDA itself now calls small farms with gross sales below $50,000 that, on average, lose money on their farming operations (USDA/ERS, 1993b).

While the number of farms has been declining steadily since the 1930s, there were by the end of the 1980s fewer owners of U.S. farmland than at any other time in this century (USDA/ERS, 1991). The skewed concentration of control over the land itself has resulted in an ownership pattern that rivals that of any oligarchy: today nearly half of all the nation's farmland is held by about four percent of all farmland owners, and over 40 percent of the 833 millions acres of private farmland in 1989 was held by owners or organizations that did not themselves farm the land (USDA/ERS, 1991).

Today most farmers and their families have to hold off-farm jobs in order to maintain their farming operations. Some 60 percent of farm operator households rely on either the farm operator or spouse—or both—to supply off-farm wage and salary income (USDA/ERS, 1993b). But despite all efforts to maintain economic viability on the farm, over 21 percent of all farm operator households in 1990 fell below the poverty threshold (USDA/ERS, 1993b).

For African-American and other minority farmers, the situation is far worse. In fact, the very survival of black farmers in the United States is at stake. Despite a 1982 U.S. Civil Rights Commission report warning that there may be no black farmers by the year 2000 (U.S. Commission on Civil Rights, 1982), little has been done at the state or national policy level to assure their survival.

> The loss of black-owned land and farming operations has been precipi-
> tous, exacerbated by racist government and private sector policies. A
> million black farm operators owned fifteen million acres of land in 1910;
> by 1987, only 2.2 million acres were left in the hands of 23,000 black
> farm operators (Federation of Southern Cooperatives, 1993). African-
> American farmers are still losing an estimated 1,000 acres of land each
> day—a loss translating conservatively into over $275 million of irre-
> placeable equity each year. (Pennick, 1992: 10)

The sweeping corporate takeover of U.S. agriculture in this period has gone virtually unchallenged outside the progressive farm and rural community. With the 1994 takeover of Congress by a conservative, pro-business Republican landslide, and with a weakened and disinterested Democratic administration, the emergence of any significant opposition to this takeover is highly unlikely in this decade. Between 1982 and 1990 there were some 4,100 food industry mergers and leveraged buyouts, tripling the industry's total debt to $270 billion at the turn of the decade (Krebs, 1992). The reason is simple: the U.S. food manufacturing industry has become the nation's most profitable industrial sector as measured by return on stockholder equity (Krebs, 1992).

According to data compiled by A.V. Krebs, the ten-year average return to the food manufacturing sector was 18.4 percent, compared with the all-industry median of 14.3 percent (Krebs, 1992). For Kellogg alone, the return on equity in this period averaged 38.9 percent, while the farm and food mega-giant ConAgra realized 21.9 percent (Krebs, 1992). Comparatively, the return to equity for farmers during this same period averaged a negative 3.79 percent (Krebs, 1993).

ConAgra and Cargill (the largest privately held corporations in the world) today control 50 percent of the nation's grain exports and, with Iowa Beef Processors, slaughter nearly 80 percent of its beef (Krebs, 1992). In virtually every sector of the food industry, these two corporations wield enormous economic power from the ground to the grocery store. A farmer today can purchase key production inputs (e.g., seed, fertilizers, chemicals) from these companies, feed for livestock that is in turn marketed through one of the companies' meatpacking plants, and then go to the grocery store and buy a company brand product (such as ConAgra's "Healthy Choice") to put back on the kitchen table.

It was during the farm crisis of the 1980s that the "Big Three" packers began to dominate the livestock industry at the farm and factory alike. Bolstered by extraordinary profits and unfettered by antitrust enforcement in the "free market" Reagan–Bush era, Cargill and ConAgra expanded their meat production and slaughter operations.

In 1986, for example, one of the worst years of the U.S. farm crisis, Cargill realized its highest level of pretax profits since 1974. And between 1981 and 1987, ConAgra's profits rose 513 percent—from $24 million to $147 million—as it consolidated its rank among the world's top five grain traders and expanded its role in meatpacking with the purchase of Monfort.

The move of both companies into hog production and slaughter was an early warning sign of the industrialization that would sweep one of the last strongholds of independent livestock production. In 1974, there were almost three-quarters of a million hog producers of all types and sizes in the United States. By the early 1990s that number had shrunk to 256,000, with predictions that by the year 2000 there will be only 100,000 producers remaining (PrairieFire, 1993). With the rapid takeover of hog production by massive confinement operations (in which large numbers of hogs are raised in factory-like facilities), more than two-thirds of the nation's total hog supply is now raised by a mere 12 percent of its hog producers (PrairieFire, 1993). In short, hog production, processing, and marketing are rapidly going the way of the nation's broiler industry: highly integrated both vertically and horizontally, and controlled by a diminishing number of corporate interests.

Local Action and Organizing

Effective counter-responses to the power of the industrialized food system must be rooted in political action from the local to the global level, and simultaneously in creative disengagement from the dominant economy.

In rural America, local action is the first bulwark against corporate takeover of the food system, and perhaps one of the most difficult to secure. For under the guise of "economic development," the alleged benefits of the new industrial food system, such as large livestock or poultry operations, often obscure their cost. Time and again, the tinsel-coated benefits—more jobs, more tax dollars returned to the community and county, more purchases of local grain, for example—hide their true costs. Tax abatements, bond sales, and a trough-full of local, state, and federal loans (many of which are tax-free for a designated period and/or completely forgivable) and grants for a variety of infrastructure "needs" are costly enticements in the competitive scramble by poor and job-hungry rural communities and counties.

The need for citizens and county leaders to conduct sound cost–benefit analysis of proposed or operating industrial food facilities has never been greater. In recent years, counties across the Midwest have taken a more assertive regulatory and monitoring role to assure, for example, the environmental integrity of large livestock operations. Rural neighborhoods are organizing to stop those operations from dispersing waste and odor, and are in turn challenging the corporate powers behind them. Zoning commissions have taken decisive action to keep industrial food and livestock operations out of counties.

From imposing new or tighter operating restrictions to refusing permits for proposed confinement facilities whose economic and environmental costs far outweigh their benefits, those counties have broken new ground in public policy development at the local level. In an era of increasing abdication of such responsibilities by state government, the county role must be strengthened in the days ahead—without falling into the trap of the corporate-dominated "wise use" movement that advocates individual property rights above all else.

State and Regional Cooperation

At the state and regional level, the challenge posed by this renewed push for industrial food operations is equally critical. Industry interests are posing both subtle and direct threats to state-level corporate farming laws —laws that prohibit large corporations from owning farmland or engaging directly in agricultural operations.

In fact, the industry is quite clear about its position on these laws that have been at the heart of state commitments to protect and preserve family farm agriculture: they must be loosened up and changed to permit expansion, for example, of industrial livestock operations. In 1993, the Des Moines, Iowa, Chamber of Commerce Federation's "Project 21" report stated that "although it is politically popular to defend and protect the concept of the family farm, legislation limiting corporate investment is economic folly" (Project 21, 1993: 102).

Enlisting the support of producer groups and other business interests, the industry is making steady headway. Laws that put limits on the size and type of corporate farm entities, restrictions on "vertical coordination" as well as "pro-debtor" legislation—namely, right of first refusal, right of redemption, bankruptcy exemptions—have been identified as barriers to expanding corporate livestock operations.

The industry has also become very adept at playing states against one another with threats of taking their operations to more "receptive" locales if they don't get their way. Such "border hopping" has already occurred, and it will occur again, particularly if farm, rural, labor, and religious organizations and coalitions within a threatened region do not work together to develop more common and consistent policies to protect independent producers, the rural economy, and the environment.

But as always, it is at the grassroots level, in our neighborhoods, communities, and counties, that the people of rural America must first speak out and exercise their rights and responsibilities for democratic decision-making, and thereby assure the preservation of family farms and the revitalization of rural communities.

The industry is, quite literally, shifting direction by the week, and it is imperative that producers and rural communities take action to counter corporate takeovers. Public policy at the state and federal levels is woefully inadequate and too out of date to effectively address it; local action is necessary and essential, coupled with new public policy initiatives and strategic legal challenges.

The Challenge at the Federal Level

Such action must be aimed, finally, at the federal level. The one fundamental that must be stated emphatically with regard to the economic well-being of rural America is this: that unless and until family farmers get a fair price and profit from their grain and livestock production, the rural economy will not recover in any sustainable manner and the corporate sector will, indeed, gain its final dominance over agriculture. The fight for fair prices, for fair federal policies that benefit independent family farm and ranch operations and not simply the transnational giants, must continue at every level.

That fight must not and cannot succumb to the potentially divisive struggle to elevate environmentally sustainable agriculture above economically sustainable agriculture, especially in the 1995 Farm Bill deliberations by a budget slashing Congress. Indeed, the former will not be achieved without assuring the latter. The bills coming due for decades of farm and food policies that have externalized the human and environmental costs of production agriculture rooted in economic concentration and chemical fixations will not be paid only by addressing the environmental side of the ledger. Economic and environmental sustainability in rural America, as Dixon Terry stated so well, are fundamentally inseparable; the shift to sustainable farming is necessary, but not sufficient unless independent farmers are also able to make the economic transition that will enable them to realize a sound return from their production.

Likewise, the struggle for economic and racial justice for black and other minority farmers must be intensified throughout the nation in both rural and urban areas alike. While passage of the Minority Farmers Act of 1990 was a major breakthrough—won by grassroots organizations across the country working together under the leadership of the Federation of Southern Cooperatives—its implementation has been less than noteworthy. Federal agencies like the Farmers Home Administration must be held accountable for their responsibilities to serve and support minority farmers.

But the struggle for black farmers must also be elevated among black leaders and organizations, many of whom have failed to see how central the land struggle is to the economic viability and revitalization of the black community. As Jerry Pennick, Director of the Land Assistance Fund of the Federation of Southern Cooperatives, wrote:

> There is hope for the survival of the black farmer, but it is the responsibility of black America to make it happen. We can no longer sit idly by and hope the government will do its job fairly and equitably.... The black land loss problem must take its rightful place alongside the more glamorous and "safe" issues, e.g., voter registration, school integration, and affirmative action.... The most logical tool to achieve a significant degree of economic independence for Blacks is through land ownership and development. (Pennick, 1992: 10)

The land-based struggle for economic justice by minority farmers also points to the overall need for a broader, communities-based land reform agenda in America. This will not be an easy task, since most Americans no longer have any direct ties to the land and are essentially oblivious to the land control problem. As historian Lawrence Goodwyn wrote:

> [L]and centralization is a process that remains obscure to most Americans, but one they feel no right to inquire into— given the fact that land centralization is sanctioned by the culture itself.... Americans no longer contest the matter." (Goodwyn, 1978: 316)

But contest the matter we must. Despite the opposition of corporate agribusiness interests, including organizations like the American Farm Bureau Federation, the need to move toward both state and federal land ownership reporting requirements is a critical first step. Laws prohibiting corporate ownership of land must be vigorously upheld and enforced in those key states where they have been enacted; in other states without such protection, new initiatives must be considered to prohibit corporate ownership. Eventually local and state efforts must focus—when the time is right politically—on developing a more comprehensive American land reform agenda at the national level. Every political and legal avenue available must be utilized in the meantime to seek a return to democratic principles fundamentally rooted in widespread distribution of the land itself.

Finally, if the corporate dominance of the nation's food system is to be successfully challenged at the federal level, antitrust laws must be enforced. It was the four-firm beef trust that controlled U.S. cattle slaughter earlier this century that led to the Consent Decree of 1920, splitting up the cattle cartel of that era. Since 1980—when levels of concentration throughout the food sector blossomed—there has been virtually no antitrust enforcement applied to the food industry by the U.S. Justice Department, despite numerous attempts by grassroots organizations since 1989 to move the Department to action. It will take continuing, increased grassroots political pressure to secure any action by the Justice Department on this particular front. Given both the complexity and the impact of corporate concentration in the food industry on farmers, workers, and consumers, it is imperative to strengthen existing coalitions if this battle is to be effectively engaged and won.

Creative Disengagement from the Dominant Economy

If family farmers and rural Americans are to survive, radical new possibilities for development and diversification must also be explored, driven by wide-open creative thinking about new directions for farming in an American economy dominated by distant capital, powerful corporations, and votes concentrated in metropolitan areas of the nation.

In short, we must imagine how to creatively disengage from the dominant economy. North Dakota populists did it decades ago, setting up state banks and state grain elevators. Southern populists of the late nineteenth century similarly disengaged by establishing cooperatives that took advantage of the opportunities in the dominant system to buy and sell, without themselves becoming dominated by that system—at least for a while.

Creative disengagement from the dominant economy means adherence to a number of principles that differ from those that normally guide our thinking and action. It means that farm and rural people exercise control over the development process and engage in acts of self-determination, rooted in a fundamental commitment to both short- and long-term community benefits.

Along with developing effective community-based cost–benefit analysis methodologies by which communities can determine the true potential of proposed economic development projects, progressive communities and organizations must begin to look at the possibilities for locally based, locally controlled capital development. In both small and significant amounts, capital is diffused and controlled by families and households, churches, labor, and farm organizations throughout rural America. The substantial capital (and land) resources controlled by an older generation of rural Americans could significantly benefit farm and rural communities through small-scale economic development and job-creation initiatives that are locally controlled by small "investors" from participating communities.

New and powerful coalitions must be established, especially with groups in urban and metropolitan America where common interests abound in both the marketplace and politics. The renewed, politically powerful farm and labor coalitions of the 1980s underscore the possibility for rural–urban coalitions in the 1990s and beyond. The political clout of family farmers and rural communities is fading rapidly, and even its elected "friends" are safely able to ignore it. Determination of common interests with other marginal people and communities is central to development of the political voice necessary for the emerging common struggles of rural and urban people in the twenty-first century.

Finally, as Dixon Terry alluded to in his 1987 speech, we must begin to forge stronger international alliances to counter the power of global capital and transnational corporations that dominate and destroy the farm and rural infrastructure everywhere. The free-trade proposals sweeping the hemisphere have been primary catalysts for such international cooperation among progressive organizations. Farm, labor, human rights, religious, and environmental groups from Canada, the United States, and Mexico forged uncommon alliances to fight the North American Free Trade Agreement, which will benefit the transnationals at the expense of farmers and workers in all three nations. Out of that common struggle must come even stronger alliances for economic, social, racial, and environmental justice in the years ahead.

From Political Cowardice to a Democratic Community of Communities

Political cowardice is a commodity in abundant supply today. The price for those who buy it is low; the price for those who pay for it is staggering. We see it everywhere, but we see it especially in the refusal to tackle the gross inequities in this nation's political economy and in the lack of concern about concentration of control over its most basic sector: food.

Historian Lawrence Goodwyn wrote that this American century may become known as one of "sophisticated deference," as in our passivity we failed to confront the consolidation of political and economic power that so directly affects our lives and undercuts democratic principles (Goodwyn, 1978: 318).

The political will to overcome such deference still lies in the hands and hearts of our people—people of the land, the small towns and cities, and the metropolises. We know what is wrong. Now it is in our hands not just to fix the wrongs, but to create anew the kind of democratic communities that assure all our neighbors—rural and urban, nearby and global—the right and opportunity to live in a society where economic, racial, political, and environmental justice is the reality, and no longer a distant possibility.

13

Sustainable Agriculture Embedded in a Global Sustainable Future: Agriculture in the United States and Cuba

Ivette Perfecto

This modern industrialized form of agriculture has frequently been cited as a miracle with yield increases of over 100 percent reported for most major commodities (Feher, 1984). But there are two main problems with this generalization. First, the increases have been achieved at an enormous social, economic, and environmental cost. Second, at least for certain commodities, there has been an actual reduction in the efficiency of agricultural production from an energetic point of view.

Introduction

The defining feature of the post-war world, the Cold War, ended in 1989. In its immediate wake, the world was seen by some as poised on the brink of unbridled freedom and happiness, and by others as falling rapidly into a cauldron of uncertainty. Just five years later the unbridled freedom and happiness seem at best somewhat elusive, and most realists count themselves amongst the uncertain ones. The fall of the Soviet Union and its ideological tenets and the loss of public confidence in the United States and its ideological tenets have generated geopolitical as well as ideological chaos, providing opportunities for the construction of a radically different world. It is within the context of this aperture that I shall attempt to analyze agricultural development as part of a strategy for developing a sustainable future. First, I will examine the context within which industrial agriculture was developed in the United States along with its social, environmental, and economic impacts. Then I will explore the conditions that led to a dramatic shift

Ivette Perfecto is an assistant professor in the School of Natural Resources and Environment of the University of Michigan. Her general research interest is in theoretical and practical aspects of agro-ecology and the interaction between agriculture and conservation. She has conducted extensive research in Nicaragua and Costa Rica, examining a variety of ecological aspects of tropical agriculture. She is also interested in broader issues of environmental justice, particularly those related to pesticides and farmworkers. She now teaches agroforestry and tropical natural resource conservation at the University of Michigan.

172

in the agricultural discourse in Cuba and the concomitant development of a philosophy of sustainable agriculture in that country. Finally, I will draw parallels between policy changes in Cuba and what I perceive to be the necessary policy and ideological changes for the development of a truly sustainable agriculture in the United States.

The Myths of Modern Agriculture
"Farming is growing peanuts.
Agriculture is turning petroleum into peanut butter."
(Lewontin,1982:12).

Lewontin captures the essence of the difference between farming and modern industrialized agriculture. The history of modern agriculture is a history of devaluation of farming, loss of control of farming activities by farmers, loss of rural societies, separation of people and nature, plundering and degradation of the conditions of production by agribusiness, and the penetration of capital primarily through mechanization and chemicalization. Equally important have been the internationalization of agriculture and its place in the international division of labor. An understanding of this history and the concrete results of this transformation provides insights for the redirection of agriculture toward a sustainable future.

The most striking change in agricultural production since the turn of the century was the change in the nature of agricultural inputs from being supplied almost exclusively from within the farm to being purchased from outside the farms. So, for example, farmers used to produce their own fertilizers from the manure produced by the animals that provided the traction power to plow the fields. Now chemical fertilizers are purchased from chemical companies and fossil fuels power tractors that replaced the oxen. Especially since World War II, machinery, pesticides, irrigation water, fertilizers, and antibiotics (in livestock production) have replaced land, diversity, and labor as the principal components of agricultural production (National Research Council, 1989).

The first step in this process was the replacement of draft animals and human labor by tractors, virtually completed by 1960 (National Research Council, 1989). In the last 30 years the use of inorganic fertilizer has increased from 7.4 million tons to 19 million tons (U.S. Department of Agriculture, 1987a); the total amount of pesticides applied on farms increased 170 percent between 1964 and 1982 (U.S. Department of Agriculture, 1984); antibiotic use for animal production increased from 440,000 pounds in 1953 to 9.9 million pounds in 1985 (National Research Council, 1989: 49). The use of groundwater for irrigation increased 160 percent in 35 years, while surface water use for irrigation increased 50 percent during the same period. Energy cost for on-farm pumping of groundwater increased 352 percent between 1974 and 1984 (U.S. Department of Agriculture, 1987b).

Today the food and fiber sector of the U.S. economy represents about 17.5 percent of the gross national product (GNP), or about $700 billion in economic activity (U.S. Department of Agriculture, 1987c). Although farming is at the center of agricultural production, it accounts for only about 2 percent of total GNP (U.S. Department of Agriculture, 1986); inputs (seeds, equipment, and agrochemicals) account for another 2 percent; and processing, marketing, and retail sales account for almost 14 percent (U.S. Department of Agriculture, 1986). In essence, farmers in the United States are caught between powerful monopsonies and monopolies representing both ends of agriculture: suppliers of agricultural inputs and corporations that control the processing, transportation, and marketing of agricultural outputs (Lewontin, 1982). This led to an accumulation of an enormous debt by farmers and the deterioration of rural communities in the 1980s (National Research Council, 1989; Buttel, 1990).

This modern industrialized form of agriculture has frequently been cited as a miracle, with yield increases of over 100 percent reported for most major commodities (Feher, 1984). But there are two main problems with this generalization. First, the increases have been achieved at an enormous social, economic, and environmental cost. Second, at least for certain commodities, there has been an actual reduction in the efficiency of agricultural production from an energetic point of view.

Social Cost

Social costs are realized as a deterioration in the quality of life, polarization of income distribution, and constraints on the decision making of economic agents (Beckenbach, 1989). In the 1950s, 24 percent of the farms in the United States were lost. An additional 11 percent were lost in the 1980s during the farm crisis. Since the total harvested acres has remained constant (340 million acres), the average farm size has almost tripled. The growth in average farm size has been largely at the expense of the small farm (National Research Council, 1989). As farmers are displaced from agriculture and their operations consolidated into larger, more efficient units, the countryside has become depopulated and rural communities have deteriorated (Bultena and Leistritz, 1992; Buttel, 1990).

Furthermore, the burden of high-input agriculture has been borne disproportionately by people of color and the poor. For example, farmworkers, 90 percent of whom are people of color, have been most affected by the use of toxic pesticides in U.S. agriculture (Perfecto, 1992a; Perfecto and Velázquez, 1992). However, since agriculture encompasses not only farming activities but also the manufacture of agricultural inputs and the processing of agricultural outputs, social effects at all levels must be considered. From the pesticide manufacturing plants to the disposal of hazardous waste generated in the process, people of color are also disproportionally affected by the contamination generated by agricultural production (Robinson, 1991; Bullard, 1990). The international dimension of this cost is frequently overlooked. The internationalization of agriculture and its place in the international division of labor facilitate the movement of useless products (e.g., banned pesticides) and waste to the periphery, putting the life of people in the Third World at risk (Center for Investigative Reporting and Moyers, 1990; Perfecto, 1992b).

Environmental Effects

In the last 50 years, a mode of production based on potentially renewable resources well contained within the production unit has expanded to a mode of production based, to a large extent, on nonrenewable resources, resulting in unprecedented environmental degradation. The detrimental environmental effects of farming under industrial agriculture were reviewed in a report of the National Research Council (1989). Farming alone is the largest nonpoint source of water pollution. Water runoff from agricultural fields carries sediments, minerals, nutrients, and pesticides into rivers, lakes, estuaries, and underground water reservoirs, affecting the quality of drinking water as well as aquatic resources in rivers, lakes, and estuaries. Between 675 million and 1 billion tons of eroded agricultural soils are deposited in the water each year (National Research Council, 1986), and between 50 and 70 percent of all nutrients reaching surface waters originate on agricultural land in the form of fertilizers and animal waste (U.S. Department of Agriculture, 1987d). In subhumid and arid regions, irrigation practices continue to deplete aquifers and cause salinization of agricultural land and water.

Approximately 500 million pounds of pesticides are applied to agricultural fields each year in the United States, and although it is estimated that less than 5 percent of these actually reach streams and lakes (Phipps and Crosson, 1986), their environmental and public health effects can be devastating. For example, detectable levels of chlorinated hydrocarbons are still found in several fish, shellfish, and bird species in the Great Lakes. Here also, people of color suffer the greatest impact of environmental pollution since, in these risk areas, people of color tend to depend to a greater degree on fish consumption as a source of protein (West, 1992). Pesticides have also been detected in the groundwater of 26 states (Williams et al., 1988). Finally, as modern agriculture converts previously diverse land-use mosaics into monocultures, genetic, biological, and ecological diversities are eroded (Soule et al., 1990).

Economic Effects

With a total net farm income of $46.3 billion and a contribution of $700 billion to the GNP, industrial agriculture would appear to be a profitable and dynamic enterprise that has contributed significantly to the prosperity of the country. But what kind of prosperity and for whom?

In 1987, direct federal subsidies reached $16.7 billion. Who benefited from these subsidies? Not farmers, who accumulated a debt of $150 billion in 1988 (National Research Council, 1989). Not consumers, who have been paying more for less and of lower quality (if pesticide residues are considered) (Lewontin, 1982). Finally, not farmworkers, whose wages are still below the federally established minimum wages, whose working conditions have improved very little in 50 years, who receive the direct impact of the application of toxic chemicals, and who are specifically excluded from the Occupational Safety and Health Act, the Fair Labor Standards Act, and the National Labor Relations Act.

Input and output capital enterprises have been the clear winners in the transformation of agricultural production in the United States. In the early 1980s, inputs purchased to produce farm outputs reached $80 billion. At the same time, agricultural products generated more income after they leave the farm than ever before in U.S. history. In a 20-year period, the economic activity of these industries rose from $235 billion to about $450 billion (U.S. Department of Agriculture, 1986).

Furthermore, to evaluate accurately the economic contribution of industrial agriculture to the U.S. economy, the social and environmental costs, which have been dismissed as externalities, should be incorporated in the calculations (Repetto, 1992). The public health cost of pesticide use, the cost of cleaning toxic waste dumps, the decline in fisheries due to water pollution or lake eutrophication, the decline in soil fertility due to soil erosion, etc., all should be incorporated into the equation that determines the real economic benefits and costs of industrial agriculture. For example, Pimentel et al. (1992) estimated an annual cost of approximately $8.1 billion, just due to pesticides. In sum, consumers, farmers, farmworkers, people of color, poor communities, and the environment are paying the real cost of agricultural production. And yet they appear to be the least benefited.

Energy Efficiency

Historically, economic development has been linked to a progressive increase in energy consumption. Not counting solar energy, the energy input into agriculture has increased more than production (Martínez-Alier, 1987). According to Pimentel and Dazhong (1990), from 1700 to 1983, energy inputs in U.S. corn production increased 15-fold; yields during this period increased only 3.5 fold. Most comparisons of peasant and industrialized agriculture are based on calculations of the productivity of land and labor, but they rarely include considerations of energy efficiency of the agricultural system (Redclift, 1987). As Redclift explains,

Agricultural systems which show the greatest dependence on commercial energy sources, such as production of apples, spinach, and tomatoes in the United States, show a relatively inefficient use of energy and often impose an irrecoverable burden on natural resources....The real cost of producing cheap spinach or tomatoes in the United States lies in depleted groundwater and increasing toxic uptake in soils and drinking water. (Redclift, 1987: 27–28)

A Movement toward a Sustainable Agriculture Based on Social, Economic, and Racial Justice

According to Levins (1990: 121), three main factors have led to the protection of harmful practices and the resistance to ecological rationality in agriculture worldwide: poverty, ignorance, and institutionalized greed. These three factors are interdependent, with the last having a lot to do with the promotion and maintenance of the other two. The development of a "sustainable agriculture" that maintains the current conditions of agricultural property and production rather than guaranteeing conditions of production for everyone would not likely result in social, economic, and environmental equity. The basic premises and ideology of the sustainability discourse have to be transformed into ones that replace greed with societal altruism, poverty with the commitment to meeting the basic needs of the population, and ignorance with knowledge through an enhanced educational system. Sustainability movements must address the question, who and what needs to be sustained? They must focus on people's social and cultural relations as well as their relations with nature, become a multicultural movement, and finally, they must explore the extent to which the agricultural crisis springs not only from the relationship between society and nature, but also from the contradictions of social relations themselves. "We should ask if sustainability is possible, much less desirable, without the elimination of patriarchy, racism, and class exploitation—all of which maintain the systems of power that reinforce nonsustainable, undesirable social relations" (Allen, 1991: 28).

A multicultural sustainable agriculture movement that includes the knowledge and experiences of those who have been subjugated and dispossessed (racial and ethnic minorities, women, farmworkers, consumers, poor communities, Third World peasants) under the totalizing discourse of capitalism, or what Wallerstein (1989) calls the geoculture of the capitalist world economy, could shape an ideological framework that could potentially serve as the basis for a truly sustainable future. In recent times, challenges to this geoculture have taken three major forms (Wallerstein, 1991).

First, there is a new intellectual focus on culture as opposed to economy or politics. In agriculture this is manifested by a criticism of the ever increasing separation of people from nature, the loss of indigenous knowledge of farming practices, and the loss of rural communities and cultures.

The second major challenge to geoculture lies in "the creation of the concepts of racism and sexism in recognition of a fundamental feature of the geoculture of the capitalist world economy: the inherent and necessary existence of racism and sexism within its structures in spite of (or even because of) its universalizing pretensions" (Wallerstein, 1991:12). In agriculture, the struggles of farmworkers and other people of color affected by the contamination generated by agro-industries against what has been termed "environmental racism" (Mohai and Bryant, 1992) best represent this challenge. This challenge is also manifested through feminists' demands for greater recognition of women's participation in agricultural production. Internationally, coalitions of environmental activists from Third World countries and the United States have criticized the racism inherent in pesticide export and toxic waste dumping policies.

Finally, the third challenge to the geoculture of the world-capitalist economy comes from challenges to science itself. The Baconian–Newtonian science that has provided the scientific bases for the development of ever-needed new technologies upon which capitalist expansion relies and depends has itself been challenged, "not in any rejection of the basic scientific enterprise—the optimal comprehension of material reality—but in the rapprochement of the scientific method (reinterpreted as an attempt to reduce complexity to minimalism) with intelligent work in the social sciences and the humanities" (Wallerstein, 1991:13). I would further argue that the challenges go far beyond the rejection of the science-versus-humanities dichotomy. Other approaches to science include dialectics (Levins and Lewontin, 1985), feminism (see for example Haraway, 1988; Shiva, 1988), metaphysical beliefs of Eastern philosophies (see for example Capra's, 1975, *The Tao of Physics* and Needham's, 1956, *Science and Civilization in China*), and the fields of non-linear dynamics, complexity, and chaos. In agriculture this has been manifested most vividly, although not exclusively, as a challenge to the research establishment of the land grant universities and its applied commodity-oriented research (Buttel, 1990), and most recently, as opposition to the increasing volume of research undertaken in private firms, especially in the area of biotechnology.

The supposed detachment of human relations from scientific development has allowed, for the sake of profit, the development of agricultural technologies that are inhumane. In agricultural research, general cultural goods are frequently claimed in order to justify public funding for commodity development. This has been possible with the assumption of universalism (in this case, a homogeneous society whose members all benefit equally from research and technological changes) and the ideological baggage of racism (Perfecto, 1992b). No example illustrates this phenomenon more clearly than the "scientific" development of hybrid corn (Lewontin and Berlan, 1990).

In agriculture these three basic challenges come from a variety of social movements, including environmental justice activists, anti-pesticide activists, biotechnology critics, Third World solidarity movements, migrant farmworkers unions, organic/sustainable agriculture movements, NAFTA and GATT critics, eco-socialists, etc. The collective intelligence of the people in these movements has to be mobilized to articulate a new agricultural discourse based on ecological and economic sustainability as well as on racial, social, and economic equity.

A powerful exercise to help visualize a truly sustainable agriculture would be to examine a real situation where a sustainable agriculture based on social, economic, and environmental justice has actually been attempted. The transformation of Cuban agriculture, especially over the last four years, provides a unique opportunity to do just that.

The "Classical Model" of Cuban Agriculture[1]

In the international socialist division of labor, Cuba's role was primarily to produce sugar and citrus for export to socialist countries. In exchange, it received products from Eastern Europe and the Soviet Union. Sugarcane production went from five million tons to ten million tons through a program of agricultural intensification and incorporation of lands previously used to produce other crops. The importation of cereals, powdered milk, and other food products from Eastern Europe resulted in the transformation of consumption patterns of the Cuban population. Interestingly enough, this division of labor was based on the neoclassical concept of comparative advantage. This division of labor made it possible for Cuba to significantly intensify agriculture and specialize in the production of certain crops, while at the same time providing the population with a diverse and nutritious diet.

The element of greed (in the sense of private profit motive) was counter to the tenets of the socialist revolution of 1959, so it did not play a significant role in the maintenance of unsustainable agricultural practices. On the other hand, poverty and ignorance were (and, to a certain extent, still are) important factors in the propagation and perpetuation of unsustainable agriculture (Levins, 1990).

The first 30 years of the Cuban Revolution were characterized by a commitment to the elimination of poverty, hunger, and illiteracy and to an equitable distribution of wealth. Caloric as well as protein consumption (based to a large degree on imported products) increased to 2,845 calories/grams per day per person and 76 g. per day per person, respectively, one of the highest in Latin America (Peréz Marín and Muñoz Baños, 1991).

Increased food consumption along with other social and health programs resulted in one of the highest life expectancies (75 years) as well as one of the lowest child mortality rates (10 in 1,000) in Latin America. Illiteracy was eliminated. But many of these achievements rested on the shaky pillars of a dependent and nonsustainable agriculture.

Cuban agriculture for the last 30 years was based on what they now call the Classical Model (Peréz Marín and Muñoz Baños, 1991). This model was based on regional specialization under the international socialist division of labor; technically, it shared many features of capitalist industrial agriculture. It centered on increasing production. But unlike industrial capitalist agriculture's goal of profit maximization, its goals were to increase the standard of living of the population as a whole. As with U.S. agriculture, Cuban agriculture experienced a dramatic increase in productivity, and as in U.S. agriculture, this increase was based to a large extent on a shift toward mechanization and agrochemical inputs. Much like in the United States in the 1940s and 1950s, tractors replaced oxen, and much of the agricultural labor force moved to urban areas in the 1960s and 1970s. Chemical fertilizers and pesticides became cornerstones of Cuban agriculture and symbols of the degree of development it had achieved. The consequences of such unsustainable agriculture were an even greater dependence on external markets, a significant pressure on natural resources and the environment in general, and an accelerated rural exodus. Because of concern with human health, the devastating effects of toxic pesticides on farmers, farmworkers, and rural communities as a whole were reduced to a minimum through strict pesticide regulations. Nonetheless, environmental effects were as rampant, or even more so, as in the United States.

The "Alternative Model" of Cuban Agriculture

Probably no other country in the Americas was more affected by the events of 1989 than Cuba. The strong alliance of Cuba with the Soviet Union was not only ideological but also economic. The collapse of the Soviet Union and other socialist countries in Eastern Europe meant to Cuba the loss of 73 percent of its total imports and a similar percentage (figure not available) of their exports (Lage, 1992). In one year Cuba found itself with less than 25 percent of its supply of fertilizers and pesticides, and with little fuel and no imported spare parts for tractors (Lage, 1992). Although Cuba was already in transition toward a lower input agriculture (Levins, 1990), this transformation had encountered many barriers and was proceeding at a slow pace. The events of 1989 served as a catalyst to that process. Now, in what Cubans call "the special period," a new and unique model of agricultural development is being invented.

The Alternative Model has four main components: appropriate technology, alternative organization of labor, alternative planning, and environmental preservation (Peréz Marín and Muñoz Baños, 1991).

Appropriate Technology

The main component of appropriate technology is the minimization or elimination of agrochemical inputs and heavy machinery in such a way that productivity is maintained as much as possible, and health and environmental damage is minimized. To achieve this goal, the Cubans have focused on ecological pest management, organic fertilizers, and animal traction.

The first significant steps toward sustainable agriculture were made in the 1980s, when the Ministry of Agriculture adopted biological pest management as one of its national priorities, after several biological control programs proved to be very successful (Levins, 1990). Thanks to this prior development, the "special period" did not represent a dramatic shift in terms of pest management, but rather an expansion and intensification of what they were already doing. Major advances in ecological pest management have been made through the development of biological control of insect pests. Today Cuba has 222 Centers for the Reproduction of Entomopathogens and Entomophagous Agents (CREE) distributed in all the provinces. These centers consist of relatively simple facilities where artisan techniques are combined with semi-industrial techniques (i.e., autoclaves, fermenters, etc.) to produce and distribute a variety of biological control agents, such as parasitic wasps and bacterial and fungal insect diseases. In 1991, the CREEs produced 764 tons of *Bacillus thuringensis*, 207 tons of *Beauveria basiana* and *Metarhizium anisopliae*, and 31 tons of *Verticillium lecanii*, all of which are entomopathogens of important pests that attack vegetables, rice, plantain, taro, sweet potatoes, potatoes, tobacco, corn, and flowers. In addition, 9.8 billion *Trichogramma* sp. (parasitic wasps) were raised and distributed for the control of insect pests in pastures and taro, and 15,300 hectares of sweet potato fields were "planted" with colonies of the ant *Pheidole megacephala* to control the main insect pest in that crop.

Weed and disease control through ecological means is more difficult to achieve than insect control for a variety of reasons that are beyond the scope of this chapter. In the last two years, four Cuban researchers have intensified their efforts to develop programs for the integrated management of weeds and diseases, with very good results. The focus of the weed control program is to view weeds as a complex community of plants that interact with one another, the crop, and their environment. Through ecological modeling and with data on the species composition in the seed bank, Cuban agronomists are able to predict accurately the composition of the weed community for the following planting season and plant crops accordingly. Disease control has focused on the use of antagonist microorganisms that displace the pathogen but do not harm the crop, but many of these initiatives (except for biological control of insect pests) are still at the level of research or initial implementation. The Cubans predict that within the next five years they will be able to control most insect pests, weeds, and diseases in agriculture through biological means (Jorge Ovies,[2] personal communication).

In general, Cuba has relatively poor soils. In the past, increasing agricultural production focused on the use of inorganic fertilizers, especially nitrogen and phosphorous. Today Cuba has engaged in probably the most ambitious program for organic fertilizers in the world. This program includes a variety of techniques ranging from the old technique of producing high-quality earthworm humus out of bulky and low-quality manure (vermiculture), to the industrial manufacturing of phosphorous-solubilizing bacteria (previously unknown on a commercial scale). The production of *Rhizobium* (nitrogen-fixing bacteria that form a symbiotic association with legumes) on a commercial scale is now standard practice and has replaced all nitrogen application on leguminous crops in the whole country. They are also using *Azotobacter* (a free-living nitrogen-fixing bacteria) as a nitrogen source. Perhaps because of a temperate-zone bias in soil science, it had always been assumed that free-living nitrogen-fixing bacteria were insignificant sources of nitrogen, and that the technology for managing this bacterium on a commercial scale was too difficult. Cuban researchers argue that in tropical soils these bacteria appear to play a more significant role than in temperate soils, and they seem to have overcome the technical problems related to large-scale production, making Cuba the only country using *Azotobacter* on a massive scale to substitute for the nitrogen fertilizers that evaporated in 1989.

Today Cubans have less than half the fossil fuel they had in 1990 for agricultural production (Rosset, 1994). The lack of fossil fuel in the countryside has been overcome by the use of animal traction. Although Cuba had almost completely eliminated oxen from the countryside in the 1970s, it has now trained 100,000 oxen and is in the process of training another 100,000. Oxen are now a common feature of the rural landscape, and farming implements are being redesigned both to fit oxen and to conserve soil.

These are but a few examples of the type of appropriate technologies that now characterize Cuban agriculture. Some represent the reimplementation of old technologies, others are clever modifications of technologies developed elsewhere, and yet others are Cuban inventions. Within this last category there are what appear to be major scientific and technological breakthroughs made possible by the investment in science and education of the Cuban Revolution during the last 30 years.

To the extent that the Cubans have adopted and modified very old techniques (vermiculture, animal traction, and others), they have done so within a new discourse under which these technologies are seen not as "backward," but rather as "cutting-edge appropriate technologies," or what Richard Levins (1990) calls "thought-intensive technologies." These guarantee Cuba's survival during a period of high uncertainties, but also are Cuba's contribution to a new, more livable future world.

Alternative Organization of Labor

An alternative organization of labor has been necessary in part because of the move toward appropriate technology. With the return of animal traction and low-input agriculture, more labor is needed in the countryside. The Cubans have faced this new challenge through a variety of policy changes that prioritize agricultural labor and provide incentives to city workers to volunteer to work in the countryside and so stimulate the re-establishment of rural communities. A volunteer program established in 1990 to solve the immediate problem of food supply to the cities is seen as a short-term solution. On the other hand, the re-establishment of rural communities (with roads, housing, schools, health centers, etc.) is regarded as the long-term solution to the labor shortage in the countryside and to the more philosophical problem of the separation of people from nature.

Significant labor reorganization occurred also within the large state farms. With the exception of those that produce sugarcane and perhaps rice, state farms constituted a mosaic of smaller production units, all managed by a central administration staff for the whole farm. Labor used to be distributed according to specialized tasks and the labor demands on the farm as a whole. So, for example, a working crew might have spent three days harvesting in one production unit and then be moved to another. Now, to stimulate a stronger link between workers and the land, each working crew is associated with only one production unit, from planting to harvesting. In that way people have a stronger attachment to the piece of land they are working and hopefully will make greater efforts to preserve its productivity. These efforts have been undertaken under a new program called Linking People with the Land (Rosset, 1994). In addition, greater efforts are being made to use local labor instead of migrant labor.

The more ecological the technology, the more site specific it has to be. To deal with this, Cuba has developed a system in which the farmers (or farmworkers) interact with the off-farm scientists to determine the most efficient way to manage the production unit and to develop appropriate technologies for it. This facilitates the interaction between those who have a detailed intimate local knowledge of their own circumstances and those who can provide the general, theoretically based, and abstract knowledge that requires some distancing from the particular (Levins, 1990). In addition, some of the technical staff, who used to sit in the central administrative office of the farm and pay only occasional visits to the production units, have been transferred to the units and have become part of the regular staff of the production unit. The same principle, that a stronger attachment to the land will foster a stronger and more direct commitment to sustainability, applies to the technical staff. But it also results in a greater degree of communication between the farmworkers who do the field tasks and the technical staff who make recommendations on what needs to be done. This is an example of a continuous flow of knowledge from the farmworkers (and peasants) to the technical personnel and vice versa. The most dramatic change in the reorganization of labor, and in a sense the culmination of the Linking People with the Land Program, occurred in 1993, when the government terminated the existence of state farms and turned them into workers cooperatives (Perfecto, 1994; Rosset, 1994).

Alternative Planning

Alternative planning reflects the urgency of the food situation in Cuba. The sudden shift to a low-input agriculture, and in some cases the complete elimination of agrochemical inputs from one season to the next, inevitably leads to some yield reduction. This, in combination with the loss of a large percentage of their imports (which included a variety of food items that had become part of Cubans' regular diet), has resulted in a food crisis. Protein intake, for example, has been reduced by 30 percent over the last four years (Pérez-Marín, personal communication). The economic blockade imposed by the United States has made a bad situation even worse; food that could be imported from Miami (only 90 miles away) has to be imported from Europe, Asia, or South America, sometimes tripling the cost of transportation. To address these problems, the Cubans have developed a variety of food programs, primarily in the cities where the food crisis is most evident, and have made some changes in land-use and agricultural planning to reflect the priority of food production during the "special period." Municipal gardens are sprouting up all over Havana. Each social center (including schools, hospitals, child care centers, factories, and state agencies) has its own production garden, which supplies vegetables, fruits, and other foods to the people at the centers. Changes in land-use planning reflect the changes in production priorities from increasing foreign exchange (or the acquisition of hard currency) to increasing food self-sufficiency. The rotation of export crops with food crops, the intercropping of export and food crops, and the adjustments of land use to crop requirements have all become standard practices in Cuban agriculture. For example, the intercropping of sugarcane with soybeans guarantees a protein source for the population (either as vegetable protein or as feed for pigs, the main meat consumed in Cuba) and at the same time maintains the production of the main export crop that generates the hard currency needed for the importation of fuel, spare parts, and other goods necessary for other sectors of the economy.

Environmental Preservation

Environmental preservation is at the center of the Alternative Model. An indigenous ecological movement in Cuba has been growing since the mid 1970s, when the Commission for Environmental Protection was created. This movement is very different from the environmental movement in the Developed World and lacks the misanthropy that characterizes the latter. According to Richard Levins (1990: 126), "Cuban ecology activists are political, committed revolutionaries who see their struggles for ecologically sound policies as part of the duties of communists in building a new society with its own relation to nature." These activists have been very influential in developing the environmental consciousness of the people through a proselytized participation in mass organizations (unions, the Women Federation, etc.). The crisis generated by the events of 1989 helped legitimize ecologists in all facets of Cuban life, but was particularly important in legitimizing sustainable agriculture.

Conclusion: Lessons from the Development
of Sustainable Agriculture in Cuba

The development of sustainable agriculture in Cuba was a response to external and internal pressures. On the one hand, the sudden loss of almost all trade with the Soviet Union and the Eastern European countries left Cuba with extreme shortages of fuel, pesticides, and fertilizers for agricultural production. On the other hand, the realization that their agricultural system, dependent on costly inputs and environmentally unsound practices, could not maintain the conditions of production much longer. This led them to invest in the development of alternative agricultural practices that facilitated the transition to low-input agriculture. The coupled effects of these events has resulted in the biggest experiment in the transformation of agriculture in recent history. Although the experiment has not been completed, preliminary results are promising.

While it is very unlikely that the United States will experience a sudden loss of agrochemical inputs, many have already recognized the unsustainable nature of industrialized agriculture and are looking for alternatives. The Cuban experiment provides a unique opportunity to examine not only the implementation of appropriate technology on a massive scale, but also the development of a sustainable agriculture within the framework of racial, economic, and social equality.

Concerns for the well-being of the population as a whole have been molding the development of agriculture in Cuba since 1959. It was this concern that initially resulted in the prohibition of the use of certain toxic pesticides and the search for alternatives. But the desire to supply the whole population with adequate nutrition, under conditions of underdevelopment and the lack of knowledge, created a sense of urgency that led to short-term solutions. This contradiction was almost always resolved by emphasizing increased production and relegating environmental and other long-term concerns to a secondary place. In that sense, the events of 1989 were eye-opening for Cuban planners. Since then, food self-sufficiency has become their number one priority.

U.S. agriculture suffers from the reverse problem. The crisis of overproduction has resulted in depressed farm-commodity prices, the accumulation of an enormous debt by farmers, the degradation of the environment, and the degradation of the rural sector. In U.S. agriculture greed, rather than poverty and ignorance, hinders the development of sustainable agriculture. Institutionalized greed makes the profitability of a technology the sufficient and only reason for its invention and promotion (Levins, 1990). Therefore, any technology that does not result in high profitability is not promoted. Greed, more than any other factor, represents the biggest barrier to the development of sustainable agriculture in the United States.

But there are other lessons to be learned from the Cuban experience. First, the re-construction of integrated rural communities appears to be an essential component of the development of sustainable agriculture. However, rather than isolated self-contained units, these communities are conceived of as interdependent, forming part of an integrated rural society. Centralized but democratic planning should prevent the anarchism and exclusionism that could spring from a purist and myopic bioregionalist approach. It was this centralized democratic planning that allowed Cuba to move to sustainable agriculture at such a rapid pace.

Second, the small-is-better ideology of some sustainable agriculture movements in the United States might not be the most appropriate for a complex modern society. We should be able to distinguish between the unit of planning and the unit of production. To take advantage of the economies of scale and to satisfy larger societal goals, the planning unit should be large. But to maintain the ecological integrity of the region and to benefit from the intimate knowledge of very local conditions, the production units should be much smaller and should form a mosaic of production systems (Levins, 1990).

Third, the interaction of farmers and farmworkers with researchers and other technical people should be continuous and should take place when the parties meet on terms of equality and mutual respect. Farmers and farmworkers possess very intimate knowledge of their surrounding environment and are continually inventing and adapting technology. This knowledge should be valued as part of the scientific enterprise.

Finally, the realization that there is not just one pathway to development is needed. The developmentalist approach led Cuba to embark on the classical model of development for the first thirty years of the revolution. This was thought to be the only possible pathway. The creation of an alternative model challenges that developmentalist ideology. Five years after Cuba engaged in this massive experiment on sustainable agriculture, it is showing the world that even though it is not an easy pathway, it is a highly rewarding one. But even more important, the transformation of agriculture provides the rest of the world with the first real test of the transition from conventional to organic agriculture on such a large scale. It will be in the interest of humanity to see the experiment succeed.

Notes

1. The information presented in this and the following section was obtained during a fact-finding mission to Cuba that took place in November 1992. The data were provided by the Cuban Ministry of Agriculture.

2. Jorge Ovies is director of the Institute of Plant Protection Research of Cuba's Ministry of Agriculture.

14

Rethinking International Environmental Policy in the Late Twentieth Century

Frederick H. Buttel

... the environmental agenda lacks an image of how the people of developing countries can achieve modernization that will enable them to achieve significant improvements in living standards.

Introduction

There is scarcely an American or international environmentalist who was not enthusiastic, or at least relieved, about the Clinton/Gore victory in November 1992.* A glance at Gore's (1992) *Earth in the Balance* leaves little doubt that the vice president has extremely strong environmental convictions, and the persons the administration has nominated for environmental policy-related cabinet and agency posts (Bruce Babbitt as secretary of the interior, and Carol Browner as administrator of EPA) suggest even more reasons to be optimistic about the course of environmental policy in the 1990s.

Not only does the current administration have a pro-environmental veneer, but Gore's *Earth in the Balance*, which exhibits considerable sophistication about environmental science, shows that Gore at least has a strongly environmental core.

*Although environmentalists were enthusiastic about the Clinton/Gore ticket and although they were pleased that a considerable number from their ranks entered the federal government at various levels, the environmental performance of the Clinton/Gore administration has been less than adequate. Considerable amounts of pressure to weaken or even do away with environmental regulations were in evidence even before the November 1994 elections.

Frederick H. Buttel is professor of rural sociology at the University of Wisconsin, Madison. He has done research on a variety of environmentally related issues and problems, including environmental attitudes, the internationalization of environmental activism, agricultural sustainability and sustainable development, energy efficiency, conservation of crop plant genetic resources, the relationship between the environmental and labor movements, and the changing role of environmental quality in national politics. He is co-author of Environment, Energy, and Society *(1986) and co-editor of* Labor and the Environment *(1984).*

In his book, and occasionally during the campaign, Gore spoke convincingly of the need for the United States to exercise "moral authority" in the service of environmental protection.

Earth in the Balance is particularly distinctive in that it clearly embraces the international or global environmental orientation that has become so prominent in the environmental movement since the late 1980s. The policies advocated by Gore in *Earth in the Balance* are largely consistent with those favored by the major organizations in the international environmental movement. Insofar as international environmental policy is almost certain to be one of the most important and the most visible, glamorous, and controversial areas of environmental policy, Gore's presence in the administration provides strong encouragement that the United States will no longer be "isolated" in international environmental negotiations. The fact that Gore will be given responsibility for coordinating federal technology as well as environmental policy is another plus. The kinds of technologies that are promoted, and the ways in which new technologies are regulated, will be crucial in the progress that can be made in environmental and conservation policies. In sum, the conditions for American leadership in international environmental policy could hardly be more propitious. A new administration with pro-environmental impulses has taken office at the apogee of international environmental awareness and will have a Democratic Congress with which to work.[1]

Despite these clear reasons for optimism about the course that environmental policy may take in the new administration, it takes no deep understanding of national and international political economy to realize that the pro-environmental impulses of persons at the top level of the new administration will be tempered by the imperative to deal with a variety of enormous, if not intractable, problems. Clinton/Gore were elected on a fairly traditional, mildly "social democratic" and social-Keynesian platform. They will mainly be held to account after four years in terms of whether they were able to promote more rapid economic growth and to utilize government resources to achieve simultaneously a social safety net and increased public investment in infrastructure that will help underwrite further growth. Unemployment, global economic stagnation, the federal budget deficit and national debt, the U.S. trade deficit, the health care crisis, "welfare reform," trade liberalization, international monetary instability, and countless other manifestations of Clinton's motto, "the economy, stupid," will in all likelihood command far more of their attention than will environmental policy. There is every indication that federal policy will be deficit-driven, meaning that environmental protection, both domestic and through foreign aid, is not likely to have a strong claim on additional funding. The environment was not really given much stress by Clinton/Gore as a campaign issue, particularly down the stretch when "promises" are taken most seriously. Bush/Quayle's ridiculing of Gore as "ozone" during the last two weeks of the campaign proved to be fairly effective and no doubt reinforced the instinct of Clinton/Gore to soft-peddle their environmental views.

Further, the United Nations Conference on Environment and Development

(UNCED, or the "Earth Summit") of June 1992, which it was hoped would set forth the mechanisms and help generate the resources for global conservation, arguably was a qualified failure. The disappointments of UNCED may signal that the momentum behind international environmental policy has peaked.

No matter how accurate the picture just painted is of a new administration with pro-environmental views and intentions, and as environmentally responsive as it can be given the other problems it has inherited, the environmental policy prospects for the next several years will be a complex matter. The progress that will be made will be largely a function of whether there is social innovation in policy strategies, in research and development strategies, and in the vision of government officials, environmental movement organizations, and other groups. Though I will not elaborate on the point here, my guess is that UNCED did not fail primarily or entirely because of Bush administration recalcitrance, but rather on account of some structural features of the world economy, geopolitics, and national politics that the Clinton/Gore administration must address if it is to earn good marks for its international environmental policy. We should also bear in mind that while government environmental scientists and agencies in most of the industrial countries were quite aware of the state of evidence on global climate change in the mid-1980s (see, for example, the considerable material on this topic in the widely circulated World Commission on Environment and Development's *Our Common Future*, published in 1987), not one nation-state was willing to publicize this knowledge and initiate a plan of response. Mass mobilization by international environmental organizations was necessary to put these issues on the public agenda. This will likely continue to be the case.

I will begin with a few analytical comments on how one should conceptualize environmental mobilization and politics in general, and the emerging international environmental politics of the last decade of the twentieth century in particular. I will then explore some of the major political, economic, and ideological factors that will shape international environmental policy during the Clinton/Gore administration. Finally, I will make some suggestions about how an administration that professes to want to make a difference in environmental policy, particularly international environmental policy, can do so and still be re-electable four years hence.

The Nature of Environmentalism and Environmental Mobilization

The past five or so years have been a period of very considerable mobilization about global environmental problems by non-governmental organizations (NGOs) and citizens. In late 1988, in the aftermath of widespread droughts and severe climatic episodes in several of the temperate industrial countries, the major groups in the international environmental community began to raise concerns about how global air pollution had already led to stratospheric ozone depletion and was almost certain to lead to global warming. Shortly thereafter a cluster of issues closely or not so closely related to ozone depletion and greenhouse gases—such as the loss of tropical biodiversity, land degradation, acid rain, desertification, and ocean pollution—came to be grouped under a common umbrella of "global environmental change." Though the vast bulk of greenhouse gases and ozone-depleting chemicals are products of fossil fuel consumption and the chemical industry in industrial countries (OECD countries, plus the former COMECON countries of Eastern Europe), the scope of global environmental change was expanded to include many of the environmental problems of the tropics. Most important in this regard was the "rainforest connection": the fact that the burning of tropical rainforests releases greenhouse gases (particularly CO_2), while at the same time causing other problems (loss of biodiversity, land degradation, and so on).

Some indicators of the significance and scope of global environmental mobilization are the fact that it culminated in the most heavily attended UN conference in world history (UNCED) in Rio de Janeiro in June 1992, and that global environmental change very soon became a pervasive buzzword within the NGO community, universities, international agencies, and the popular press. Another indicator is that the international environmental movement created a climate in which an otherwise mainstream American politician such as Al Gore was prompted to write *Earth in the Balance*.

Global environmental mobilization and the widespread institutionalization of its symbols and occasionally its substance are conventionally thought of as having been a process of enlightenment about the environmental realities of the late twentieth century. There has been enlightenment in terms of more widespread recognition of the scientific facts revealed by the environmental, planetary, ecological, and evolutionary sciences. The rise of global environmental mobilization is also widely hailed as a step forward in creating greater awareness of the fact that all of us in the global village have a moral obligation to protect the biosphere for the use and enjoyment of future generations.

There is much to be said for the rise of global environmental consciousness having been a logical step toward enlightenment about the facts of, and our obligations to, the biosphere. But these phenomena also need to be examined in a broader perspective about how environmental issues are framed. I would argue that a more realistic and useful perspective on international environmental issues must see these phenomena in much more variegated terms.

Consider briefly some of the distinctive aspects of environmental issues and some of the implications for how we define global environmental problems and identify solutions. Most social movements, such as feminism, the working-class movement, civil rights, and others, involve an identifiable constituency that stands to benefit if movement goals are achieved. Environmentalism, particularly international environmentalism, does not have a "natural" or enduring constituency that anchors its base of support. There are, in other words, no a priori bearers of the environmental agenda.[2] There are manifold ways in which almost any social group can find its interests being consistent with a "pro-environmental" position, or alternatively that it would oppose a particular environmental policy. What the agenda and implications of environmentalism are at any given point is a social product.

Environmental issues are distinctive in several other respects: (1) Environmental issues are ubiquitous, in that there is scarcely a social relationship or social process that does not involve some implication for resource use, pollution, ecosystem processes, or the biosphere. (2) Because environmental issues are ubiquitous, the forums at which environmentally related decisions must be influenced and where environmental struggles must be waged are innumerable; as a result, the environmental movement must come up with master, all-encompassing strategies and powerful symbols that will be persuasive and effective, and will enable energies to be focused on a few forums in which environmentalists can make the biggest difference. (3) Because the referent of environmentalism is the human relationship to the natural world, environmentalism may be enhanced or legitimated by natural-scientific reasoning and evidence, or it may be undermined by contrary natural-science data (Buttel, 1992; Yearley, 1991).

Environmental issues as a social product must be conceptualized and understood in two quite different respects. The first dimension is one of environmental quality or integrity being a social end which, if achieved, will confer no particular privately appropriable benefits to those who advocate for environmental quality. Many environmental goals are public goods, the benefits of which would go to environmentalists and non-environmentalists alike. Such goals (e.g., the notion that it is important to leave a wholesome environment for future generations, to conserve all biodiversity) are often intangible or diffuse when viewed from the eyes of a typical North American household struggling to make ends meet. The rationales presented for achieving such goals are usually moral or ethical in nature. In this sense, although environmental protection has a universal constituency, it may, because of the diffuse, public-goods nature of such an objective, have no particular constituency.

The second, or situational, dimension of environmental issues concerns the fact that these issues invariably involve concerns and material interests that are extra-environmental or non-environmental in nature. In other words, environmental issues and conflicts tend to be shaped in highly situational and contingent ways. Virtually every environmental policy issue is nested within other social issues, interests, and motivations. International environmental issues, in particular, are typically characterized by the superimposition of environmental motives and claims upon longstanding political, economic, and social struggles and policy questions (e.g., who benefits from development programs? Is colonization of frontiers by poor people desirable or undesirable? Can or should the planet feed several billion more human residents? Is rural-to-urban migration desirable? Is a raw-materials-export-oriented development policy a viable strategy to achieve Third World modernization?). Thus, while environmental issues as a whole cannot be tied in any universal way to the interests and concerns of particular social groups, most concrete environmental issues will involve clear-cut distributional implications and specific material interests. Various groups support or oppose environmental policies because of how these policies would affect their incomes and profits, economic security, property values, workplace safety, and public health (what Sunderlin, 1992, has called "instrumental environmentalism"). This means that over the long term, successful environmental mobilization will require coalition partners—in other words, non-environmentalist allies who support environmental protection because it will generally benefit the allies in concrete ways. At the same time, environmentalists can be sure that a broad agenda of environmental conservation will attract an array of opponents.

Recognizing these organizing dilemmas, environmental movements have continually been compelled to seek out new ways of packaging their agendas and claims that, they hope, would be persuasive and effective. Well before the rise of global environmental change, these strategies tended to be based on globally oriented scientific reasoning (and ethical-moral appeals), because of the advantages such reasoning affords in dealing with the difficulties of environmental mobilization (ubiquity, multiple forums, the need for scientific legitimacy). Historically, these have included "the population bomb" (a notion from population biology and demography codified in popular terms by Ehrlich in 1968); the "limits to growth" (a notion from the systems dynamics school of operations research engineering, codified in popular terms by Meadows et al., 1972); and now "global environmental change" and "global warming" (originally codified by a range of scientist-environmentalists, especially Schneider, 1976; Myers and Myers, 1982; and WCED, 1987). Each was a comprehensive, essentially global, framework that justified the need for a global approach to more comprehensive environmental protection. Each did so by forecasting global disruption, predicting that if environmental conservation at a global scale was neglected, the future of humanity and the biosphere would be in peril. From each of these scientific-ideological vantage points, a strong case was made for concerted international responses; in so doing, the multiple forums of environmental problems can be dealt with because global agreements and regulations will override politics as usual on national and local levels. It merits mention, however, that each of the previous global formulas was ultimately de-legitimated to such a degree that the environmental community had to largely abandon the approach and look for a new one (Buttel et al., 1990; Taylor and Buttel, 1992).

Toward a Sympathetic Critique of Global Environmentalism: Implications for International Environmental Policy

While the international environmental movement has done the world a great service in putting global environmental change on the public policy agenda, scholars and policymakers need to be sympathetically critical of how global environmental issues have been framed through movement efforts. We must be sympathetic, in that the efforts of the environmental community have had to confront some formidable opposition to effective environmental mobilization. Due to their activities, the U.S. electorate and other citizens of the planet are now much more aware of the realities of environmental degradation than they were five years ago. Even in this era of fairly widespread awareness of global environmental issues, nation-states are not likely to be any more proactive toward international environmental policy than they were in the mid 1980s. Environmentalist mobilization and pressure will be essential to keeping global environmental problems on the agendas even of those governments that have better than average track records on environmental protection.

But now that mobilization around global environmental change has peaked, and may well be in decline, there is a need for a fresh approach. We must be candid about how limited the definitions of these problems by the international environmental community and environmental scientists have been. Some of the limits and vulnerabilities of the global thrust to solve environmental problems include the following.

Much of the scientific basis of global environmental change is now being cast in doubt. Some well-known climate scientists have stated that global circulation models are not adequate to predict a significant level of global warming five or six decades into the future (e.g., Bryson, 1990; see Pearce, 1992a). Human-induced desertification is coming to be recognized as a near myth (Pearce, 1992b).[3] Many scientists reject the notion that loss of tropical biodiversity seriously threatens the global biosphere (see Mann, 1991). Efforts to address global environmental change face, therefore, a slow but steady de-legitimization of the scientific bases of their agendas.[4]

Global environmental change has been presented in a singular, undifferentiated way that may stand in the way of identifying priorities and developing realistic solutions. We need to keep in mind that global environmental change is as much a social construction as it is a natural phenomenon. Global warming (and later, global environmental change) was constructed within the environmental community as a comprehensive environmental rationale, essentially an umbrella under which most of the movement's pre-existing priorities (such as habitat preservation, protection of endangered species, industrial pollution control) could be placed. But as noted earlier, this imagery—which represents scientifically documented threats to the biosphere and to humanity that must be addressed globally and collectively—is itself being chipped away by science. In addition to some of the scientific questioning of global environmental change noted earlier, other scientific arguments can undermine the traditional agenda. For example, we know that some regions (the temperate breadbaskets, coastal areas) would be adversely affected by global warming, while others (northern temperate areas) would be affected very little or might even benefit (Stern et al., 1992). The highly variable regional effects of global environmental problems not only undermine the imagery of a world community facing a (uniform or undifferentiated) shared peril, but can also divide nations according to how much they might be hurt or might benefit from global environmental change. The argument of some economists that we may be able to "mitigate" global warming more cheaply than we can stop it (see the summary in Stern et al., 1992) can be persuasive to many.

To deal more effectively with the world's environmental problems, a more fine-grained view of these problems is needed; one that considers global environmental issues as affecting the disruption of either (1) globally functioning systems such as the atmosphere and oceans (some global environmental problems are more global than others)[5] or (2) "local" (nation-state, regional, community) systems requiring a geopolitical strategy.[6] Table 14.1 presents types of global environmental issues based on these distinctions. The typology suggests that some ostensibly global environmental problems are actually fairly localized problems in terms of the ecological systems that are disrupted. Saying that they are "global" problems may undermine the integrity of the concept of global environmental change. Also, many environmental problems that have a widespread ("global") incidence will in all likelihood need to be solved through national or other local action. It should also be kept in mind that the vast bulk of actions needed to address such global environmental problems as atmospheric disruption have as strong a rationale, or even a stronger one, at the national/local level. For example, reducing greenhouse gases can reduce smog and the discomfort and health problems due to air pollution, reduce energy imports and the trade deficit, provide insurance against future energy shortfalls or price increases, increase industrial efficiency, and generate more export revenues from sales of improved technologies.

Major environmental groups, in striving to popularize global environmental issues and make the message as palatable as possible, have tended to emphasize certain issues (e.g., putting disproportionate blame on Third World countries for their rainforest destruction; putting emphasis on bringing other countries to heel through international agreements) and to de-emphasize others (e.g., the need for drastic energy conservation in the industrial countries). This approach has alienated many Third World countries, put too many eggs in the UNCED basket, and left an awareness gap among Western publics in terms of the degree to which energy conservation must be achieved in the industrial countries. In addition, little has been said about the possibility that reducing greenhouse gases without also achieving significant energy conservation could lead to greater reliance on nuclear power, and thus to further electrification of and risk in the energy system (Buttel et al., 1990).

International environmental mobilization has also tended to succumb to "rainforest fundamentalism." Destruction of primary rainforests was often exaggerated as a source of greenhouse gases, while the degree to which greenhouse

Table 14.1. Types of Global-Scale Environmental Problems

Appropriate or Likely Solutions Are Likely to Be at:	Environmental Problems Affect Globally Functioning Systems (Yes, are "Systemic"; No, are "Cumulative")[a]	
	Systemic	Cumulative (Local)
The "local" (primarily national) policy level	Land-use emissions of greenhouse gases Industrial and consumer emissions of greenhouse gases	Toxic wastes
International policy level	Industrial emissions of ozone-depleting chemicals	Third World land degradation problems requiring innovative agri-cultural research

[a]This distinction is based on Turner et al. (1990).

gases derive from industrial and fossil fuel combustion sources in the developed industrial countries has often been understated. International development assistance has been shifted from the problems of agriculturists and nonrainforest zones toward the problems of rainforest dwellers and primary rainforest ecosystems.

Searching for levers to affect the environmental practices of tropical developing countries, the international environmental movement has elected to work closely with the World Bank/IMF complex. The implicit threat that adjustment, bridging, and project loans might be terminated by the Bank and IMF has proven to be a significant lever to increase Third World attention to the environmental effects of their development strategies. But the working relationship between environmental groups and the major institutions of international finance and supervision of debt repayment has no doubt caused the environmentalists to pull their punches about how the Third World debt crisis is a direct and indirect cause of Third World environmental degradation (Buttel, 1992; Daly and Cobb, 1989: 231). It is arguably the case that substantial debt forgiveness would be more efficacious in alleviating Third World environmental degradation than would the biodiversity and forest conventions prepared for ratification at UNCED.

For a variety of reasons, Western environmental groups are experiencing decreased support, and occasionally considerable hostility, from Third World people. Much of the Third World intelligentsia believes that developing countries are being unfairly blamed for global environmental problems (e.g., Center for Science and Environment, 1990). Peasants and the rural poor are troubled by environmental group alliances with (often hated) police and security forces to restrict their access to forests (Peluso, 1991). Tropical timber exploiters and mining firms as well as state architects of ambitious export-led development strategies are unhappy that this obvious option for generating foreign exchange is opposed by environmental organizations and restricted by the very organizations (the World Bank, IMF, and International Development Association) that have imposed structural adjustment plans. Many Third World people continue to bristle when they see more neo-Malthusian rhetoric from environmental groups. Most important, there seems to be growing Third World antagonism to international environmentalism. This may be splitting the world community more than it is uniting it.[7]

The major environmental responses to Third World economic and development problems have been inadequate. Sustainable development, though a promising idea, is almost entirely rural in its orientation (even though in many developing countries upwards of 60 percent of the population is urban). Sustainable development in its current version has little to say about the Third World's urban environmental and socioeconomic problems (a very notable exception to which is the work of the Worldwatch Institute). As noted earlier, sustainable development programs are targeted disproportionately at rainforest zones, typically lead to decreased access to land, and often tend to look upon agriculture as being an environmentally destructive practice. Furthermore, the environmental agenda lacks an image of how the people of developing countries can achieve modernization that will enable them to achieve significant improvements in living standards.

Rethinking International Environmental Action:
The Context

I would argue that a productive strategy for international environmental action and policy must be based on a very clear understanding of its context, and of the options and limits this context presents. The milieu of international environmental action and policy is a mixed one, with some definite opportunities and some major problems. My estimation of the nature of this context is as follows.

Protracted global stagnation. The world economy is in an extended phase of economic stagnation, with average annual rates of GNP growth being less than 2 percent. It should be noted in this regard that the anemic rates of economic growth, and thus growth of resource consumption of the past two decades, have not been far away from those advocated by Meadows et al. (1972) in *The Limits to Growth*, which was written at the end of a long era in which rates of about 4 percent per annum were typical. This long phase of stagnation has not diminished the responsibility for economic stewardship to which electorates hold their state officials. Quite the contrary. There is every indication that elections are contested more specifically over strategies to bolster national economic viability than was the case 10, 20, or 30 years ago.

Though this is unlikely to occur during the time of a Clinton/Gore administration, even if there is a second one, global stagnation (relative to the expectations of mid-century) could be liberating as far as environmental protection is concerned. The twentieth century in which heavy industrial-led growth of national product led to rising real wages—and to sufficient surplus for expansion of social-Keynesian spending, reinvestment, and further industrial growth—is probably a thing of the past (Lipietz, 1992). In the twentieth century industrial countries have had to choose between economic growth and environmental protection (Schnaiberg, 1980). In the future they may not have that choice; that is, inattention to environmental protection may no longer deliver the economic gains achieved at mid-century, and instead may increasingly undermine economic security.

The Declining Material Basis of Social-Keynesianism and Thus of Social Democracy

The technical, fiscal, and social structural basis of social-Keynesianism has declined significantly. Since social-Keynesianism no longer delivers the goods of full employment, rising real wages, and government fiscal stability, social democracy is decreasingly persuasive at the ballot box. Most regimes in the Western world, regardless of the party in power, are centrist (e.g., Clinton/Gore) or center-right (e.g., Major) governments. They are, in other words, neo-conservative regimes that want to unleash market forces, constrain the share of state revenues going to state dependents, rein in "unnecessary regulation," and so on. Essentially all of the industrial countries have serious fiscal problems. Much as will be the case in the Clinton/Gore administration, their public programs are increasingly deficit-driven. But as I will stress later, fiscal crises will probably open up new opportunities to implement "green taxes" that could simultaneously generate revenue and increase the incentive to conserve resources.

An Integrated and Divided World Economy

It is widely recognized that the world economy is increasingly tightly integrated, mainly through mobility of financial capital and other financial services, and also through trade in raw materials and manufactured goods. This integration is only partial, however, in that the three contending industrial powers, the United States, Japan, and Western Europe, tend to emphasize trade and financial relations among themselves and within the regional trade spheres they dominate (the Americas, East Asia, and the remainder of Europe and Asia plus parts of Africa, respectively; Gilpin, 1987). A handful of "stronger," "upper-income" developing countries, typified by the Asian newly industrialized countries, have prospered, but in the Third World as a whole there has been increased economic differentiation (see the extensive and impressive empirical documentation of this point in UNDP, 1992).[8] The least developed third or so of Third World nations are in aggregate worse off than they were 20 years ago in terms of living standards. Such large sections of the Third World are faring so poorly that some scholars (e.g., McMichael, 1992) now talk of a "post-developmentalist era," or even of the "end of development"; they say the prospects of developmental modernization are so grim, we should stop pretending that development efforts are accomplishing anything positive.

As noted earlier, the Third World debt crisis remains a huge problem, being mainly responsible for a roughly $50 billion annual net capital drain from the developing to the industrial countries (UNDP, 1992). Heavy public (and private) debts have led to structural adjustment policies being imposed on the developing countries by the multilateral international finance agencies in order to ensure debt repayment. These policies typically include deregulation, expansion of exports, and reduction of state social spending so as to free hard currency reserves for loan repayment. For Third World countries to balance their accounts, they must lower their labor costs so that their exports are more internationally competitive, and reduce consumption so that their imports decline. Social welfare declines under these circumstances (Lipietz, 1992; Canak, 1989). In addition to the hardships these policies cause, particularly in poorer and weaker developing countries, their environmental implications are generally adverse.

Environmental Regulations May Be Redefined As Trade Barriers

A major global trade agreement (GATT) is in the final stages of ratification and several major regional trade agreements (NAFTA, EC) are in various stages of implementation. Several of these agreements in their current forms would make some national environmental and health regulations illegal restraints to trade. Trade agreements involving Third World signatories may increase their imperative to export, and thus may cause their agricultural and forest lands to be cultivated more intensively (and destructively). These environmentally threatening provisions of trade agreements, however, were ones that were negotiated under the leadership of the Reagan and Bush administrations and their U.S. trade representatives. These agreements could be modified through leadership of the Clinton/ Gore administration to be more environmentally benign (e.g., permitting tariffs on environmentally sensitive products such as tropical hardwoods and export taxes on military hardware). Since most countries have a strong incentive to achieve greater access to world markets, perhaps trade agreements could be written to include minimal environmental protection standards as a condition of participation, and to exempt most existing national environmental and health standards from lists of nonpermissible nontariff barriers.

End of the Cold War

The Cold War is more or less over. Waning East–West rivalry will likely reduce the impulse by Western nations to spend on foreign aid. But the end of East–West rivalry will open up new possibilities for the redesign of international economic and geopolitical arrangements. Overseas development assistance in the form of military assistance can be reduced sharply; in 1989, for example, Third World expenditures on imported armaments were over $90 billion (UNDP, 1992). There is an ongoing reduction of military spending across most of the world. But there is room for a great deal more reduction in military spending in the developed and developing worlds, and realizing them could yield peace dividends that could go toward debt reduction, environmental protection, and other social investments. Considerable foreign aid for social development and environmental protection could be freed through the demilitarization of American foreign assistance.

Strategies for Implementing International Environmental Policies

There is a great deal of fascination right now with pursuing international environmental agreements as the core strategy for dealing with global environmental problems. Environmental groups and government officials with environmental responsibilities should leave no stone unturned in pursuing such agreements. The Rio Declaration of 27 principles and the Agenda 21 document are very positive statements. By signing the Biodiversity Convention, the Clinton/Gore administration increased its moral and financial support for the climate change and forest agreements. Since the immediate years after UNCED will be critical in sustaining whatever momentum was generated there, the U.S. government's lending a strong, clear voice to the framework convention on climate change, the convention on biodiversity, and the "forest principles" would be helpful.

There are, however, several indications that UNCED and post-UNCED international agreements will not be the magic bullet that will solve global environmental problems. For most developing countries, foreign aid will be crucial to their ability to make progress in environmental protection. Already, though, the governments of several industrial countries that were relatively supportive of the UNCED initiatives (Germany, Britain) have essentially reneged on some of their promised support for the Global Environmental Facility and the Earth Increment program at the International Development Association, due to growing fiscal problems. Several countries (e.g., Britain and even Sweden, the world's most generous aid donor) are rumored to be in the process of paring their foreign aid programs, with some of the savings to come out of environmentally related initiatives. Britain, which holds the presidency of the European Community, proposed a cut of about $225 million in the Community's aid budget, the bulk of which would come from tropical rainforest conservation aid (*The Economist*, 1994).

It should be recognized at the outset that the international arena is a difficult one within which to encourage environmental responsibility. Both main institutions of global society—international trade and the interstate system—are environmentally problematic and provide strong centrifugal forces to efforts to utilize international arrangements to enhance environmental quality. The basic thrust of world trade arrangements is a system of international competition that may compel environmentally destructive practices in order to remain competitive in the international market. The interstate system, based on the principle of state sovereignty, gives nation-states the prerogative to degrade their environments if they see fit.

In general, international agreements (or "international regimes") tend to reflect rather than to restructure power relations among nations (Gilpin, 1987). International agreements generally emerge when a dominant power or power bloc of nations is able to impose an agreement or when an agreement is mutually beneficial to a wide range of parties. That the world currently lacks a single dominant economic and military power that can forge international agreements, and that there is disarray in world power arrangements, was clearly apparent at the Earth Summit. Also, the moral fervor for protecting the global environment that was nurtured on the road to Rio was not sufficient to override the fact that there was insufficient mutual benefit to make meaningful agreements possible. In general, this boiled down to the fact that (1) Third World countries saw too little foreign aid and technical assistance forthcoming from the industrial world to justify surrender of their sovereignty over natural resource policy[9]; (2) the dominant developed countries were too divided on their commitment to global environmental protection to be able to leverage resources from one another, or to put enough on the table to generate reciprocal interest by the South; and (3) in the current global environment of economic insecurity and fiscal stress, most nations concluded that these problems took precedence over achieving global environmental protection, even if aggressive conservation might ultimately be necessary to avert ecological catastrophe.

While not abandoning the international environmental agreement route, environmental groups and the Clinton/Gore administration must pursue complementary strategies. The following are some suggestions to this end.

Those who are committed to solving global environmental problems should be encouraged by the fact that most measures that will help to address global environmental problems will confer national benefits as well. This suggests a needed change of emphasis in justifying or "selling" environmental policies. Rather than relying on scientific arguments implying that new policies need to be implemented primarily to achieve intangible goals (averting global-scale human and biospheric catastrophe), more, but by no means exclusive, stress should be placed on implementing policies primarily because of their national benefits. If these policies should ultimately help to avert international environmental calamities, all the better.

Government fiscal crisis means that new revenue sources must be explored. Ideally, the generation of new revenues should accomplish social purposes other than deficit reduction. One of the most obvious such sources of tax revenues is that of "green taxes" (taxes on natural resources that are consumed, pollution-produced, and so on) to encourage conservation behavior (see Pearce et al., 1989; Repetto et al., 1992). There is a particularly strong rationale for fossil fuel energy taxes in the form of "carbon taxes." These policies exist already in Sweden, the Netherlands, and Finland, and their successful implementation in Northern Europe creates a stronger case that they can be successful here. Carbon taxes at the level of 80 percent or so of final-use cost would help to conserve energy (and, in the U.S. context, sharply reduce the trade deficit) and reduce urban and global air pollution over the short to medium term. Perhaps more significant would be the long-term (10 to 20 years hence) stimulus to the development of technologies that would significantly reduce fossil energy consumption in industry, commerce, households, transport, and so on. The revenues generated should be targeted thoughtfully—a portion to deficit reduction (which would likely be the major rationale for a carbon tax), a portion to alleviate social disruptions caused by the fact that carbon taxes would be regressive, and a portion to development of "green technology."

As Gore (1992) stressed in *Earth in the Balance*, the new administration must do a much better job of funding and coordinating environmentally related research. There is a sound rationale to create a National Institutes for the Environment (NIE), to give them the lead role in U.S. environmental research, and to charge them with emphasizing work on global environmental problems. This recommendation is made, however, with the proviso that the NIE would be primarily mission- and/or policy-oriented or, in other words, that the experience with some earlier ecology research programs that led to little practical knowledge is not repeated. The needed reemphasis on federally funded applied research should place "green technology" agendas, such as energy conservation, alternative fuels, renewable energy, and sustainable agriculture, at the top of the list of applied research topics that demand more support. In addition to fuel-related research, emphasis should be placed on "industrial ecology" R&D that enables a shift from linear to cyclical production methods in industry. Cyclical production processes would enable producers to take "cradle to grave" responsibility for their products and for pollution caused in the production process. While some have claimed that environmentally related business will create jobs and offer huge global-profit-making opportunities (Brown et al., 1993), the green business will be substantial only if there is sufficient public R&D investment to make it happen. Pollution taxes, according to a polluter-pays principle, would reinforce eventual adoption of these technologies. In addition to the domestic benefits from developing these technologies, their availability in the future would make an enormous difference in generating confidence by other nations that more ambitious international environmental targets could be achieved. More research on identifying potentially useful secondary metabolite substances from tropical species would provide further impetus to conserving tropical biodiversity.

Following the 1972 Stockholm UN Conference on the Environment, most developing countries established ministries of the environment. The United States is now among a minority of world nations that do not have a chief environmental "minister" in their cabinets; however, this is expected to change in the near future. There should also be discussion of whether to emulate an innovative Third World environmental policy. Some developing countries have created ministries of science, technology, and environment. Implementing a cabinet position or a White House office with responsibility for environmental protection and technological development would help place environmental protection higher on the priority list of federally supported R&D. In light of the end of the Cold War, the time is ripe to remove the U.S. Agency for International Development (AID) from the Department of State. AID should be relocated to create a more independent American overseas development assistance agency that emphasizes meeting human needs over achieving immediate geopolitical ends (see Lipschutz, 1989, for a useful critique of overseas development assistance programs that have been derived from industrial countries' geopolitical ambitions).

And now for the biggest challenge for Clinton/Gore, that of reshaping the world order in directions that will permit global cooperation and full citizenship for all in the global village. Global society today is essentially an uninviting, if not hostile, environment for international cooperation on the tasks that need to be accomplished as we look toward the twenty-first century. The forces of international economic competition have been unleashed with a scope unprecedented in world history. There is every indication that the tripartite economic rivalry among the United States, Europe, and Japan will intensify. The expression "international competitiveness" is uttered so often nowadays that most people in the world see other countries mainly as competitors posed to take their markets and jobs. Capital mobility and global economic restructuring are undermining the national type of economy in which nation-states have primary control over economic policy. The debt burden, the South-to-North capital drain, the stagnation of overseas economic development assistance, and the end of the Cold War are dividing the developed and developing worlds. The flow of environmental and economic refugees within the South, and from South to North, continues to increase. There is even speculation that the East–West conflict of mid-century could be replaced with a comparable North–South nuclear-weapons-oriented conflict in the twenty-first century. The entire continent of Africa is being economically disenfranchised and condemned to grinding poverty, widespread infectious disease, chronic malnutrition, decreased life expectancy, and so on. This kind of global environment, essentially a coercive one coupled with despair about the future, is not conducive to protecting the biosphere.

I agree with the basic thrust of the UNDP's Human Development Report 1992 that the time has come for world nations to realize that these trends must not continue, and to dedicate themselves to working together to develop a "new global compact." In an industrial world in which most heads of state have considerably less than widespread popularity at home, there is only one such person, Bill Clinton, who is likely to be in a position to initiate the negotiation of this new global compact.

Borrowing liberally from the UNDP report, this new social compact might look something like the following: The industrial countries have a need to come to the table because many of the problems they currently face—drug trafficking, pollution, immigration pressures, and nuclear threats—require cooperation with the developing world. The developing countries are also host to valuable genetic resources that the industrial world covets. Developing countries could bring to the table a commitment to reducing their military expenditures, to nuclear disarmament, to democratic principles and human rights, to stemming the flow of illegal drugs, to reduction of corruption, to environmental protection, to stressing poverty alleviation in development programs, and so on.

Resources to make a new compact work could come from several sources. First, an agreement by world nations to reduce military expenditures would over time free up an enormous peace dividend that could be used to meet human and environmental-protection needs. If, for example, there was a 3 percent decline in military expenditures each year in all world nations in the 1990s, the peace dividend by the year 2000 would be about $1.5 trillion (or about three times the largest number yet mentioned by UNEP as the estimated total cost of implementing the UNCED conventions and agreements).[10] About one-third of the amount would accrue to the developing nations, and this amount would be increased by 50 percent if as little as 12 percent of the industrial world's peace dividend went to environmental foreign aid. A major write-down of developing country debt (and 100 percent debt forgiveness for the poorest developing countries), in which the burden would be shared among official donors, commercial banks, and multilateral institutions, would free up tens of billion dollars annually for use in social development and environmental protection programs. UNDP (1992: 84) has also suggested means of raising revenues to simultaneously encourage conservation of global resources and fund sustainable development programs. Various taxes or levies on users of the global commons (oceans, Antarctica, space), the bulk of which would be paid by the industrial countries, could be implemented to protect these commons resources as well as to raise funds earmarked for conservation programs.

Other revenue sources for sustainable development programs could include tradable greenhouse gas permits, taxes on weapons expenditures, pollution taxes, and fossil fuel consumption taxes. Each of these taxes would simultaneously create incentives for conservation (in both North and South) and make most developing countries the net beneficiaries. Other resources could be freed up by shifting foreign aid from military assistance to development assistance, tying foreign aid to reduction of military expenditure, and restricting arms sales. Promoting and subsidizing North-to-South transfer of "green technologies" would need to become a major emphasis in overseas development assistance.

Also important to generating a global climate supportive of social development and environmental protection is the need to address the issue of property rights in tropical biodiversity (including cultivated plants as well as nonagricultural species). Third World countries that continually hear messages about how valuable their tropical genetic resources are will be unlikely to accede to agreements that involve giving away those resources to the North, while being obligated to respect First World patents on products containing tropical genetic materials. Some system of compensation, in which taxes on appropriate products such as seeds and pharmaceuticals sold are collected in the North for investment in genetic resources conservation in the South, will be needed.

The specifics concerning the origin of resources and the programs to be supported through this covenant, however, are less important than the overall need, which is to create the conditions for a more equitable and cohesive world community. Those conditions, in fact, may need to be achieved before the kinds of agreements that the environmental community pursued on the road to Rio can be brought to fruition.

Concluding Comments
Clinton/Gore cannot be expected to pursue the international and domestic environmental agenda laid out here on their own volition. As noted at the outset, Clinton/Gore were elected on a fairly traditional platform that emphasized a mild renaissance of social-Keynesianism and social democracy. They made no major environmental promises. Whether they give priority to the environment will thus depend on the pressure that the environmental community and its allies place on them to do so.

The position that the environmental movement takes and the kind of allies it cultivates will make a big difference. The environmental community, in my view, is already a few meters down the slippery slope of aligning themselves with forces such as the international development finance establishment, developing country security forces, and the U.S. State Department (through AID funding) that could stand in the way of working toward a more equitable and cooperative world order. The world's environmental community has an increasingly large set of responsibilities. It must create awareness of and support for actions that would conserve environmental resources around the globe. And if the environmental community should decide that it is necessary to line up support for a world summit on a new social development and environmental protection order, the Clinton/Gore administration might be the key to success.

The coalitions that the environmental community elects to construct will indirectly influence the world order that emerges in the future. In my view, the environmental community must place the Third World debt crisis, the "debt regime," and the world monetary order at the very top of its priority list. Until there is a substantial write-down of Third World debt, most conservation and sustainable development programs in the Third World will be little more than rearranging the deck chairs on the *Titanic*. Unless environmentalists side with the debtor nations, they will have implicitly aligned themselves with the forces that perpetuate global and national inequality. Further, as Daly and Cobb (1989) have stressed, the international monetary system in which huge short-term accumulations of money capital from trade and exchange imbalances lead to large debtor–creditor disparities, is undesirable from an American national viewpoint on both economic and environmental grounds. Put somewhat differently, environmental policy must be recognized for what it is—broad social policy.

Notes

1. Governing with a Democratic Congress can be a plus in two senses: A Democratic Congress reduces the gridlock of a divided government, in which the legislative branch is controlled by one party and the executive by another, and there has been a longstanding trend for Democrats in Congress (and statehouses) to be more supportive of environmental legislation than are Republicans.

2. Research on environmental movement activists and supporters has found that they have particular social characteristics: high levels of education, liberal political outlooks, a tendency (or preference) not to work in corporate-industrial milieus, and so on. Note, however, that locally oriented environmental groups have much more diverse memberships and officers than do the larger, internationally oriented ones (Mitchell et al., 1992; Freudenberg and Steinsapir, 1992; Portney, 1992).

3. One of the outcomes of UNCED was a request to the General Assembly of the UN to establish a negotiating committee for the preparation of a convention to combat desertification.

4. This should not be taken as an implication that many or most of the claims of the international environmental community are false, but rather that in the terms in which the claims are presented, there is an enormous burden placed on the data

that can be generated by environmental and planetary scientists. It is, for example, far easier to assert that global circulation models are shaky or incompletely developed than it is to say that there is conclusive proof that there will be a global greenhouse warming of 4 to 5°C by the middle of the twenty-first century. Exploiting scientific uncertainty is a well-developed tactic by industrial firms resisting environmental regulation.

5. See Turner et al. (1990) for a useful discussion of the distinction between systemic and cumulative global environmental change. The former is global environmental change that affects globally functioning systems, and the latter is global environmental change that reflects a global cumulation of local environmental disruption.

6. As the industrial world's major environmental groups have placed increased emphasis on global environmental issues, several problems and antagonisms have emerged between them and other groups (particularly local environmental organizations and "deep ecologists"). For example, Reich's (1991) study of citizen mobilization against toxic waste contamination found that, more often than not, major American environmental organizations were not interested in these problems. The major environmental organizations became involved only after there was sufficient citizen mobilization so that the toxic problem could not be ignored. There are occasional antagonisms between international and local environmental groups, with the latter often feeling that issues of local relevance such as toxics, groundwater contamination, and land-use regulation do not receive sufficient interest among the major groups. The major international environmental groups often see local ones as being parochial, pushing NIMBY agendas that relocate rather than solve environmental problems (Mitchell et al., 1992; Freudenberg and Steinsapir, 1992).

7. Another reason for disillusion and hostility is that many Third World leaders had expected that the agreements to be signed in association with UNCED would lead to a significant infusion of "fresh" green foreign aid funds. Environmental groups and Third World officials were probably unrealistic in this regard. The current foreign aid systems of most of the industrial countries were largely outgrowths of the Cold War and of the East–West struggle for hearts and minds. Now that the Cold War is over, there is little geopolitical rationale even to maintain foreign aid at current levels. UNCED led to commitments for less than $10 billion of fresh environmental foreign aid for implementation of Agenda 21, compared with the $100–$200 billion that the UNCED Secretariat had indicated was the minimum amount needed and the $500 billion figure now floated by the UN Development Program, which has lead-agency responsibility for "capacity-building" under Agenda 21. It is not clear how much of this will be made available. Indeed, there is every indication (*The Economist*, 1994) that only a few months after

the Earth Summit there already was backsliding by the industrial countries on the small amounts they had pledged for the Global Environmental Facility and the Earth Increment to the International Development Association. Further, the bulk of this fresh foreign aid will be administered through the Global Environmental Facility located in the First World–dominated World Bank, rather than through the UN system that is regarded as being more sympathetic to the developing countries. Later I will stress how a new vision for global economic partnership, and thus for the foreign aid system, should be a centerpiece of the agenda for the new administration.

8. It is interesting to note that in this world of increased differentiation among developing countries, the Group of 77 (expanded to include the 128 developing countries) demonstrated such an effective and coherent bargaining power at UNCED. United by the desire to maintain state sovereignty and increase the amount of Western overseas development assistance, the Group of 77 proved to be more coherent and disciplined at UNCED than was the developed world.

9. Developing countries also generally lack the resources and technical capability to participate in and report on compliance related to international environmental agreements.

10. Note that this was the actual average annual rate of decline in global military expenditures (–2.3 percent per annum in developing countries, –3.1 percent per annum in industrial countries) from 1987 to 1990 (UNDP, 1992).

Summary

Bunyan Bryant

...we must be clear that participatory research is not intended to lead to the extrapolation of the findings to a larger population. The purpose of participatory research is to solve the problem at hand—not to test new theories, or to extend them, or to establish causality, or to necessarily use conventional forms of statistical significance. Although community groups are already doing this kind of research, sometimes referred to as "action research" (Lewin, 1946) or "popular epidemiology" (Brown, 1992), more legitimacy should be given to its importance.

Although the post–World War II economy was designed when environmental consideration was not a problem, today this is no longer the case; we must be concerned enough about environmenal protection to make it a part of our economic design. Today, temporal and spatial relations of pollution have drastically changed within the last 100 years or so. A hundred years ago we polluted a small spatial area and it took the earth a short time to heal itself. Today we pollute large areas of the earth—as evidenced by the international problems of acid rain, the depletion of the ozone layer, global warming, nuclear meltdowns, and the difficulties in the safe storage of spent fuels from nuclear power plants. Perhaps we have embarked upon an era of pollution so toxic and persistent that it will take the earth in some areas thousands of years to heal itself.

To curtail environmental pollutants, we must build new institutions to prevent widespread destruction from pollutants that know no geopolitical boundaries. We need to do this because pollutants are not respectful of international boundaries; it does little good if one country practices sound environmental protection while its neighbors fail to do so. Countries of the world are intricately linked together in ways not clear 50 years ago; they find themselves victims of environmental destruction even though the causes of that destruction originated in another part of the world. Acid rain, global warming, depletion of the ozone layer, nuclear accidents like the one at Chernobyl, make all countries vulnerable to environmental destruction.

The cooperative relations forged after World War II are now obsolete. New cooperative relations need to be agreed upon—cooperative relations that show that pollution prevention and species preservation are inseparably linked to economic development and survival of planet earth. Economic development is linked to pollution prevention even though the market fails to include the true cost of pollution in its pricing of products and services; it fails to place a value on the destruction of plant and animal species. To date, most industrialized nations, the high polluters, have had an incentive to pollute because they did not incur the cost of producing goods and services in a nonpolluting manner. The world will have to pay for the true cost of production and to practice prudent stewardship of our natural resources if we are to sustain ourselves on this planet. We cannot expect Third World countries to participate in debt-for-nature swaps as a means for saving the rainforest or as a means for the reduction of greenhouse gases, while a considerable amount of such gases come from industrial nations and from fossil fuel consumption.

Like disease, population growth is politically, economically, and structurally determined. Due to inadequate income maintenance programs and social security, families in developing countries are more apt to have large families not only to ensure the survival of children within the first five years, but to work the fields and care for the elderly. As development increases, so do education, health, and birth control. In his chapter, Buttel states that ecological development and substantial debt forgiveness would be more significant in alleviating Third World environmental degradation (or population problems) than ratification of any UNCED biodiversity or forest conventions.

Because population control programs fail to address the structural characteristics of poverty, such programs for developing countries have been for the most part dismal failures. Growth and development along ecological lines have a better chance of controlling population growth in developing countries than the best population control programs to date. Although population control is important, we often focus a considerable amount of our attention on population problems of developing countries. Yet there are more people per square mile in Western Europe than in most developing countries. "During his/her lifetime an American child causes 35 times the environmental damage of an Indian child and 280 times that of a Haitian child" (Boggs, 1993: 1). The addiction to consumerism of highly industrialized countries has to be seen as a major culprit, and thus must be balanced against the benefits of population control in Third World countries.

Worldwide environmental protection is only one part of the complex problems we face today. We cannot ignore world poverty; it is intricately linked to environmental protection. If this is the case, then how do we deal with world poverty? How do we bring about lasting peace in the world? Clearly we can no longer afford another Somalia; we can no longer afford a South Africa as it was once organized, or ethnic cleansing by Serbian nationalists. These types of conflicts bankrupt us morally and destroy our connectedness with one another as a world community. Yet, we may be headed on a course where the politically induced famine, poverty, and chaos of Somalia today will become commonplace and world peace more difficult, particularly if the European Common Market, Japan, and the United States trade primarily among themselves, leaving Third World countries to fend for themselves. Growing poverty will lead only to more world disequilibrium to wars and famine—as countries become more aggressive and cross international borders for resources to ward off widespread hunger and rampant unemployment. To tackle these problems requires a quantum leap in global cooperation and commitment of the highest magnitude; it requires development of an international tax, levied through the United Nations or some other international body, so that the world community can become more involved in helping to deal with issues of environmental protection, poverty, and peace.

Since the market system has been bold and flexible enough to meet changing conditions, so too must public institutions. They must, indeed, be able to respond to the rapid changes that reverberate throughout the world. If they fail to change, then we will surely meet the fate of the dinosaur. The Soviet Union gave up a system that was unworkable in exchange for another one. Although it has not been easy, individual countries of the former Soviet Union have the potential of reemerging looking very different and stronger. Or they could emerge looking very different and weaker. They could become societies that are both socially and environmentally destructive or they can become societies where people have decent jobs, places to live, educational opportunities for all citizens, and sustainable social structures that are safe and nurturing. Although North Americans are experiencing economic and social discomforts, we too will have to change, or we may find ourselves engulfed by political and economic forces beyond our control. In 1994, the out-sweeping of Democrats from national offices may be symptomatic of deeper and more fundamental problems. If the mean-spirited behavior that characterized the 1994 election is carried over into the governance of the country, this may only fan the flames of discontent. We may be embarking upon a long struggle over ideology, culture, and the very heart and soul of the country. But despite all the political turmoil, we must take risks and try out new ideas—ideas never dreamed of before and ideas we thought were impossible to implement. To implement these ideas we must overcome institutional inertia in order to enhance intentional change. We need to give up tradition and "business as usual." To view the future as a challenge and as an opportunity to make the world a better place, we must be willing to take political and economic risks.

The question is not growth, but what kind of growth, and where it will take place. For example, we can maintain current levels of productivity or become even more productive if we farm organically. Because of ideological conflicts, it is hard for us to view the Cuban experience with an unjaundiced eye; but we ask you to place political differences aside and pay attention to the lyrics of organic farming and not to the music of Communism. In other words, we must get beyond political differences and ideological conflicts; we must find success stories of healing the planet no matter where they exist—be they in Communist or non-Communist countries, developed or underdeveloped countries. We must ascertain what lessons can be learned from them, and examine how they would benefit the world community. In most instances, however, we will have to chart a new course. Continued use of certain technologies and chemicals that are incompatible with the ecosystem will take us down the road of no return. We are already witnessing the catastrophic destruction of our environment and disproportionate impacts of environmental insults on communities of color and low-income groups. If such destruction continues, it will undoubtedly deal harmful blows to our social, economic, and political institutions.

As a nation, we find ourselves in a house divided, where the cleavages between the races are in fact getting worse. We find ourselves in a house divided where the gap between rich and the poor has increased. We find ourselves in a house divided where the gap between the young and the old has widened. During the 1980s, there were few visions of healing the country. In the 1990s, despite the catastrophic economic and environmental results of the 1980s, and despite the conservative takeover of both houses of Congress, we must look for glimmers of hope. We must stand by what we think is right and defend our position with passion. And at times we need to slow down and reflect and do a lot of soul searching in order to redirect ourselves, if need be. We must chart out a new course of defining who we are as a people, by redefining our relationship with government, with nature, with one another, and where we want be as a nation. We need to find a way of expressing this definition of ourselves to one another. Undeniably we are a nation of different ethnic groups and races, and of multiple interest groups, and if we cannot live in peace and in harmony with ourselves and with nature it bodes ominously for future world relations.

Because economic institutions are based upon the growth paradigm of extracting and processing natural resources, we will surely perish if we use them to foul the global nest. But it does not have to be this way. Although sound environmental policies can be compatible with good business practices and quality of life, we may have to jettison the moral argument of environmental protection in favor of the self-interest argument, thereby demonstrating that the survival of business enterprises is intricately tied to good stewardship of natural resources and environmental protection. Too often we forget that short-sightedness can propel us down a narrow path, where we are unable to see the long-term effects of our actions.

The ideas and policies discussed in this book are ways of getting ourselves back on track. The ideas presented here will hopefully provide substantive material for discourse. These policies are not carved in stone, nor are they meant to be for every city, suburb, or rural area. Municipalities or rural areas should have flexibility in dealing with their site-specific problems. Yet we need to extend our concern about local sustainability beyond geopolitical boundaries, because dumping in Third World countries or in the atmosphere today will surely haunt the world tomorrow. Ideas presented here may irritate some and dismay others, but we need to make some drastic changes in our lifestyles and institutions in order to foster environmental justice.

Many of the policy ideas mentioned in this book have been around for some time, but they have not been implemented. The struggle for environmental justice emerging from the people of color and low-income communities may provide the necessary political impulse to make these policies a reality. Environmental justice provides opportunities for those most affected by environmental degradation and poverty to make policies to save not only themselves from differential impact of environmental hazards, but to save those responsible for the lion's share of the planet's destruction. This struggle emerging from the environmental experience of oppressed people brings forth a new consciousness—a new consciousness shaped by immediate demands for certainty and solution. It is a struggle to make a true connection between humanity and nature. This struggle to resolve environmental problems may force the nation to alter its priorities; it may force the nation to address issues of environmental justice and, by doing so, it may ultimately result in a cleaner and healthier environment for all of us. Although we may never eliminate all toxic materials from the production cycle, we should at least have that as a goal.

Although traditional environmentalists have been successful in getting environmental legislation passed, they have so far failed to embrace the needs of those suffering most from environmental oppression and abject poverty. People of color and low-income groups, oppressed by the sickness and anxiety that come from uncertainty, believe they have a better chance than average to succumb to cancer or other toxic-induced or toxic-aggravated diseases. As people of color and low-income groups become more aware of the dangers of toxins, we can expect their resistance to increase around the country. To improve the possibility of achieving pollution prevention and a cleaner and healthier environment, it behooves traditional environmental organizations to get behind the grassroots movement in order to give it their fullest support. This will undoubtedly provide a coalition to weaken the wise use movement and other groups that attempt to delegitimize the environmental movement and reverse the last 20 years of environmental regulations. Neither the environmental justice movement nor the traditional environmental movement can go it alone. Traditional environmental organizations can start by supporting the social justice policies put forth in this book.

Participatory Research

To deal with immediate demands of certainty and solution requires that community people become intricately involved in participatory research. Participatory research does not mean that certainty will be established, but it may provide a working milieu where trust and mutual respect can be fostered and where everyone can give their best effort to find meaningful and agreeable solutions. Although policies will probably be crafted in the absence of certainty, these policies may gain acceptance by community groups, particularly if such groups are involved in their formulation. Although participatory research emerged from work with oppressed peoples in the Third World (Brown and Tandon, 1983), it is also useful to communities in developed countries engaged in the struggle to find environmental solutions. For participatory research to be effective, scientists must become closely involved with communities, not remain detached from them. Scientists must help people to formulate not only questions for research, but to help them gather and analyze data; both parties must be involved in the process every step of the way. Community groups are an important resource and in many instances they have worked with professional/technical people on environmental and health issues (Freudenberg, 1984; DiPerna, 1985; Brown, 1992). Policymakers and scientists alike should not be afraid to be open about the extent of their knowledge and to present scientific information in a way that nonexperts can readily understand.

In addition, community groups should be part of any programs that reduce pollution. They should be part of any discussion that emphasizes reduction of potential risks and any compensation measures that emphasize redistribution through compensation for taking on the burden of uncertainty. It should be clear that involving people in the decision-making process to deal with uncertainty and immediacy of solution is only a temporary solution. We cannot afford to keep producing chemicals, toxics, and hazardous wastes while asking people to assume high risks. Also, such uncertainty should be equally distributed so that no one group is more concerned than another about the potential exposures to hazardous waste. The ultimate goal is to have a society where no group is at risk from life-threatening toxic exposures. To reach that goal we must begin to look at long-range strategies now, using our best brainpower for creative solutions. We need to revamp our institutions, to tread where we have not dared to tread before.

Participatory research is important because the locus of control rests with those who generate the data and not with outside agencies such as governments or corporations. Sampling procedures become key to quantitative research because they empower outside agencies to extrapolate information from a population subset to a larger one. The ability to extrapolate research results to the larger population is the preferred basis for policymaking. However, we must be clear that participatory research is not intended to lead to the extrapolation of the findings to a larger population. The purpose of participatory research is to solve the problem at hand—not to test new theories, or to extend them, or to necessarily establish causality, or to use conventional forms of statistical significance. The involvement of professional and community activists in the repetitive and rigorous process of planning, action, observation, and reflection until desired outcomes are obtained perhaps is a research methodology to help them find immediate solutions. This process ensures that control not only rests with communities, but that the process itself provides opportunities for scientists and community groups to work together in order to help one another better understand the complexity of issues to be researched within a social context. Although community groups are already doing this kind of research, sometimes referred to as "action research" (Lewin, 1946) or "popular epidemiology" (Brown, 1992), more legitimacy should be given to its importance. As the environmental justice movement gains momentum, it will influence scientific thinking; it may force traditional science to give way to a different research paradigm in order to deal with immediate demands for certainty and solution.

If key stakeholders agree to work hand in hand to solve local community problems the questions to be answered are: Can stakeholders or agencies relate to participatory research in ways that are helpful to community groups affected by environmental crises? Can government agencies and universities as a whole accept and make room for nontraditional participatory research? Can stakeholders stand by results from participatory research? Can they withstand the criticism from academics for supporting such research? More specifically can key stakeholders stand up to the heavy onslaught of criticism similar to that leveled at the Harvard study that trained and used community people of Woburn, Massachusetts, to collect data on health problems? These are questions not only for the various government agencies to answer, but for universities as well, particularly as environmental justice research centers become a part of the academic landscape. Participatory research will have a difficult time unless considerable pressure is brought to bear that shows its usefulness and legitimizes its research methodologies and other ways of knowing.

The Information Highway

Because of the new information age we are embarking upon (some refer to it as the information highway), information retrieval may become easier and more readily available. Although some groups will fail to have access to this technology, we must work hard to make sure that such technology is evenly distributed according to income and race. Such technology may make public schools and universities obsolete. Through computers and other forms of mass media, information can be democratized in ways never before thought possible. Perhaps, universities will no longer have a monopoly on knowledge as they do today. Such technology will allow us to gather information on the harmful effects of pesticides, agricultural run-off, and groundwater contamination. This information can be quickly retrieved to help us better understand soil erosion, euthrophication, the effects of global warming, greenhouse gases, desertification, acid rain, depletion of the rainforest, biodiversity, and land degradation. Information can be quickly retrieved to help us to research and understand the concentration of corporate power (e.g., the monopoly of seed, fertilizer, and chemical companies), the role of race, poverty, and the disproportionate impacts of environmental hazards on high-risk populations.

Information retrieval will serve as a basis for making recommendations for policy decisions. Examples of such recommendations reflected in previous chapters are: (1) placing limits on the number and amount of corporate farms owned, (2) fossil fuel consumption tax, (3) worker control of the work place and decentralized industries, (4) new sources of energy based upon renewable sources and recycling programs, (5) elimination of subsidies to energy companies and the abolition of government sales of timber and minerals of all forms, (6) pollution prevention strategies, (7) the cleanup of our communities to make them lead free and the cleanup of other toxic chemicals, creating decent paying and safe jobs. We do not all have to become expert in all areas, but we should know where to obtain knowledge and we should have an understanding of the interrelationships of social, economic, and political forces that determine the quality of our health and our environment.

An Example of Working Together

In the previous two sections we have discussed participatory research and the information highway. At this point I shift the discussion and give an example of where community people and federal agencies were able to work together. On June 9, 1993, the National Institute for Environmental Health Research (NIEHS), the Agency for Toxic Substance and Disease Registry (ATSDR), and the Environmental Protection Agency (EPA) sponsored a meeting in Research Triangle Park, North Carolina, to prepare a symposium on environmental justice research for July 1993. After long and intense debate over the extent of community involvement in the design of a research symposium on environmental justice, the July symposium was postponed to give community participants more time to play a significant role in the design of the symposium. At a planning meeting, it was decided that the symposium was to be held at some future date. It was clear at the outset that government officials had clear notions about how the symposium should be designed and implemented.

To the dismay of government officials, the environmental justice participants wanted more than a token involvement in planning and conducting the symposium. They claimed the research by government agencies was often worthless to them and their communities, and demanded that government officials become more accountable. After much discussion it was decided that grassroots activists would be an integral part of the symposium planning, implementation, and participation.

In February of 1994, approximately 1200 people, one-third of whom were grassroots people, along with numerous university professors, government policymakers, scientists, and some business people, came to the Washington, D.C., area to participate in a three-day Symposium on Health Research and Needs to Ensure Environmental Justice. This symposium was highly participatory. Many professionals were awestruck by the technical knowledge shown by the grassroots people. From this symposium came over three hundred recommendations; an executive summary has been written to be forwarded to EPA and the Interagency Working Group to implement the Environmental Justice Executive Order 12898.

(The Executive Order on Environmental Justice was signed on February 11, 1994 at the White House during the time of the symposium.) These recommendations will hopefully serve as a basis for designing environmental justice strategies for agencies throughout the government. A major theme of the symposium was the involvement of community people at all levels of community research.

The Challenge

Even though the social and economic problems are massive, we should not despair. We should view environmental conditions as a challenge. One does not have to look far to find needed answers or activities that can make a significant difference in our communities and the world at large. To make that difference we must renew our commitment and responsibility to one another, and to building communities where individuals can interact within a safe and a nurturing environment, and where people can have decent health care, clothing, and food. We must develop our spiritual well-being and develop loving and caring relationships that are valued more highly than material possessions. We must build a system based on fairness and justice, to ensure that people have decent jobs and opportunities to develop and express their skills and creativity. We must make sure that housing and equal educational opportunities exist as basic rights for all and not a privilege for the few. We can build a society that is truly democratic and extend democracy into the workplace, where workers spend approximately one third of their waking hours. We can spread social costs and benefits as evenly as possible to everyone without distinctions based on race, sex, or religion. We can build communities where desire for personal relationships replaces the drive for consumerism, where cooperation at the community level is the rule rather than the exception, and where people are not forced into hierarchical relationships based on race, sex, class, and age. We can exercise our basic rights not in ways that exploit, demean, or oppress others, but in ways to develop people's talents to their highest potential and in ways to help us organize for meaningful social change. We can live in harmony with nature by protecting and conserving our highly cherished natural resources to be used prudently to serve human needs and future generations. We can learn to live in a world where biodiversity is respected and cultural diversity is celebrated. We can become planetary citizens so that all people can enjoy equally the highest quality of life possible within the context of a nurturing and sustainable environment. To reach our highest positive potential as a world community, we must answer these challenges.

To take up the challenge of environmental justice requires us to understand that immediate demands for certainty and solution fail to provide long-term solutions, as do the 3Rs or pollution prevention policies. While the latter offer more hope, they are still inadequate because they fail to deal with distributive justice. They fail to deal with equal opportunities for people of color and women or with mounting issues of poverty and racism here at home and abroad. In other words, we can have a clean, healthy, and safe environment as a result of pollution-prevention policies, yet many people will still be without health insurance, jobs, homes, and an adequate education to make them competitive. People will still live in abject poverty and in areas infested with crime and delinquency. The solutions to social and environmental problems require us to move beyond thinking about environmental and social problems in conventional terms. We must begin thinking about them not as separate from one another, but in terms of their intricate relationship with one another. We can no longer afford to champion the rights of trees and nonhuman life without also championing the rights of all people, regardless of race, sex, income, or social standing. We can no longer afford to treat certain categories of people as if they were not a part of a biodiverse community. We need to think of ourselves and nature in ways that increase the quality of human life and in ways that make it possible for nonhuman life not only to exist, but to be revered.

To solve the complex social and environmental problems we face today requires an interdisciplinary approach by universities, governmental agencies, and communities. Such problems do not organize themselves along the patterns determined by academic specialities or governmental agencies or departments. An environmental problem in one area has problematic implications for other areas. For instance, although lead poisoning is a health problem, it is also a housing problem and educational problem, and ultimately perhaps a criminal justice problem. Often those affected by lead poisoning cannot compete as children or as adults, and out of frustration they may commit delinquent or criminal acts; they may never be able to compete for the better jobs in life and are thus more likely to become marginal citizens. Other instances of toxic-induced or -aggravated disease may have multiple social, environmental, and health impacts that require a coordinated, multiple-agency, interdisciplinary approach for solutions. Anything short of an integrated and coordinated approach will be less than adequate.

To date, the environmental justice movement has provided the impetus for a federally coordinated effort to solve these critical social and environmental problems. People of color and low-income communities are not only demanding a coordinated effort on the part of governmental agencies to achieve equal protection against toxic and hazardous waste, they are also demanding in many instances that the government stop industries from producing more toxic and hazardous waste. At no time in our history since the New Deal has there been such a comprehensive movement to deal with the issues of environmental, social, economic, and political problems. Present-day agencies should not attempt to defang or resist this movement. They should view this movement as a challenge to improve the quality of life of all residents of this country. They should tap into this energy to imbue governmental bureaucrats at all levels with a new ethic—an ethic that is more comprehensive than those that have preceded it.

The Clinton administration joined the Environmental Justice Movement by signing the Environmental Justice Executive Order 12898, by establishing the President's Council of Sustainable Development, Executive Order 12852, and by creating the National Environmental Justice Advisory Council (NEJAC) within USEPA. Executive Order 12898 is the first of its kind for developing environmental justice strategies throughout a number of government agencies. This Order promotes the enforcement of all health and environmental statutes in areas of high-risk populations, ensures greater public participation, improves research data collection relating to health and environmental factors of high-risk populations, identifies differential patterns of natural resource consumption among high-risk populations, and a timetable for implementation. Two important points in Executive Order 12898 should be highlighted here: (1) coordination of government agencies in addressing environmental justice problems and (2) the support of grassroots community participation in human health research, including data collection and analysis where practical and appropriate. (For more information on Executive Order 12898, see the appendix.)

The President's Council on Sustainable Development, the first executive order of its kind, adopted a definition of its work to include the meeting of needs of this generation without compromising the ability of future generations to fully meet their own needs. While including high-ranking representatives from industry, government, environmental, labor, and civil rights organizations, the 25 member council cannot carry out its charge of new approaches to integrate economic and environmental policies without having a task force on environmental justice. This task force on environmental justice will undoubtedly play a key role to help shape sustainable development. The National Environmental Justice Advisory Council is also the first of its kind in federal government; it has brought together people from the grassroots community, academia, industry, nongovernment organizations, state, tribal and local agencies, and environmental organizations to advise the EPA administrator on environmental justice concerns.

While the Executive Orders and NEJAC are important and a step forward, we cannot afford to rest on our laurels as we did with the passage of the 1964 Civil Rights Act and the 1965 Voters Rights Act. Many of us rolled down our sleeves and thought that the passage of civil rights legislation meant that our job was finished. We found that it was only the beginning. We cannot afford to make that mistake again with the Executive Orders or with NEJAC, particularly in light of the conservative Republican takeover of the House and Senate. Grassroots people, academics, and others have worked long and hard to bring into existence these Executive Orders and NEJAC; both the Clinton administration and the environmental justice groups must take on the challenge of making them effective. Although this challenge will take much energy, time, creativity, and commitment, we must be ready to make the sacrifice. We can start the process of making them work by having the Interagency Working Group on Environmental Justice established by Executive Order 12898, the President's Council on Sustainable Devel-

opment established by Executive Order 12852, and NEJAC adopt and/or implement the recommendations from the 1994 Symposium on Health Research and
Needs to Ensure Environmental Justice. (See Appendix 2 for information on
recommendations.) Both the Clinton administration and the environmental justice
groups should set up a monitoring system to make sure that the goals of the
Executive Orders and recommendations from NEJAC are implemented. We
should revisit the Executive Orders and the work of NEJAC five years from now
to give the government a score card to indicate the extent of its success. We must
make a conscious effort to correct our mistakes, continue to make recommendations, and to work to make sure those recommendations are carried out.

   We also have to move well beyond the Executive Orders or the work of NEJAC.
Additionally, we must move well beyond immediate demands and solutions of
community groups. We must reorder our priorities to get government agencies to
embrace an industrial policy to provide safe, decent paying, and environmentally
benign jobs to all those who need or want them. We must ensure that environmental
education, including environmental justice, is incorporated into the public schools.
We must create plans for sustainable communities where distributive justice
prevails. We must deal with the issue of land use, housing, banking, energy,
effective national health care, and the indigenous people's needs. We must also
take environmental justice to the international arena and to help build sustainable
communities in both the industrialized and developing countries. Over the next
decade we can expect to experience powerful resistance as we engage in activities
to enhance environmental justice. We must persevere and the victory will be well
worth it to us and future generations.

Appendix 1

EXECUTIVE ORDER 12898

February 11, 1994

*FEDERAL ACTIONS TO ADDRESS ENVIRONMENTAL JUSTICE
IN MINORITY POPULATIONS AND LOW-INCOME POPULATIONS*

By the authority vested in me as President by the Constitution and the laws of the United States of America, it is hereby ordered as follows:

Section 1-1. Implementation.

1-101. Agency Responsibilities. To the greatest extent practicable and permitted by law, and consistent with the principles set forth in the report on the National Performance Review, each Federal agency shall make achieving environmental justice part of its mission by identifying and addressing, as appropriate, disproportionately high and adverse human health or environmental effects of its programs, policies, and activities on minority populations and low-income populations in the United States and its territories and possessions, the District of Columbia, the Commonwealth of Puerto Rico, and the Commonwealth of the Mariana Islands.

1-102. Creation of an Interagency Working Group on Environmental Justice. (a) Within 3 months of the date of this order, the Administrator of the Environmental Protection Agency ("Administrator") or the Administrator's designee shall convene an interagency Federal Working Group on Environmental Justice ("Working Group"). The Working Group shall comprise the heads of the following executive agencies and offices, or their designees: (a) Department of Defense; (b) Department of Health and Human Services; (c) Department of Housing and Urban Developing; (d) Department of Labor; (e) Department of Agriculture; (f) Department of Transportation; (g) Department of Justice; (h) Department of the Interior; (i) Department of Commerce; (j) Department of Energy; (k) Environmental Protection Agency; (l) Office of Management and Budget; (m) Office of Science and Technology Policy; (n) Office of the Deputy Assistant to the President for Environmental Policy; (o) Office of the Assistant to the President for Domestic Policy; (p) National Economic Council; (q) Council of Economic Advisers; and (r) such other Government officials as the President may designate. The Working Group shall report to the President through the Deputy Assistant to the President for Environmental Policy and the Assistant to the President for Domestic Policy.

(b) The Working Group shall;

(1) provide guidance to Federal agencies on criteria for identifying disproportionately high and adverse human health or environmental effects on minority populations and low-income populations;

(2) coordinate with, provide guidance to, and serve as a clearinghouse for, each Federal agency as it develops an environmental justice strategy as required by section 1-103 of this order, in order to ensure that the administration, interpretation and enforcement of programs, activities and policies are undertaken in a consistent manner;

(3) assist in coordinating research by, and stimulating cooperation among, the Environmental Protection Agency, the Department of Health and Human Services, the Department of Housing and Urban Development, and other agencies conducting research or other activities in accordance with section 3-3 of this order;

(4) assist in coordinating data collection, required by this order;

(5) examine existing data and studies on environmental justice;

(6) hold public meetings as required in section 5-502(d) of this order; and

(7) develop interagency model projects on environmental justice that evidence cooperation among Federal agencies.

1-103. Development of Agency Strategies. (a) Except as provided in section 6-605 of this order, each Federal agency shall develop an agency-wide environmental justice strategy, as set forth in subsections (b) - (e) of this section that identifies and addresses disproportionately high and adverse human health or environmental effects of its programs, policies, and activities on minority populations and low-income populations. The environmental justice strategy shall list programs, policies, planning and public participation processes, enforcement, and/ or rulemakings related to human health or the environment that should be revised to, at a minimum: (1) promote enforcement of all health and environmental statutes in areas with minority populations and low-income populations; (2) ensure greater public participation; (3) improve research and data collection relating to the health of and environment of minority populations and low-income populations; and (4) identify differential patterns of consumption of natural resources among minority populations and low-income populations. In addition, the environmental justice strategy shall include, where appropriate, a timetable for undertaking identified revisions and consideration of economic and social implications of the revisions.

(b) Within 4 months of the date of this order, each Federal agency shall identify an internal administrative process for developing its environmental justice strategy, and shall inform the Working Group of the process.

(c) Within 6 months of the date of this order, each Federal agency shall provide the Working Group with an outline of its proposed environmental justice strategy.

(d) Within 10 months of the date of this order, each Federal agency shall provide the Working Group with its proposed environmental justice strategy.

(e) Within 12 months of the date of this order, each Federal agency shall finalize its environmental justice strategy and provide a copy and written description of its strategy to the Working Group. During the 12 month period from the date of this order, each Federal agency, as part of its environmental justice strategy, shall identify several specific projects that can be promptly undertaken to address particular concerns identified during the development of the proposed environmental justice strategy, and a schedule for implementing those projects.

(f) Within 24 months of the date of this order, each Federal agency shall report to the Working Group on its progress in implementing its agency-wide environmental justice strategy.

(g) Federal agencies shall provide additional periodic reports to the Working Group as requested by the Working Group.

1-104. Reports to the President. Within 14 months of the date of this order, the Working Group shall submit to the President, through the Office of the Deputy Assistant to the President for Environmental Policy and the Office of the Assistant to the President for Domestic Policy, a report that describes the implementation of this order, and includes the final environmental justice strategies described in section 1-103(e) of this order.

Sec. 2-2. Federal Agency Responsibilities for Federal Programs. Each Federal agency shall conduct its programs, policies, and activities that substantially affect human health or the environment, in a manner that ensures that such programs, policies, and activities do not have the effect of excluding persons (including populations) from participation in, denying persons (including populations) the benefits of, or subjecting persons (including populations) to discrimination under, such programs, policies, and activities, because of their race, color, or national origin.

Sec. 3-3. Research, Data Collection, and Analysis.

3-301. Human Health and Environmental Research and Analysis. (a) Environmental human health research, whenever practicable and appropriate, shall include diverse segments of the population in epidemiological and clinical studies, including segments at high risk from environmental hazards, such as minority populations, low-income populations and workers who may be exposed to substantial environmental hazards.

(b) Environmental human health analyses, whenever practicable and appropriate, shall identify multiple and cumulative exposures.

(c) Federal agencies shall provide minority populations and low-income populations the opportunity to comment on the development and design of research strategies undertaken pursuant to this order.

3-302. Human Health and Environmental Data Collection and Analysis. To the extent permitted by existing law, including the Privacy Act, as amended (5

U.S.C. section 552a): (a) each Federal agency, whenever practicable and appropriate, shall collect, maintain, and analyze information assessing and comparing environmental and human health risks borne by populations identified by race, national origin, or income. To the extent practical and appropriate, Federal agencies shall use this information to determine whether their programs, policies, and activities have disproportionately high and adverse human health or environmental effects on minority populations and low-income populations;

(b) In connection with the development and implementation of agency strategies in section 1-103 of this order, each Federal agency, whenever practicable and appropriate, shall collect, maintain and analyze information on the race, national origin, income level, and other readily accessible and appropriate information for areas surrounding facilities or sites expected to have a substantial environmental, human health, or economic effect on the surrounding populations, when such facilities or sites become the subject of a substantial Federal environmental administrative or judicial action. Such information shall be made available to the public, unless prohibited by law; and

(c) Each Federal agency, whenever practicable and appropriate, shall collect, maintain, and analyze information on the race, national origin, income level, and other readily accessible and appropriate information for areas surrounding Federal facilities that are: (1) subject to the reporting requirements under the Emergency Planning and Community Right-to-Know Act, 42 U.S.C. section 11001-11050 as mandated in Executive Order No. 12856; and (2) expected to have a substantial environmental, human health, or economic effect on surrounding populations. Such information shall be made available to the public, unless prohibited by law.

(d) In carrying out the responsibilities in this section, each Federal agency, whenever practicable and appropriate, shall share information and eliminate unnecessary duplication of efforts through the use of existing data systems and cooperative agreements among Federal agencies and with State, local, and tribal governments.

Sec. 4-4. Subsistence Consumption of Fish and Wildlife.

4-401. Consumption Patterns. In order to assist in identifying the need for ensuring protection of populations with differential patterns of subsistence consumption of fish and wildlife, Federal agencies, whenever practicable and appropriate, shall collect, maintain, and analyze information on the consumption patterns of populations who principally rely on fish and/or wildlife for subsistence. Federal agencies shall communicate to the public the risks of those consumption patterns.

4-402. Guidance. Federal agencies, whenever practicable and appropriate, shall work in a coordinated manner to publish guidance reflecting the latest scientific information available concerning methods for evaluating the human health risks associated with the consumption of pollutant-bearing fish or wildlife.

Agencies shall consider such guidance in developing their policies and rules.

Sec. 5-5. Public Participation and Access to Information. (a) The public may submit recommendations to Federal agencies relating to the incorporation of environmental justice principles into Federal agency programs or policies. Each Federal agency shall convey such recommendations to the Working Group.

(b) Each Federal agency may, whenever practicable and appropriate, translate crucial public documents, notices, and hearings relating to human health or the environment for limited English speaking populations.

(c) Each Federal agency shall work to ensure that public documents, notices, and hearings relating to human health or the environment are concise, understandable, and readily accessible to the public.

(d) The Working Group shall hold public meetings, as appropriate, for the purpose of fact-finding, receiving public comments, and conducting inquiries concerning environmental justice. The Working Group shall prepare for public review a summary of the comments and recommendations discussed at public meetings.

Sec. 6-6. General Provisions.

6-601. Responsibility for Agency Implementation. The head of each Federal agency shall be responsible for ensuring compliance with this order. Each Federal agency shall conduct internal reviews and take such other steps as may be necessary to monitor compliance with this order.

6-602. Executive Order No. 12250. This Executive order is intended to supplement but not supersede Executive Order No. 12250, which requires consistent and effective implementation of various laws prohibiting discriminatory practices in programs receiving Federal financial assistance. Nothing herein shall limit the effect or mandate of Executive Order No. 12250.

6-603. Executive Order No. 12875. This Executive order is not intended to limit the effect or mandate of Executive Order No. 12875.

6-604. Scope. For purposes of this order, Federal agency means any agency on the Working Group, and such other agencies as may be designated by the President, that conducts any Federal program or activity that substantially affects human health or the environment. Independent agencies are requested to comply with the provisions of this order.

6-605. Petitions for Exemptions. The head of a Federal agency may petition the President for an exemption from the requirements of this order on the grounds that all or some of the petitioning agency's programs or activities should not be subject to the requirements of this order.

6-606. Native American Programs. Each Federal agency responsibility set forth under this order shall apply equally to Native American programs. In addition, the Department of the Interior, in coordination with the Working Group, and, after consultation with tribal leaders, shall coordinate steps to be taken pursuant to this order that address Federally-recognized Indian Tribes.

6-607. Costs. Unless otherwise provided by law, Federal agencies shall assume the financial costs of complying with this order.

6-608. General. Federal agencies shall implement this order consistent with, and to the extent permitted by, existing law.

6-609. Judicial Review. This order is intended only to improve the internal management of the executive branch and is not intended to, nor does it create any right, benefit, or trust responsibility, substantive or procedural, enforceable at law or equity by a party against the United States, its agencies, its officers, or any person. This order shall not be construed to create any right to judicial review involving the compliance or noncompliance of the United States, its agencies, its officers, or any other person with this order.

WILLIAM J. CLINTON

THE WHITE HOUSE
February 11, 1994

Appendix 2

EXECUTIVE SUMMARY OF THE RECOMMENDATIONS:
from the Symposium on Health Research
and Needs to Ensure Environmental Justice

INTRODUCTION

On February 10–12, 1994, six government agencies with the support of community and academic leaders convened the first federal symposium on environmental justice. This symposium on Health Research and Needs to Ensure Environmental Justice was a working meeting. Its goal included formulation of recommendations by community leaders, workers, business and academic representatives, diverse government personnel, and people from the broader scientific community.

More than a thousand symposium participants worked in small core groups that met three times throughout the symposium for facilitated discussions. These groups provided opportunities to discuss substantive issues raised in breakout groups and plenary sessions and answer specific questions related to health research and needs. Core group discussions also provided opportunities for individuals to share different experiences and to debate, integrate, and summarize key symposium issues. Within core groups, everyone shared expertise or information from plenary and breakout sessions and from personal and professional experiences. The core group format allowed each person to become teacher and learner, and increased the level of participation.

A major theme of the symposium was the importance of involving grassroots organizations in education and research activities in their communities, and in making sure that communities benefit from these activities. Another major theme was the need for federal agencies to work together and avoid contradictory policies and duplication of services.

Core groups recommended that the federal government and other environmental justice stakeholders empower communities, increasing their self-determination and enhancing their interaction, collaboration, and communication with a more responsive, reinvented government. Specific requests included:

I.   Conduct meaningful health research
II.   Promote disease prevention and pollution prevention strategies
III. Set up new ways for interagency coordination
IV.   Provide outreach, education, and communications
V.   Design legislative and legal remedies

Sections I through V of this executive summary provide an overview of recommendations crafted by symposium participants. The appendices to the executive summary provide specific recommendations and other symposium products.*

I. Conduct meaningful health research in support of people of color and low-income communities. Preventing disease in all communities and providing universal access to health care are major goals of health care reform. Effective preventive measures cannot be equitably implemented in the absence of a targeted process that addresses the environmental health research needs of high-risk workers and communities, especially communities of color.

1. Develop new models for occupational and environmental science research that involve high risk communities and workers as *active participants* in every part of research, including:
   a. making and testing of hypotheses
   b. planning and putting into action creative research strategies and methodologies
   c. interpreting and communicating research results
   d. translating research results into disease prevention and pollution prevention action

2. Assure that new models include examination of the ethics and social responsibility of research, standards of evidence, and the history of worker and community involvement in research and policy making.

3. New models of studying people must be developed that address:
   a. exposures and diseases among only small numbers of people
   b. exposures to low levels of a hazard
   c. exposures to many different occupational and environmental hazards over a short period of time and over a lifetime
   d. the knowledge and experiences of community members and workers about their diseases and exposures

---

*Appendix A identifies questions posed to each core group, specific recommendations based in part on these questions, and recommendations from more specialized caucuses and environmental justice networks. Appendix B describes the difficulties and rewards of the core group process. Appendix C summarizes the evaluation of the symposium by its participants. Appendix D contains letters from federal sponsors of the symposium regarding these recommendations.

4. Target the development of new molecular technologies and tools to serve the at-risk workers and communities. These technologies and tools should serve the community in risk assessment, disease etiology, and policy formation.

5. Federally funded research centers should prepare well-thought-out plans for partnerships with local communities of color. (These plans should be made available to community groups on request.) Community and worker representatives in these partnerships must be *active participants* in all stages of research, and partnerships must lead to timely and effective public health actions. The plans and results of the partnerships and public health actions should be evaluated in the same peer review and site visitation process as the more traditional research parts of the project.

6. Where high-risk workers and communities are underserved, create new local/regional occupational and environmental health research centers.

7. Community-based research needs to be conducted in ways that strengthen ties among community-based organizations, public health agencies, and educational institutions.

II. Promote disease prevention and pollution prevention strategies. While treating disease and cleaning up environmental problems are essential, long-term solutions must rely upon truly preventive approaches.

8. Build a stronger base for occupational and environmental health.
    a. Increase the emphasis on occupational and environmental health in curricula and training programs for health care providers. This should include training to gather information on occupational and environmental exposures as part of medical histories.
    b. Increase clinical studies in affected communities to provide people at risk with effective surveillance, monitoring, and treatment of adverse health effects.
    c. Initiate where necessary and fund birth and disease registries for all states.

9. Increase Department of Health and Human Services funding through the Public Health Service (including ATSDR, CDC, NIEHS, and NIOSH) for prevention research that addresses occupational and environmental disease problems in communities of color and other high-risk populations.

10. Direct a major part of ongoing and new NIH disease prevention research funding through NIEHS for prevention of environmental and occupational disease in communities of color.

11. Promote communities that have been successful in eliminating or reducing pollutants from the environment as models for research on disease and pollution prevention.

12. Use tax and government buying policies to promote sustainable and safer technologies that improve product stewardship.

13. EPA should support regional pollution prevention networks involving government, community, and industry associations to investigate, develop and put in place alternate, less polluting technologies.

14. Funds should be available to help workers and communities make transitions when plants temporarily or permanently shut down for purposes of improving technology. Use military conversion to stimulate new technology for preventing pollution in the future.

III. Promote interagency coordination to ensure environmental justice. While at-risk communities and workers are most threatened by occupational and environmental hazards, government agencies (federal, regional, state, local, and tribal) are also important stakeholders. Unfortunately, environmental problems are not organized along departmental lines. Solutions require many agencies to work together effectively and efficiently.

15. Educate stakeholders about functions, roles, jurisdictions, structures, and enforcement powers of government agencies and the needs and concerns of low-income and people of color communities. Research projects must identify environmental justice issues and needs in a particular community, and how to meet those needs through the responsible agencies.

16. Establish interagency working groups at all levels to address and coordinate issues of environmental justice.

17. Agency attitudes need to change and agency staff need exposure to the community's perspective.

    a. Agencies should actively provide information about the government's role as the community identifies short- and long-term economic and environmental needs and health effects.

    b. Train staff to support inter- and intra-agency coordination, and make them aware of the resources needed for such coordination.

    c. Government agencies should make available staff who are trained in culturally appropriate language and communication.

    d. Tribal, local, state, and federal governments need to recognize and rectify problems when other levels of government are not effectively doing so.

    e. Support research agencies operating in the public interest by increasing or protecting their budgets.

    f. Hold workshops, seminars, and other meetings to develop partnerships between agencies, workers, and community groups.

IV. Provide effective outreach, education, and communications. Findings of community-based research projects need to be produced and shared with community members and workers in ways that are sensitive and respectful to race, ethnicity, gender, language, culture, and in ways to promote public health action.

18. Government agencies, including ATSDR, CDC, EPA, NIEHS, and others, should visit affected communities and workers, and provide information about (a) research goals, objectives, and policy; (b) the organization of each agency; and (c) the specific agency's mandate. Such visits should also promote a better understanding of worker and community needs.

19. CDC, DOE, EPA, and NIH should develop and/or increase funding for community/academic research partnerships (such as the NIOSH Education Resource Centers) in order to provide research services to address environmental justice concerns. They should review existing community/worker research partnerships and develop guidelines to be used in forming partnerships at federally funded centers. Make environmental justice issues part of the curricula of schools of public health. Include environmental justice in the accreditation process of institutions of higher learning. Assure that environmental justice is an integral part of any ATSDR, CDC, DOE, EPA, NIEHS, and NIOSH research and training grant.

20. Recruit, retain, and promote people of color and members of affected communities in scientific research and education. In particular promote scientific research and education at historical black colleges and universities (HBCUs) and other minority institutions.

21. Design and carry out education efforts tailored to specific communities and problems. Increase the involvement of ethnic caucuses, religious

groups, the press, and legislative staff in resolution of health and environmental justice issues.

22. Train workers and communities to understand the links between health and pollution and to pose meaningful questions to researchers.
    a. Expand the NIEHS hazardous waste worker training program to include other workers and communities. Make disease and pollution prevention part of the training curriculum.
    b. Fund community training programs through a portion of pollution permit fees.

23. Assure *active participation* of affected communities in the decision-making process for outreach, education, training, and communication programs—including representation on advisory councils and review committees.

24. Revise EPA's Superfund Technical Assistance Grant procedures to eliminate federal procurement requirements for those grants and to establish federally funded, state-based, community coordinators to promote and facilitate community participation.

25. Encourage federal staff to change bureaucratic processes to be more responsive to community needs and to provide training to enhance environmental justice awareness.

V. Design legislative and legal remedies.

26. Incorporate private attorney rights-of-action clauses into regulatory laws, making it easier to bring suits and, if successful, to recover costs and attorney fees.

27. Strengthen whistleblower protection laws so that agency staff can identify problems and initiate actions to protect affected communities.

28. Government agencies should use Title 6 of the Civil Rights Act of 1964 in their enforcement of environmental justice.

29. Enact, strengthen, and/or enforce legislation such that it provides equal protection of the law to all people against environmental problems.
    a. Increase civil and/or criminal penalties for violators.
    b. Strengthen legislation (such as the Federal Insecticide, Fungicide and Rodenticide Act, which regulates pesticides, the Clean Water

Act, the Clean Air Act, and the Superfund law) coming up for re-authorization in 1994 to protect vulnerable or at-risk populations.

c. Redefine "action levels" to accurately reflect the needs of sensitive subpopulations, such as children and communities exposed to many different hazards and/or exposed at many different times and places.

d. Authorize and appropriate funds to address issues of environmental justice (e.g., prevention, cleanup, and health care), and make grassroots participation mandatory.

References

Introduction

Alston, D. and N. Brown. 1993. "Global Threats to People of Color." In Robert D. Bullard (Ed.), *Confronting Environmental Racism: Voices from the Grassroots*. Boston: South End Press: 179–195.

Miller, G.T. 1988. *Living in the Environment: Fifth Edition*. Belmont, CA: Wadsworth Publishing Company.

Mypanya, M. 1992. "The Dumping of Toxic Waste in African Countries: A Case of Poverty and Racism." In B. Bryant and P. Mohai (Eds.), *Race and the Incidence of Environmental Hazards: A Time for Discourse*. Boulder, CO: Westview Press, pp. 204–214.

Chapter 1

Alston, D. and N. Brown. 1993. "Global Threats to People of Color." In Robert D. Bullard (Ed.), *Confronting Environmental Racism: Voices from the Grassroots*. Boston: South End Press: 179–195.

Anderson, H.A. 1985. "Evolution of Environmental Epidemiologic Risk Assessment." *Environmental Health Perspectives* 62: 389–392.

Aronowitz, S. 1988. *Science as Power: Discourse and Ideology in Modern Society*. Minneapolis, MN: University of Minnesota Press.

Becker, H. 1967. "Whose Side Are You On?" *Social Problems* 14: 239–247.

Blumberg, L. and R. Gottlieb. 1989. *War on Waste: Can America Win Its Battle with Garbage?* Washington, DC: Island Press.

Boggs, G.L. 1993. "Preparing People to Work for Social Change." An unpublished paper presented at the Steering Committee, Neighborhood Academy, June: 7.

Brown, L.D. and R. Tandon. 1983. "Ideology and Political Economy in Inquiry: Action Research and Participatory Research." *The Journal of Applied Behavioral Science* 19(3): 277–294.

Brown, P. 1992. "Popular Epidemiology and Toxic Waste Contamination: Lay and Professional Ways of Knowing." *Journal of Health and Social Behavior* 33 September: 267–281.

Bryant, B. and P. Mohai (Eds.). 1992. *Race and the Incidence of Environmental Hazards: A Time for Discourse*. Boulder, CO: Westview Press.

Bullard, R.D. 1983. "Solid Waste Sites and the Black Houston Community."
      Sociological Inquiry 53: 273–288.
_____. 1984. "Endangered Environs: The Price of Unplanned Growth in
      Boomtown Houston." *California Sociologist* 7: 85–101.
_____. 1990. *Dumping in Dixie: Race, Class, and Environmental Qual-
      ity*. Boulder, CO: Westview Press.
_____. 1993. *Confronting Environmental Racism: Voices from the
      Grassroots*. Boston: South End Press.
Bullard, R.D. and B.H. Wright. 1986. "The Politics of Pollution: Implications for
      the Black Community." *Phylon* 47: 71–78.
_____. 1987a. "Environmentalism and the Politics of Equity: Emergent
      Trends in the Black Community." *Mid-American Review of Sociology* 12:
      21–38.
_____. 1987b. "Environmentalism, Economic Blackmail, and Civil Rights:
      Competing Agendas Within the Black Community." Paper presented at the
      Annual Meeting of the Society for the Study of Social Problems.
_____. 1987c. "Blacks and the Environment." *Humboldt Journal of
      Social Relations* 14: 165–184.
_____. 1987d. "Implications of Toxics in Minority Communities." Pro-
      ceedings of Conference on Community Toxic Pollution Awareness for
      Historically Black Colleges and Universities. Tallahassee, FL: Legal Envi-
      ronmental Assistance Foundation.
Burke, L.M. 1993. "Race and Environmental Equity: A Geographic Analysis in
      Los Angeles." *GEO Info System* 3(9) October: 44–48.
Carr, W. and S. Kemmis. 1983. *Becoming Critical: Knowing Through Action
      Research*. Victoria, Australia: Deakin University Press.
Carson, R. 1960. "Silent Spring." *The New Yorker*. Later published by Houghton
      Mifflin, Boston.
Chambers, R. 1983. *Rural Development: Putting the Last First*. New York:
      Longman.
Cloward, R. and F. Piven. 1975. *The Politics of Turmoil: Essays on Poverty, Race
      and the Urban Crisis*. New York: Vintage.
Commoner, B. 1976. *The Poverty of Power: Energy and the Economic Crisis*. New
      York: Alfred A. Kopf.
_____. 1992. "Pollution Prevention: Putting Comparative Risk Assess-
      ment in Its Place." An unpublished paper presented at a conference on
      Setting National Environmental Priorities: The EPA Risk-Based Paradigm
      and its Alternatives. The Historic Inns of Annapolis, Annapolis, Maryland.
      Sponsored by the Center for Risk Management, Resources for the Future.
      November, pp. 15–17.
Cook, G. 1990. "Getting the Lead Out." *Maryland in Baltimore* 4(2): 2–7.
Costner, P. and J. Thornton. 1990. *Playing with Fire*. Washington, DC: Greenpeace.
Crampton, L.S.W. 1991. "Environmental Equity Communication Plan." An Inter-

nal Memorandum to Gordon L. Binder, Chief of Staff of the Environmental Protection Agency.

Davis, H. 1992. "The Environmental Voting Record of the Congressional Black Caucus." In B. Bryant and P. Mohai (Eds.), *Race and the Incidence of Environmental Hazards: A Time for Discourse.* Boulder, CO: Westview Press, pp. 55–63.

DeGannes, K., et al. 1991. "Sumpter Township Study: The Effects of Two Incinerator Ash Facilities on a Community." An unpublished paper. University of Michigan School of Natural Resources and Environment.

Dickerson, D. 1984. *The New Politics of Science.* New York: Pantheon Books.

DiPerna, P. 1985. *Cluster Mystery: Epidemic and the Children of Woburn, Massachusetts.* New York: The C.V. Mobsby Company.

Dunlap, R.E. 1987. "Polls, Pollution, and Politics Revisited: Public Opinion on the Environment in the Reagan Era." *Environment* 29(July/August): 6–11, 31–37.

Edelstein, M.R. 1987. *Contaminated Communities: The Social and Psychological Impacts of Residential Toxic Exposure.* Boulder, CO: Westview Press.

Ellis, T. 1993. "Work and Slavery: A Gaian Perspective." In B. Bryant (Ed.), *The Future: Images for the 21st Century.* Ann Arbor, MI: University of Michigan Office of the Vice Provost of Minority Affairs and the Environmental Equity Institute.

Epstein, S., L.O. Brown, and C. Pope. 1983. *Hazardous Waste in America.* San Francisco: Sierra Club Books.

Fals-Borda, O. 1982. "Participatory Research and Rural Social Change." *Journal of Rural Cooperation* X(1): 25–40.

Flavin, C. and N. Lenssen. 1990. "Beyond the Petroleum Age: Designing a Solar Economy." *Worldwatch Paper 100.* Washington, DC: Worldwatch Institute.

Franklin, B.A. 1986. "In the Shadow of the Valley." *Sierra* 71 May/Jun: 38–44.

Freidson, E. 1971. "Professionalism: The Doctor's Dilemmas." *Social Policy* January: 35–40.

Freudenberg, N. 1984. "Citizen Action for Environmental Health: Report on a Survey of Community Organizations." *American Journal of Public Health* 74(5) May: 444–448.

Funnye, C. 1970. "The Militant Black Social Worker and the Urban Hustle." *Social Work* 15(2): 5–12.

Gale, R.P. 1983. "The Environmental Movement and the Left: Antagonists or Allies." *Sociological Inquiry* 53(Spring): 179–199.

Gaventa, J. 1991. "Participatory Research in North America." Prepared for a volume on participatory research. O. Fals-Borda and A. Rahman (Eds.), Knoxville, TN: University of Tennessee, Department of Sociology and Highlander Center, New Market, TN: 1–15.

Gaventa, J. and H. Lewis. 1991. "Participatory Education and Grassroots Development: Current Experiences in Appalachia U.S.A." Unpublished paper, Knoxville, TN: University of Tennessee, Department of Sociology and Highlander Center, New Market, TN: 1–18.

Geiser, K. and G. Waneck. 1983. "PCB and Warren County." *Science for the People* 15: 13–17.

Gelobter, M. 1986. The Distribution of Outdoor Air Pollution by Income and Race: 1970–1986. Master's Thesis. Energy and Resource Group. Berkeley: University of California.

_____. 1992. "Toward a Model of 'Environmental Discrimination'." In B. Bryant and P. Mohai (Eds.), *Race and the Incidence of Environmental Hazards: A Time for Discourse*. Boulder, CO: Westview Press, pp. 64–81.

Geschwind, S.A., et al. 1992. "Risk of Congential Malformations Associated with Proximity to Hazardous Waste Sites." *American Journal of Epidemiology* 135(11): 1197–1207.

Gianessi, L., H.M. Peskin, and E. Wolff. 1979. "The Distributional Effects of Uniform Air Pollution Policy in the U.S." *Quarterly Journal of Economics* (May): 281–301.

Goggin, M.L. 1986. *Governing Science and Technology in a Democracy*. Knoxville, TN: University of Tennessee Press.

Goldfield, D.R. 1987. *Promised land: The South Since 1945*. Arlington Heights, IL: Harlan Davidson.

Goldman, B. and Fitton, L. 1994. "Toxic Waste and Race Revisited: An Update of the 1987 Report in the Racial and Socioeconomic Characteristics of Communities with Hazardous Waste Sites." Center for Policy Alternatives, National Association for the Advancement of Colored People, and the United Church of Christ Commission for Racial Justice.

Goldman, B.A. 1991. *The Truth about Where You Live: An Atlas for Action on Toxins and Mortality*. New York: Times Books/Random House.

Goodman, R. 1982. *The Last Entrepreneurs: American's Regional Wars for Jobs and Dollars*. Boston: South End Press.

Gottlieb, R. and H. Ingram. 1988. "The New Environmentalists." *The Progressive* 52: 14–15.

Gouldner, A. 1968. "The Sociologist as Partisan: Sociology and the Welfare State." *American Sociologist* 3(2): 103–116.

Gregory, R. and H. Kunreuther. 1990. "Successful Siting Incentives." *Civil Engineering* 60(April): 73–75.

Grossman, K. 1992. "From Toxic Racism to Environmental Justice." *E: The Environmental Magazine* 3(June): 28–35.

Grossman, R. and G. Daneker. 1977. *Jobs and Energy*. Washington, DC: Environmentalists for Full Employment.

Gyorgy, A. and Friends. 1979. *No Nukes: Everyone's Guide to Nuclear Power*. Boston: South End Press.

Hamilton, L. 1985. "Concern about Toxic Waste: Three Demographic Predictors." *Sociological Perspective* 28: 463–486.

Hare, N. 1970. "Black Ecology." *The Black Scholar* 1(April): 2–8.

Haug, M.P. and M.B. Sussman. 1969. "Professional Autonomy and the Revolt of the Client." *Social Problems* 17: 153–159.

Hayes, D. 1976. "Energy: The Case for Conservation." *World Watch Paper 4.* Washington, DC: Worldwatch Institute.

Hays, S.P. 1987. *Beauty, Health, and Permanence: Environmental Politics in the United States, 1955–1985.* Cambridge, MA: Cambridge University Press.

Hershey, M.R. and D.B. Hill. 1977–78. "Is Pollution 'a White Thing'? Racial Differences in Pre-adults' Attitudes." *Public Opinion Quarterly* 41: 439–458.

Higgins, R. 1993. "Race and Environmental Equity: An Overview of Environmental Justice Issues in the Policy Process." *Polity* XXVI(2): 281–300.

Hornstein, D.T. 1992. "EPA's Use of the Risk–Based Paradigm Procedural Concerns." An unpublished paper presented at a conference on Setting National Environmental Priorities: The EPA Risk-Based Paradigm and its Alternatives. The Historic Inns of Annapolis, Annapolis, Maryland. Sponsored by the Center for Risk Management, Resources for the Future. November 16.

Human Environment Center. 1981. *Minority Education for Environmental and Natural Resources Professions: Higher Education.* Washington, DC: Human Environment Center.

Humphrey, C. R. and F. H. Buttel. 1982. *Environment, Energy and Society.* Belmont, CA: Wadsworth.

Johnson, H. 1992. Speech made at a Student Environmental Action Coalition Conference held at the University of Michigan. October.

Jordan, V. 1978. "Energy Policy and Black People." *Vital Speeches of the Day* XLIV(11) March 15: 341–344.

_____. 1980. "Sins of Omission." *Environmental Action* 11: 26–30.

Kazis, R. and R. Grossman. 1983. *Fear at Work: Job Blackmail, Labor, and the Environment.* New York: The Pilgrim Press.

Kozol, J. 1991. *Savage Inequalities: Children in America's Schools.* New York: Crown Publishers.

Krimsky, S. and A. Plough. 1988. *Environmental Hazards: Communicating Risks as a Social Process.* Dover, MA: Auburn House Publishing Company.

Kruvant, W.J. 1975. "People, Energy and Pollution." In D. Newman and D. Dawn (Eds.), *The American Energy Consumer.* Cambridge, MA: Ballinger, pp. 125–67.

Kushner, J.A. 1980. *Apartheid in America: A Historical and Legal Analysis of Contemporary Racial Segregation in the United States.* Arlington, VA: Carrollton Press, Inc.

LaBalme, J. 1987. *A Road to Walk: A Struggle for Environmental Justice.* Durham, NC: The Regulator Press.

Latour, B. 1987. *Science in Action: How to Follow Scientists and Engineers Through Society.* Cambridge, MA: Harvard University Press.

Laurell, A.C. et al. 1992. "Participatory Research on Workers' Health." *Social Science Medicine* 34(6): 603–613.

Lavelle, M. and M. Coyle. 1992. "Unequal Protection: The Racial Divide in Environmental Law." *The National Law Journal* 15(3) September 21: 1–43.

Levine, A. 1982. *Love Canal: Science, Politics, and People.* Lexington, MA: Lexington Books.

Lewin, K. 1946. "Action Research and Minority Problems." *Journal of Social Issues* 2(4): 34–46.

Logan, J. R. and H. Molotch. 1987. *Urban Futures: The Political Economy of Place.* Berkeley: University of California Press.

Lovins, A. 1976. "Energy Strategy: The Road Not Taken?" *Foreign Affairs* 55: 1.

McCaull, J. 1975. "Discriminatory Air Pollution: If the Poor Don't Breathe." *Environment* 19: 26–32.

Miller, G.T., Jr. 1975. *Living in the Environment: Concepts, Problems, and Alternatives.* Belmont, CA: Wadsworth Publishing Company.

_____. 1982. *Living in the Environment: Third Edition.* Belmont, CA: Wadsworth Publishing Company.

_____. 1988, *Living in the Environment: Fifth Edition.* Belmont, CA: Wadsworth Publishing Company.

Mitchell, M. and W. Stapp. 1990. "A Creative Way of Educating Children: A Watershed Monitoring Program Design to Improve Water Quality, Education, and the Lives of People." In B. Bryant (Ed.), *The Future: Images for the 21st Century.* Ann Arbor, MI: University of Michigan, Office of the Vice Provost for Minority Affairs and the Environmental Equity Institute.

Mitchell, R.C. 1979. "Silent Spring/Solid Majorities." *Public Opinion* 2: 16–20.

Mitroff, I.V. 1974. *The Subjective Side of Science: A Philosophical Inquiry into the Psychology of the Apollo Moon Scientists.* New York: American Elsevier Publishing Company.

Mohai, P. 1985. "Public Concern and Elite Involvement in Environmental Conservation." *Social Science Quarterly* 66: 820–838.

_____. 1990. "Black Environmentalism." *Social Science Quarterly* 71(4): 744–765.

Mohai, P. and B. Bryant. 1992a. "Environmental Injustice: Weighing Race and Class as Factors in the Distribution of Environmental Hazards." *University of Colorado Law Review* 63(4): 921–932.

_____. 1992b. "Race, Poverty and the Environment: The Disadvantaged Face Greater Risks." *EPA Journal* 18(1) March/April: 6–8.

_____. 1992c. "Environmental Racism: Reviewing the Evidence." In B. Bryant and P. Mohai (Eds.), *Race and the Incidence of Environmental*

Hazards: A Time for Discourse. Boulder, CO: Westview Press, pp. 163–176.

Momeni, J.A. 1986. *Race, Ethnicity, and Minority Housing in the United States.* Westport, CT: Greenwood Press.

Morell, D. 1987. "Siting and the Politics of Equity." In R.W. Lake (Ed.), *Resolving Locational Conflict.* New Brunswick, NJ: Rutgers University Center for Urban Policy Research, pp. 117–36.

Morell, D. and C. Magorian. 1982. "Risk, Fear, and Local Opposition: 'Not in My Back Yard'." In D. Morell, and C. Magorian (Eds.), *Siting Hazardous Waste Facilities: Local Opposition and the Myth of Preemption.* Cambridge, MA: Ballinger, pp. 21–46

Morrison, D. E. 1980. "The Soft Cutting Edge of Environmentalism: Why and How the Appropriate Technology Notion Is Changing the Movement." *Natural Resources Journal* 20: 275–298.

_____. 1986. "How and Why Environmental Consciousness Has Trickled Down." In A. Schnaiberg, N. Watts, and K. Zimmermann (Eds.), *Distributional Conflict in Environmental Resource Policy.* New York: St. Martin's Press, pp. 187–220.

Morrison, D.E. and R.E. Dunlap. 1986. "Environmentalism and Elitism: A Conceptual and Empirical Analysis." *Environmental Management* 10: 981–989.

Mulkay, M. 1991. *Sociology of Science: A Sociological Pilgrimage.* Bloomington: Indiana University Press.

Neiman, M. and R.O. Loveridge. 1981. "Environmentalism and Local Growth Control: A Probe into the Class Bias Thesis." *Environment and Behavior* 13: 759–772.

Nelkin, D. 1985. *The Language of Risk.* Beverly Hills, CA: Sage Publications.

Nichter, M. 1984. "Project Community Diagnosis: Participatory Research as a First Step Toward Community Involvement in Primary Health Care." *Social Science Medicine* 19(3): 237–252.

Odum, H. and E. Odum. 1976. *Energy Basis for Man and Nature.* New York: McGraw-Hill Book Company.

O'Hare, M., L. Bacow, and D. Sanderson. 1983. *Facility Siting and Public Opposition.* New York: Van Nostrand Reinhold.

Packard, V. 1960. *The Waste Makers.* New York: D. McKay Co.

Peattie, L.R. 1968. "Reflections on Advocacy Planning." *AIP Journal* March: 81.

Perfecto, I. 1992. "Pesticide Exposure of Farm Workers and the International Connection." In B. Bryant and P. Mohai (Eds.), *Race and the Incidence of Environmental Hazards: A Time for Discourse.* Boulder, CO: Westview Press, pp. 177–203.

Pollack, S., J. Grozuczak and P. Taylor. 1984. *Reagan, Toxics and Minorities.* Washington, DC: Urban Environment Conference, Inc.

Reed, A.L., Jr. 1989. *The Jesse Jackson Phenomenon.* New Haven, CT: Yale University Press.

Rothman, K.J. 1986. *Modern Epidemiology.* Boston: Little, Brown and Company.

Russell, D. 1989. "Environmental Racism: Minority Communities and Their Battle Against Toxics." *Amicus Journal* 11(2) Spring: 22–32.

Schnaiberg, A. 1980. *The Environment: From Surplus to Scarcity.* New York: Oxford University Press.

Schneider, L. 1993. "New View Calls Environmental Policy Misguided." *New York Times* March 21: 1.

_____. 1983. "Redistributive Goals Versus Distributive Politics: Social Equity. Limits in Environmentalism and Appropriate Technology Movements." *Sociological Inquiry* 53: 200–219.

Silver, K. 1984. "Minorities and Toxics." *Exposure* January/February: 36–37.

Stapp, W. and M. Mitchell. 1990. *Field Manual for Water Quality and Monitoring: An Environmental Education Program for Schools.* Dexter, MI: Thomson-Shore, Inc.

Taylor, D.E. 1993. "A Redefinition of the Environment: New Voices, New Visions." In B. Bryant (Ed.), *The Future: Images for the 21st Century.* Ann Arbor, MI: University of Michigan, Office of the Vice Provost for Minority Affairs and the Environmental Equity Institute: 77–88.

_____. 1989. "Blacks and the Environment: Toward an Explanation of the Concern and Action Gap between Blacks and Whites." *Environment and Behavior* 21: 175–205.

Taylor, R.A. 1982. "Do Environmentalists Care about the Poor." *U.S. News and World Report* 96(April): 51–52.

Tesh, S.N. 1990. *Hidden Arguments: Political Ideology and Disease Prevention Policy.* New Brunswick, NJ: Rutgers University Press.

Thorton, J. 1991. *The Product Is the Poison: The Case for a Chlorine Phase-out.* Toronto: The Greenpeace Great Lakes Project.

Thurow, L. 1992. *Head to Head: The Coming Economic Battle among Japan, Europe, and America.* New York: William Morrow and Company, Inc.

Truax, B. 1990. "Minorities at Risk." *RE:Sources Environmental Action* January/February: 20.

Unger, D.G., A. Wandersman, and W. Hallman. 1992. "Living Near a Hazardous Waste Facility: Coping with Individual and Family Distress." *American Journal Orthopsychiatry* 62(1) January: 55–70.

United Church of Christ, Commission for Racial Justice. 1987. *Toxic Wastes and Race: A National Report on the Racial and Socioeconomic Characteristics of Communities with Hazardous Wastes Sites.* New York: United Church of Christ.

U.S. Environmental Protection Agency (EPA). 1992. *Environmental Equity; Reducing Risk for All Communities.* 2 Vols. EPA230-R-92-008 and EPA230-

R-92-008A. Washington, DC: Policy, Planning and Evaluation, U.S. Environmental Protection Agency.

U.S. General Accounting Office. 1983. *Siting of Hazardous Waste Landfills and Their Correlation with Racial and Economic Status of Surrounding Communities*. Washington, DC: GAO/RCED 83-168, June 1.

Urban Environment Conference, Inc. 1985. *Taking Back Our Health: An Institute on Surviving the Threat to Minority Communities*. Washington, DC: Urban Environment, Inc.

Van Liere, K. and R.E. Dunlap. 1980. "The Social Bases of Environmental Concern: A Review of Hypotheses, Explanations, and Empirical Evidence." *Public Opinion Quarterly* 44: 181–197.

Vir, A.K. 1988. "Africa Says No to Toxic Dumping Schemes." *Environmental Action* November–December: 26–28.

Vyner, H.M. 1988. *Invisible Trauma. The Psychological Effects of Invisible Environmental Contaminants*. Lexington, MA: D.C. Heath and Company.

Wernette, D.R. and L.A. Nieves. 1991. "Minorities and Air Pollution: A Preliminary Geodemographic Analysis." Presented at the Socioeconomic Research Analysis Conference. June 27–28.

West, P.C., J.M. Fly, F. Larkin and R.W. Marans. 1992. "Minority Anglers and Toxic Fish Consumption: Evidence of the State-Wide Survey of Michigan." In B. Bryant and P. Mohai (Eds.), *Race and the Incidence of Environmental Hazards: A Time for Discourse*. Boulder, CO: Westview Press, pp. 100–113.

Wolf, A. 1970. "The Perils of Professionalism." *Change* September–October: 51–54.

Wright, B.H. 1986. "Rethinking the Circle of Poison: The Politics of Pesticide Poisoning among Mexican Farm Workers." *Latin American Perspectives* 13: 26–59.

Zinn, H. 1980. *A People's History of the United States*. New York: Harper & Row.

Zwerdling, D. 1973. "Poverty and Pollution." *The Progressive* 37: 25–29.

Chapter 2

Alabama Department of Environmental Management (ADEM). 1993. Public Notice, Renewal and Modification of the Operational Permit for the North Montgomery Landfill. February 26, 1993. Montgomery, Alabama: Alabama Department of Environmental Management.

Bailey, C. and C.E. Faupel. 1992. "Environmentalism and Civil Rights in Sumter County, Alabama." In B. Bryant and P. Mohai (Eds.), *Race and the Incidence of Environmental Hazards: A Time for Discourse*. Boulder, CO: Westview Press, pp. 140–152.

Bailey, C., C.E. Faupel, and J.H. Gundlach. 1993. "Environmental Politics in Alabama's Blackbelt." In R.D. Bullard (Ed.), *Confronting Environmental Racism: Voices from the Grassroots.* Boston: South End Press, pp. 107–122.

Black, J.S. 1991. "Recent Changes in Superfund Community Relations: Bringing More 'Community' In." Paper presented at the 1991 Meetings of the Rural Sociological Society, August 1991, Columbus, OH.

Bryant, B. and P. Mohai (Eds.). 1992. *Race and the Incidence of Environmental Hazards: A Time for Discourse.* Boulder, CO: Westview Press.

Bullard, R.D. 1990. *Dumping in Dixie: Race, Class, and Environmental Quality.* Boulder, CO: Westview Press.

Haug, M.R. and M.B. Sussman. 1969. "Professional Autonomy and the Revolt of the Client." *Social Problems* 17(2) Fall: 153–161.

Korton, F.F. and R.Y. Siy, Jr. 1988. *Transforming a Bureaucracy.* West Hartford, CT: Kumarian Press.

Littrell, D.W. 1985. "An Introduction to Action Research in Community Development." *Research in Rural Sociology and Development* 2: 187–195.

Suro, R. 1993. "Pollution-Weary Minorities Try Civil Rights Tack." *New York Times* January 11: p. A1.

United Church of Christ, Commission for Racial Justice. 1987. *Toxic Wastes and Race: A National Report on the Racial and Socioeconomic Characteristics of Communities with Hazardous Wastes Sites.* New York: United Church of Christ.

U.S. Environmental Protection Agency (EPA). 1992. *Environmental Equity; Reducing Risk for All Communities.* 2 Vols. EPA230-R-92-008 and EPA230-R-92-008A. Washington, DC: Policy, Planning and Evaluation, U.S. Environmental Protection Agency.

——————. 1974. *Disposal of Hazardous Wastes; Report to Congress.* SW-115. Washington, DC: Office of Solid Waste Management Programs, U.S. Environmental Protection Agency.

U.S. General Accounting Office (GAO). 1983. *Siting of Hazardous Waste Landfills and Their Correlation with Racial and Economic Status of Surrounding Communities.* Washington, DC: GAO/RCED 83–168, June 1.

Wolf, A. 1970. "The Perils of Professionalism." *Change* 2(5) September–October: 51–54.

Chapter 3

Allenby, Braden R. and Deanna J. Richards (eds). 1994. *The Greening of Industrial Ecosystems.* Washington, DC: National Academy Press.

Amdur, M.A., J. Doull, and C. Klaassen (Eds.). 1991. *Casarett and Doull's*

Toxicology: The Science of Poisons. New York: Pergamon Press, Inc.

Colborn, T. and C. Clement. 1992. *Chemically Induced Alterations in Sexual and Functional Development: The Wildlife/Human Connection.* Advances in Modern Environmental Toxicology XXI. Princeton, NJ: Princeton Scientific Publishing Co., Inc.

The Conservation Foundation. 1987. *State of the Environment: A View Toward the Nineties.* Washington, DC: The Conservation Foundation.

DeRosa, C. and M. Dourson. 1988. "Risk Assessment Initiatives for Non-Cancer Endpoints: Implications for Risk Characterization of Mixtures." Presentation & Conference Abstract. International Symposium on Chemical Mixtures: Risk Assessment and Management. June 7–9, 1988, Cincinnati, OH.

Douglas, M. and A. Wildavsky. 1982. *Risk and Culture.* Berkeley: University of California Press.

Head, L. 1994. SouthWest Organizing Project. Personal Conversation. October 23, 1994. Albuquerque, NM.

_____. 1992. SouthWest Organizing Project. Personal Conversation. November 1, 1992. Albuquerque, NM.

Head, L. and M. Guerrero. 1991. "Fighting Environmental Racism." *New Solutions* 1(3): 38–42.

Jackson, R.J. 1992. California Department of Health Services. Personal conversation. December 18, 1992. Berkeley, CA.

Klapp, M.G. 1992. *Bargaining with Uncertainty: Decision-Making in Public Health, Technological Safety and Environmental Quality.* New York: Auburn House.

Krimsky, S. and A. Plough. 1988. *Environmental Hazards: Communicating Risks as a Social Process.* Dover, MA: Auburn House Publishing Company.

Lavelle, M. and M. Coyle. 1992. "Unequal Protection: The Racial Divide in Environmental Law." *The National Law Journal* 15(3): S1–S12.

Nadakavukaren, Anne. 1990. *Man & Environment* (Third Edition). Prospect Heights, IL: Waveland Press, Inc.

National Center for Small Communities (NCSC) [A program of the National Association of Towns and Townships/NATT and the National Center for Hazard Communication.] 1990. *Accidents Will Happen.* Washington, DC: National Association of Towns and Townships.

National Research Council (Committee on Pesticides in the Diets of Infants and Children; Board of Agriculture and Board on Environmental Studies and Toxicology; Commission on Life Sciences). 1993. *Pesticides in the Diet of Infants and Children.* Washington, DC: National Academy Press

Plutchik, R. 1968. *Foundations of Experimental Research.* New York: Harper & Row, Publishers.

Schoeny, R. and E. Margosches. 1988. "Evaluating Relative Potencies: Developing Approaches to Risk Assessment of Chemical Mixtures." Presentation and Conference Abstract. International Symposium on Chemical Mixtures: Risk Assessment and Management. June 7–9, 1988, Cincinnati, OH.

Starke, Linda (Ed.). 1994. *State of the World 1994: A Worldwatch Institute Report on Progress Toward a Sustainable Society.* New York, London: W.W. Norton & Company.

United Church of Christ, Commission for Racial Justice, Center for Policy Alternatives and the National Association for the Advancement of Colored People (NAACP). 1994. *Toxic Wastes and Race Revisited.* New York, NY: United Church of Christ.

United Church of Christ, Commission for Racial Justice. 1987. *Toxic Wastes and Race: A National Report on the Racial and Socioeconomic Characteristics of Communities with Hazardous Wastes Sites.* New York: United Church of Christ.

U.S. Environmental Protection Agency (EPA). 1994. *The 1992 Toxics Release Inventory: Public Data Release.* EPA #745-R-94-001. Washington, DC: United States Environmental Protection Agency, Office of Toxic Substances/U.S. Government Printing Office.

U.S. Environmental Protection Agency (EPA). 1991. *Toxics in the Community: National and Local Perspectives. The 1989 Toxics Release Inventory National Report.* Prepared by Hampshire Research Associates, Inc. under Contract Numbers: 68-DO-0165, 68-D9-0169. Washington, DC: U.S. Environmental Protection Agency, Office of Toxic Substances.

U.S. Office of Technology Assessment (OTA). 1984. *Acid Rain and Transported Air Pollutants: Implications for Public Policy.* Congress of the United States. Washington, DC: U.S. Government Printing Office.

_____. 1981. *Assessment of Technologies for Determining Cancer Risks in the Environment.* Congress of the United States. Washington, DC: U.S. Government Printing Office.

The White House, Office of the Press Secretary. February 11, 1994. Executive Order 12898: "Federal Actions to Address Environmental Justice in Minority Populations and Low-Income Populations." Washington, DC: The White House.

Chapter 4

Agency for Toxic Substances and Disease Registry. 1988. *The Nature and Extent of Lead Poisoning in Children in the United States: A Report to Congress.* Atlanta: U.S. Department of Health and Human Services.

Bullard, R.D. 1983. "Solid Waste Sites and the Black Houston Community." *Sociological Inquiry* 53(Spring): 273–288.

Bullard, R.D. and J.R. Feagin. 1991. "Racism and the City." In M. Gottdiener and

C.G. Pickvance (Eds.), *Urban Life in Transition*. Newbury Park, CA: Sage, pp. 55–76.

Bullard and Wright. 1985. "Endangered Environs: Dumping Groups in a Sunbelt City." *Urban Resources* 2: 37–39.

_____. 1986. "The Politics of Pollution: Implications for the Black Community." *Phylon* 47: 71–78.

Cerrell Associates, Inc. 1984. *Political Difficulties Facing Waste-to-Energy Conversion Plant Siting*. Los Angeles: California Waste Management Board.

Costner, P. and J. Thornton. 1990. *Playing with Fire*. Washington, DC: Greenpeace.

Florini, K., et al. 1990. *Legacy of Lead: America's Continuing Epidemic of Childhood Lead Poisoning*. Washington, DC: Environmental Defense Fund.

Gelobter, M. 1988. "The Distribution of Air Pollution by Income and Race." Paper presented at the Second Symposium on Social Science in Resource Management, Urbana, IL. June.

_____. 1990. "Toward a Model of Environmental Discrimination." In Bryant, B. and P. Mohai (Eds.), *The Proceedings of the Michigan Conference on Race and the Incidence of Environmental Hazards*. Ann Arbor, MI: University of Michigan, School of Natural Resources, pp. 87–107.

Geschwind, S.A., et al. 1992. "Risk of Congenital Malformations Associated with Proximity to Hazardous Waste Sites." *American Journal of Epidemiology* 135(11): 1197–1207.

Hilts, P.J. 1991. "White House Shuns Key Role in Lead Exposure." *The New York Times* August 24, p. 14.

Jasanoff, S. 1992. "Acceptable Evidence in a Pluralistic Society." In D.G. Mayo and R.D. Hollander (Eds.), *Acceptable Evidence: Science and Values in Risk Management*. New York: Oxford University Press, pp. 29–47.

Moses, M. 1989. "Pesticide Related Health Problems and Farmworkers." *American Association of Occupational Health Nurses Journal* 37: 115–130.

Perfecto, I. 1990. "Pesticide Exposure of Farm Workers and the International Connection." In B. Bryant and P. Mohai (Eds.), *The Proceedings of the Michigan Conference on Race and the Incidence of Environmental Hazards*. Ann Arbor, MI: University of Michigan, School of Natural Resources, pp. 87–218.

Slovic, P. 1991. "Beyond Numbers: A Broader Perspective on Risk Perception and Risk Communication." In D.G. Mayo and R.D. Hollander (Eds.), *Acceptable Evidence: Science and Values in Risk Management*. New York: Oxford University Press, 48–65.

Stark, R. 1992. *Sociology*. Belmont, CA: Wadsworth.

United Church of Christ, Commission for Racial Justice. 1987. *Toxic Wastes and Race: A National Report on the Racial and Socioeconomic Characteristics of Communities with Hazardous Wastes Sites.* New York: United Church of Christ.

U.S. Environmental Protection Agency (EPA). 1992. *Environmental Equity: Reducing Risk for All Communities.* 2 Vols. EPA230-R-92-008 and EPA230-R-92-008A. Washington, DC: Policy, Planning and Evaluation, U.S. Environmental Protection Agency.

U.S. General Accounting Office (GAO). 1983. *Siting of Hazardous Waste Landfills and Their Correlation with Racial and Economic Status of Surrounding Communities.* Washington, DC: GAO/RCED 83–168, June 1.

Wasserstrom, R. and R. Wiles. 1985. *Field Duty, U.S. Farm Workers and Pesticide Safety.* Study 3. Washington, DC: World Resources Institute, Center for Policy Research.

Wernette, D.R. and L.A. Nieves. 1992. "Breathing Polluted Air." *EPA Journal* 18(March/April): 16–17.

Chapter 5

Atlanta Journal. February 29, 1988: 1E

Bryant, B. and P. Mohai (Eds.), 1990. *The Proceedings of the Michigan Conference on Race and the Incidence of Environmental Hazards.* Ann Arbor, MI: University of Michigan, School of Natural Resources

Commoner, B. 1987. "A Reporter at Large (The Environment)." *The New Yorker* 63(17) June 15: 46–71.

Dowie, M. 1992. "American Environmentalism: A Movement Courting Irrelevance." *World Policy Journal* Spring: 67–92.

Gelobter, M. 1990. "Toward a Model of Environmental Discrimination." In B. Bryant and P. Mohai (Eds.), *The Proceedings of the Michigan Conference on Race and the Incidence of Environmental Hazards.* Ann Arbor, MI: University of Michigan, School of Natural Resources, pp. 87–107.

Lavelle, M. and M. Coyle. 1992. "Unequal Protection: The Racial Divide in Environmental Law." *The National Law Journal* 15(3) September 21: S1–S12.

McClosky, M. 1991. "Twenty Years of Change in the Environmental Movement: An Insider's View." *Society and Natural Resources* 4: 273–284.

United Church of Christ, Commission for Racial Justice. 1987. *Toxic Wastes and Race: A National Report on the Racial and Socioeconomic Characteristics of Communities with Hazardous Wastes Sites.* New York: United Church of Christ.

U.S. Environmental Protection Agency (EPA). 1978. *Our Common Future.* (A brochure.)

U.S. General Accounting Office (GAO). 1983. *Siting of Hazardous Waste Land-*

fills and Their Correlation with Racial and Economic Status of Surrounding Communities. Washington, DC: GAO/RCED 83–168. June 1.

Chapter 6

Bryant, B. and P. Mohai (Eds.). 1992. *Race and the Incidence of Environmental Hazards: A Time for Discourse.* Boulder, CO: Westview Press.

Bullard, R.D. 1987. *Invisible Houston: The Black Experience in Boom and Bust.* College Station, TX: Texas A&M University Press.

_____. 1990. *Dumping in Dixie: Race, Class, and Environmental Quality.* Boulder, CO: Westview Press.

_____. 1991. *In Search of the New South: The Black Urban Experience in the 1970s and 1980s.* Tuscaloosa, AL: University of Alabama Press.

_____. 1992. "Urban Infrastructure: Social, Environmental and Health Risks to African Americans." *The State of Black America.* New York: National Urban League.

_____. 1993. *Confronting Environmental Racism: Voices from the Grassroots.* Boston: South End Press.

Bullard, R.D. and J.R. Feagin. 1991. "Racism and the City." In M. Gottdiener and C.G. Pickvance (Eds.), *Urban Life in Transition.* Newbury Park, CA: Sage.

Bullard, R.D., J.E. Grigsby, and C. Lee. 1995. *Residential Apartheid: The American Legacy.* Los Angeles: UCLA Center for Afro-American Studies Publications.

Bullard, R.D. and B.H. Wright. 1986. "The Politics of Pollution: Implications for the Black Community." *Phylon* 47(March): 71–78.

_____. 1987. "Environmentalism and the Politics of Equity: Emergent Trends in the Black Community." *Mid-American Review of Sociology* 12: 21–38.

_____. 1990. "Toxic Waste and the African American Community." *The Urban League Review* 13(Spring): 67–75.

Cerrell Associates Inc. 1984. *Political Difficulties Facing Waste-to-Energy Conversion Plant Siting.* Los Angeles: California Waste Management Board.

Darden, J.T. 1989. "The Status of Urban Blacks 25 Years after the Civil Rights Act of 1964." *Sociology and Social Research* 73: 160–173.

Denton, N.A. and D.S. Massey. 1988. "Residential Segregation of Blacks, Hispanics, and Asians by Socioeconomic Status and Generation." *Social Science Quarterly* 69: 797–817.

Feagin, J.R. 1990a. *Building American Cities: The Urban Real Estate Game.* Englewood Cliffs, NJ: Prentice Hall.

Feagin, J.R. 1990b. *Racial and Ethnic Relations.* Third Edition. Englewood Cliffs, NJ: Prentice Hall.

Feagin, J.R. and C.B. Feagin. 1986. *Discrimination American Style: Institutional Racism and Sexism.* Malabar, FL: Robert E. Krieger Publishing Co.

Feldman, P. 1989. "Suit Charged Large Apartment Firm with Racial Bias in Rentals." *Los Angeles Times,* October 26.

Foust, D. 1987. "Leaning on Banks to Lend to the Poor." *Business Week,* March 2, p. 76.

Glastris, P. and S. Minerbrook. 1989. "A Housing Program That Really Works." *U.S. News and World Report* 106 (February 27): 26–27.

Gottdiener, M. 1988. *The Social Production of Urban Space.* Austin: University of Texas Press.

Hacker, A. 1992. *Two Nations: Black and White, Separate, Hostile, Unequal.* New York: Scribner's.

James, F.J., B.I. McCummings, and E.A. Tynan. 1984. *Minorities in the Sunbelt.* New Brunswick, NJ: Rutgers University Center for Urban Policy Research.

Jaynes, G.D. and R.M. Williams, Jr. 1989. *A Common Destiny: Blacks and American Society.* Washington, DC: National Academy Press.

Jones, J.M. 1972. *Prejudice and Racism.* Reading, MA: Addison-Wesley.

_____. 1981. "The Concept of Racism and Its Changing Reality." In Bowser, B.P. and R.G. Hunt (Eds.), *Impact of Racism on White Americans.* Beverly Hills: Sage, pp. 27–49.

Kay, J. 1991. "Fighting Toxic Racism: L.A.'s Minority Neighborhood Is the 'Dirtiest' in the State." The *San Francisco Examiner,* April 1, p. A1.

Kazis, R. and R. Grossman. 1983. *Fear at Work: Job Blackmail, Labor, and the Environment.* New York: The Pilgrim Press.

Kelly, E.D. 1988. "Zoning." In So, F.S. and J. Getzels (Eds.), *The Practice of Local Government Planning.* 2nd ed. Washington, DC: International City Management Association, pp. 251–284.

Kerner Commission. 1967. *Report of the National Advisory Commission on Civil Disorders.* New York: Bantam Books.

Kushner, J.A. 1980. *Apartheid in America: A Historical and Legal Analysis of Contemporary Racial Segregation in the United States.* Arlington, VA: Carrollton Press, Inc.

Logan, J. R. and H. L. Molotch. 1987. *Urban Fortunes: The Political Economy of Place.* Berkeley: University of California Press.

Mann, E. 1991. *L.A.'s Lethal Air: New Strategies for Policy, Organizing, and Action.* Los Angeles: Labor/Community Strategy Center.

Marshall, P.G. 1989. "Not in My Back Yard." *Editorial Research Reports* 1(June 9): 306–319.

Massey, D.S. and N.A. Denton. 1987. "Trends in the Residential Segregation of Blacks, Hispanics, and Asians, 1970–1980." *American Sociological Review* 52: 802–825.

_____. 1993. *American Apartheid and the Making of the Underclass.* Cambridge, MA: Harvard University Press.

Murray, S. 1992. "Clear and Present Danger: The Decay of America's Physical Infrastructure." In *The State of Black America 1992*. New York: National Urban League.

Ong, P. and E. Blumenberg. 1990. *Race and Environmentalism*. Graduate School of Architecture and Urban Planning, UCLA.

Plotkin, S. 1987. *Keep Out: The Struggle for Land Use Control*. Berkeley: University of California Press.

Rosenblatt, R.A. and J. Bates. 1991. "High Minority Mortgage Denial Rates Found." *The Los Angeles Times*, October 22. pp. A1, A25.

Udansky, M.L. 1991. "By the Numbers, Tracking Segregation in 219 Metro Areas." *USA Today*, November 11: 13.

Updegrade, W.L. 1989. "Race and Money." *Money* 18: 152–172.

U.S. Bureau of the Census (1991). *Census of Population and Housing*. Washington, D.C.: U.S. Department of Commerce.

Wernette, D.R. and L.A. Nieves. 1992. "Breathing Polluted Air." *EPA Journal* (March/April): 16–17.

Chapter 7

Alliance to Save Energy, American Council for an Energy-Efficient Economy, Natural Resources Defense Council, and Union of Concerned Scientists. 1991. *America's Energy Choices: Investing in a Strong Economy and a Clean Environment*. Washington, DC.

Basta, N. 1991. *The Environmental Career Guide: Job Opportunities with the Earth in Mind*. New York: John Wiley & Sons, Inc.

Bezdek, R.H. 1992. "Employment and Business Opportunities in the Environmental Protection Area during the 1990s." Paper presented at Environment and Employment Symposium, Ottawa, Canada, February.

Bezdek, R.H, et al. 1982. "National Goals for Solar Energy: Economic and Social Implications." *Natural Resources Journal* 22(2) April: 337–360.

Bezdek, R.H. and B.W. Cone. 1980. "Federal Incentives for Energy Development." *Energy—The International Journal* 5(5) May: 389–406.

Bezdek, R. H and F. Kreith. 1983. "Can Industry Afford Solar Energy?" *Mechanical Engineering* 105(3) March: 35–41.

Bezdek, R.H and F.T. Sparrow. 1981. "Solar Subsidies and Economic Efficiency." *Energy Policy* (December): 289–300.

Bezdek, R.H and R.M. Wendling. 1992. "Environmental Market Opportunities." Chapter 9 in Thomas F.P. Sullivan (Ed.), *The Greening of American Business*. Rockville, Maryland: GII Press, pp. 196–224.

_____. 1993. "Costs and Results of Federal Incentives for Commercial Nuclear Energy." *Energy Systems and Policy* (15) October/December: 269–293.

Bezdek, R.H, R.M. Wendling, and J.D. Jones. 1989. "The Economic and Employment Effects of Investments in Pollution Abatement and Control Technologies." *Ambio* XVIII(5): 274–279.

Borman, F.H. and S.R. Keller. 1991. *Ecology, Economics, Ethics: The Broken Circle*. New Haven: Yale University Press.

Bradley, R.A., E.C. Watts, and E.R. Williams. 1991. *Limiting Net Greenhouse Gas Emissions in the United States*. Washington, DC: U.S. Department of Energy.

Clark, M., I. Goodman, M. Anthony, and P. Kelly-Detwiler. 1992. *A Comparison of the Employment Creation Effects of the AES-Harriman Cove Coal-Fired Generating Station and Maine Demand-Side Management*. Boston: The Goodman Group.

Clark, W. 1975. *Energy for Survival: The Alternative to Extinction*. Garden City, NY: Anchor Books.

Coase, R.H. 1960. "The Problem of Social Cost." *The Journal of Law and Economics* 3 October: 1–44.

Cook, A.A. and J.D. Rosenberg. 1986. "The Ohio Story: The Economic and Employment Benefits of Controlling Acid Rain." *Amicus Journal* 8 (2): 5–8.

Cooper, M.H. 1992. "Jobs vs. Environment." *CQ Researcher* 2(18) May 15: 409–432.

Council on Economic Priorities. 1979. *Jobs and Energy: The Employment and Economic Impacts of Nuclear Power, Conservation, and Other Energy Options*. New York: Council on Economic Priorities

Coy, D.G. 1992. "Environment This Month." September 25. "Clean Air Act Update." March 12. County NatWest/Washington Analysis Co., Washington, DC.

Cropper, M.L. and W.E. Oates. 1992. "Environmental Economics: A Survey." *Journal of Economic Literature* XXX(June): 675–740.

Dower, R.C., and M.B. Zimmerman. 1992. *The Right Climate for Carbon Taxes: Creating Economic Incentives to Protect the Atmosphere*. Washington, DC: World Resources Institute.

Environmental Business Journal. 1991. IV(4) April.

Environmental Business Journal. 1992. V(4) April.

EPA Journal. 1992. "Special Issue: Environmental Protection—Has It Been Fair?" March/April.

Fischetti, M. 1992. "Green Entrepreneurs." *Technology Review* (April): 39–45.

Fisher, A.C. and V.K. Smith. 1982. "Economic Evaluation of Energy's Environmental Costs with Special References to Air Pollution." In J.M. Hollander (Ed.), *Annual Review of Energy, 1982*. Palo Alto, CA: Annual Reviews, Inc., pp. 1–36.

Fortune. 1992. "The Fortune 500: Special Report." April 20. pp. 211–316.

Gaines, L., R.S. Berry and T.V. Long II. 1979. *TOSCA: The Total Social Cost of Coal and Nuclear Power.* Cambridge, MA: Ballinger.

Geller, H., J.P. Harris, M.D. Levine, and A.H. Rosenfeld. 1987. "The Role of Federal Research and Development in Advancing Energy Efficiency: A $50 Billion Contribution to the U.S. Economy." In J.M. Hollander (Ed.), *Annual Review of Energy, 1987,* Palo Alto, CA: Annual Reviews, Inc., pp. 357–395.

Geller, H.S., et al. 1991. *Getting America Back on the Energy-Efficient Track: No-Regrets Policies for Slowing Climate Change.* Washington, DC: American Council for an Energy-Efficient Economy.

Geller, H., J. DeCicco and S. Laitner. 1992. *Energy Efficiency and Job Creation: The Employment and Income Benefits from Investing in Energy Conserving Technologies.* Washington, DC: American Council for an Energy-Efficient Economy.

Gordon, A. and D. Suzuki. 1990. *It's a Matter of Survival.* Cambridge, MA: Harvard University Press.

Gore, A. 1991. *Earth in the Balance.* New York: Houghton Mifflin.

Grossman, R. and G. Daneker. 1979. *Energy, Jobs, and the Economy.* Boston: Alyson Publications, Inc.

H & W Management Science Consultants. 1992. *Employment in the Air Pollution Control Industry.* Alexandria, VA: Report Prepared for the Industrial Gas Cleaning Institute.

Hazilla, M. and R.J. Koop. 1990. "Social Cost of Environmental Quality Regulations: A General Equilibrium Analysis." *Journal of Political Economy* 98(4): 853–873.

Heede, H.R., R.E. Morgan and S. Ridley. 1985. *The Hidden Costs of Energy.* Washington, DC: Center for Renewable Resources.

Hong, P. and D.J. Yang. 1992. "Tree-Huggers vs. Jobs: It's Not That Simple." *Business Week* October 19: 108–109.

ICF Resources, Inc. and Smith Barney, Harris Upham & Co., Inc. 1992. *Business Opportunities of the New Clean Air Act: The Impact of the CAAA of 1990 on the Air Pollution Control Industry.* August.

Jaccard, M. and D. Sims. 1991. "Employment Effects of Electricity Conservation: The Case of British Columbia." *Energy Studies Review* 3(1): 35–44.

Jorgensen, D.W. and P.J. Wilcoxen. 1990. "Environmental Regulation and U.S. Economic Growth." *RAND Journal of Economics* 21(2) Summer: 314–340.

_____. 1992. "Impact of Environmental Legislation on U.S. Economic Growth, Investment, and Capital Costs." In *U.S. Environmental Policy and Economic Growth: How Do We Fare?* March. Washington, DC: American Council for Capital Formation.

Kneese, A.V. and C.L. Schultze. 1975. *Pollution, Prices, and Public Policy.* Washington, DC: The Brookings Institution.

Labor Committee for Safe Energy and Full Employment. 1981. *Our Jobs, Our Health, Our Lives, Our Fight.* Washington, DC: Labor Committee for Safe Energy and Full Employment.

Lee, T. 1990. "Here Comes the Pink Slip." *American Demographics* 12(3): 46–49.

Leonard, H.J. 1988. *Pollution and the Struggle for World Product.* Cambridge, England: Cambridge University Press.

Linden, E. 1992. "The Green Factor." *Time* October 12: 57–60.

Lord, M., et al. 1992. "1993 Career Guide." *U.S. News and World Report* October 26: 72–110.

Lovins, A. 1977. *Soft Energy Paths.* Cambridge, MA: Ballinger Publishing Co.

Lovins, A. and L.H. Lovins. 1982. *Brittle Power: Energy Strategy for National Security.* Andover, MA: Brick House Publishing Co.

Management Information Services, Inc. (MISI) 1986a. *Economic and Employment Benefits of Investments in Environmental Protection.* Washington, DC: Management Information Services, Inc.

_____. 1986b. *Impact of Acid Rain Abatement Legislation on States and Electric Utility Company Costs and Rates.* Washington, DC: Management Information Services, Inc.

_____. 1987. *Net Costs and Benefits to Each State and the Nation of Acid Rain Abatement Legislation.* Washington, DC: Management Information Services, Inc.

_____. 1992a. *Environment and Employment in Canada: The Final Report of an Interactive Symposium of Labour, Business and Environmentalists.* April. Ottawa: Canada Employment and Immigration Advisory Council.

_____. 1992b. *The Economic and Employment Implications of RCRA-Related Solid and Hazardous Waste Control Programs in the U.S. and International Markets.* November. Washington, DC: Management Information Services, Inc.

_____. 1992c. *U.S. 1992 Environmental Protection Spending Totals $170 Billion and Creates 4 Million Jobs.* December. Washington, DC: Management Information Services, Inc.

Manne, A.S. and R.G. Richels. 1990. "CO_2 Emissions Limits: An Economic Cost Analysis for the USA." *The Energy Journal* 11(2) (April).

_____. 1992. *Buying Greenhouse Insurance: The Economic Costs of CO_2 Emission Limits.* Cambridge, MA: MIT Press.

Meyer, S.M. 1992. "Environmentalism and Economic Prosperity: Testing the Environmental Impact Hypothesis." A study by the Massachusetts Institute of Technology, Project on Environmental Policies and Policy. October.

Mullins, M.L. 1992. Letter to William G. Rosenberg, February 7. Chemical Manufacturers Association, Washington, DC.

New York Times. 1992. "Phillips Petroleum Says It Cut 1,350 Jobs." April 4. p. 41.

Peskin, H.M., P.R. Portney and V. Knesse (Eds.). 1981. *Environmental Regulation and the U.S. Economy.* Baltimore, MD: Johns Hopkins University Press.

Porter, M.E. 1990. *The Competitive Advantage of Nations.* New York: The Free Press.

—————. 1991. "America's Green Strategy." *Scientific American* April: 168.

Portney, P.R. 1982. "How *Not* to Create a Job." *Regulation* November/December: 35–38.

—————. 1990. "Economics and the Clean Air Act." *Journal of Economic Perspectives* 4: 173–181.

Portney, P.R. and D. Burtraw. 1991. "Environmental Policy in the United States." In D. Helm (Ed.), *Economic Policy Towards the Environment.* Oxford: Blackwell Publishers, pp. 289–320.

Ramsay, W. 1979. *Unpaid Costs of Electrical Energy: Health and Environmental Impacts from Coal and Nuclear Power.* Baltimore, MD: Johns Hopkins University Press.

Renner, M.G. 1992. *Saving the Earth, Creating Jobs.* Washington, DC: WorldWatch Institute.

Rutledge, G.L. and M.L. Leonard. 1991. "Pollution Abatement and Control Expenditures, 1987–89." *Survey of Current Business* September: 46–50.

Schine, E. 1992. "Cleaning Up at Fluor." *Business Week* October 5: 112–113.

Shirley, J. 1992. *Jobs and the Environment.* Sacramento, CA: Planning and Conservation League Foundation.

Silverstein, M. 1992a "In Economics 'Green Is Gold'." *The Christian Science Monitor* February 18: 19.

—————. 1992b. "Bush's Polluter Protectionism Isn't Pro-Business." *The Wall Street Journal* May 28: A19.

Silvestri, G. and J. Lukasiewicz. 1991. "Occupational Employment Projections." *Monthly Labor Review* 114(11) November: 64–94.

Tennis, M.W., I. Goodman and M. Clark. 1991. "Employment Impacts of New York State Energy Options." Boston: The Goodman Group.

Tobey, J.A. 1990. "The Effects of Domestic Environmental Policies on Patterns of World Trade: An Empirical Test." *KYKLOS* 43(2): 191–209.

U.S. Council on Environmental Quality. 1992. *Environmental Quality.* Washington, DC.

U.S. Department of Energy. 1991. *Environmental Restoration and Waste Management: Five Year Plan, Fiscal Years 1993–1997.* August. Washington, DC.

U.S. Environmental Protection Agency. 1990. *Environmental Investments: The Cost of a Clean Environment.* Washington, DC: USEPA.

U.S. Office of Technology Assessment. 1984. *Acid Rain and Transported Air Pollutants: Implications for Pubic Policy.* June. Washington, DC: U.S. Government Printing Office.

Van Leer, L. 1992. "Manufacturers Caught Between Economy, Laws." *The New Jersey Home News* August 17: A1, A2.

Walter, I. 1982. "Environmentally Induced Industrial Relocation in Developing Countries." In S.J. Rubin and T. R. Graham (Eds.), *Environment and Trade.* Totowa, NJ: Allanheld, Osmun, and Co., pp. 67–101.

Walter, I. and J. Ugelow. 1979. "Environmental Policies in Developing Countries." *Ambio* 8: 102–109.

Wendling, R.M. and R.H. Bezdek. 1989. "Acid Rain Control: Net Costs and Benefits." *International Journal of Management Science* 17(3): 251–261.

Wirth, T.E. 1992. "Lighten Up, Loggers—Environmentalism Actually Creates Jobs." *Washington Post* October 4: C.1.

Zimmerman, M.B. 1992. "Assessing the Costs of Reducing Greenhouse Gas Emissions: Comparing Modelling Approaches." Washington, DC: Alliance to Save Energy.

Chapter 8

Bookser-Feister, J. and L. Wise. 1986. "The Politics of Economic Development." *Southern Exposure* XIV(5–6): 2–3.

George, A. and P. Smith. 1988. "The Dumping Grounds." *South* August 1988: 1, 4.

Gibbs, L.M. 1982. *Love Canal, My Story.* Albany, NY: State University of New York Press, Albany.

Hegel, G.W.F. 1956. *Philosophy of History.* New York: Dover.

Henderson, H. 1981. *The Politics of the Solar Age, Alternatives to Economics.* New York: Anchor Press/Doubleday.

Kennedy, E. (Ed.). 1975. *The Negritude Poets.* "Return to My Native Land." Aime Cesaire, "Prayer to the Masks," Leopold Senghor. New York: Viking Press.

Labor/Community Strategy Center. 1993. *Reconstructing Los Angeles from the Bottom Up.* Los Angeles: Labor Community Strategy Center.

Lappe, F.M. and J. Collins. 1978. *World Hunger: Ten Myths.* San Francisco: Institute for Food and Developing Policy.

Marcuse, H. 1961. *Eros and Civilization: A Philosophical Inquiry into Freud.* New York: Vintage.

Meadows, D. et al., 1972. *The Limits to Growth.* Report of the Club of Rome's Project on the Predicament of Mankind. New York: Universe Books.

Merchant, C. 1981. *The Death of Nature.* San Francisco: Harper & Row.

Newman, O. 1970. *Design Guidelines for Creating Defensible Space.* Washington, DC: National Institute of Law Enforcement and Criminal Justice, Law Enforcement Assistance Administration, U.S. Department of Justice.

O'Connor, J. 1989. "Uneven and Combined Development and Ecological Crises: A Theoretical Introduction." *Race and Class* 30(3), January–March.

Rensenbrink, J. 1988. "What Marx Forgot, Liberals Have Never Known and Conservatives Find Frightening: The Ecology of Democracy." Unpublished paper delivered at American Political Science Association meeting, Washington, DC.

Robertson, J. H. 1983. *The Sane Alternative*. London: Riverbasin Press.

Rostow, W. 1978. *Getting from Here to There*. New York: McGraw-Hill.

Sklar, H. (Ed.). 1980. *Trilateralism: The Trilateral Commission and Elite Planning for World Management*. Boston: South End Press.

United Church of Christ, Commission for Racial Justice. 1987. *Toxic Wastes and Race: A National Report on the Racial and Socioeconomic Characteristics of Communities with Hazardous Wastes Sites*. New York: United Church of Christ.

World Commission on Environment and Development (WCED). 1987. *Our Common Future*. Oxford, New York: Oxford University Press.

Chapter 9

Ballard, C. L. and D. Fullerton. 1992. "Distortionary Taxes and the Provision of Public Goods." *Journal of Economic Perspectives* 6(3): 117–131.

Ballard, C.L., J.B. Shoven and J. Whalley. 1985. "General Equilibrium Computations of the Marginal Welfare Costs of Taxation in the U.S." *American Economic Review* 75(1) March: 128–138.

Baumol, W.J. and W. Oates. 1975. *The Theory of Environmental Policy*. Englewood, NJ: Prentice-Hall.

Bowes, M.D. and J.V. Krutilla. 1989. *Multiple-Use Management: The Economics of Public Forestlands*. Washington, DC: Resources for the Future, p. 18–19.

Browning, E.K. "On the Marginal Welfare Cost of Taxation." *American Economic Review* 77(1) March: 11–23.

Congressional Budget Office (CBO). 1993. *Reducing the Deficit: Spending and Revenue Options*. February. Washington, DC: Congress of the U.S./CBO.

Energy Information Administration (EIA). 1990. "Energy Consumption and Conservation Potential: Supporting Analysis for the NES." NES Service Report #2 (SR.NES/90-02), December 21. Washington, DC: Department of Energy/EIA.

Fickett, A.P., C.W. Gellings and A.B. Lovins. 1990. "Efficient Use of Electricity." *Scientific American* 263 September: 64–68.

Fullerton, D. and Y. Henderson. 1989. "The Marginal Excess Burden of Different Capital Tax Instruments." *Review of Economics and Statistics* 71(3) August: 431–442.

Jorgenson, D. and K. Yun. 1990. "The Excess Burden of Taxation in the United States." Mimeo. November. Cambridge, MA: Harvard Institute for Economic Research.

Killingsworth, M.R. and J.J. Heckman. 1986. "Female Labor Supply." In O. Ashenfelter and R. Layard (Eds.), *Handbook of Labor Economics, Vol.1.* New York: Elsevier Science Publishers BV, pp. 103–200.

Moffitt, R.A. and K.C. Kehrer. 1981. "The Effect of Tax and Transfer Programs on Labor Supply: The Evidence from Income Maintenance Experiments." In R.G. Ehrenberg (Ed.), *Research in Labor Economics.* Greenwich, CT: JAI Press, pp. 103–50.

Organization for Economic Co-operation and Development (OECD). 1981. *Economic Instruments in Solid Waste Management.* Paris.

Pencavel, J. 1986. "Labor Supply of Men: A Survey." In O. Ashenfelter and R. Layard (Eds.), *Handbook of Labor Economics, Vol.1.* New York: Elsevier Science Publishers BV, pp. 5–102.

Portney, P. (Ed.). 1990. *Public Policies for Environmental Protection: Resources for the Future.* Baltimore, MD: Johns Hopkins Press.

Repetto, R. 1988. "Subsidized Timber Sales from National Forests in the United States." In R. Repetto and M. Gillis (Eds.), *Public Policies and the Misuse of Forest Resources.* New York: Cambridge University Press.

Repetto, R., R.C. Dower, R. Jenkins, and J. Googhegan. 1992. *Green Fees: How a Tax Shift Can Work for the Environment and the Economy.* Washington, DC: World Resources Institute.

Stavins, R.N. (Ed.) 1991. *Project 88-Round II: Incentives for Action: Designing Market-Based Environmental Strategies.* A Public Policy Study Sponsored by Senator Timothy E. Wirth, Colorado, and Senator John Heinz, Pennsylvania. Washington, DC, December.

Tietenberg, T.H. 1988. *Environmental and Natural Resource Economics.* Second Edition. Glenview, IL: Scott, Foresman and Company.

Trostel, P.A. 1991. "Taxation in a Dynamic General Equilibrium Model with Human Capital." Ph.D. Dissertation. Dept. of Economics. Texas A&M University.

U.S. Bureau of the Census. 1992. *Statistical Abstract of the United States: 1992.* 112th Edition. Washington, DC.

Chapter 10

Humphrey, H. 1976. *Evaluation of Changes of the Level of Polychlorinated Biphenyls (PCBs) in Human Tissue.* Final report to on FDA Contract 223-73-2209. Lansing, MI: Michigan Dept. of Public Health.

_____. 1983. *Evaluation of Humans Exposed to Waterbourne Chemicals in the Great Lakes.* Final report to the EPA Cooperative Agreement CR-807192. Lansing, MI: Michigan Dept. of Public Health.

Javitz, H. 1980. "Seafood Consumption Data Analysis: Final Report." Prepared for USEPA by SRI International: Menlo Park, CA, September.

U.S. Environmental Protection Agency (USEPA). 1992. *Consumption Surveys for Fish and Shellfish: A Review and Analysis of Survey Methods.* EPA Contract No. 68-C9-0013. Washington DC: U.S. Environmental Protection Agency, Office of Water Quality and Office of Science and Technology.

West, P.C. 1992a. "Invitation to Poison? Detroit Minorities and Toxic Fish Consumption from the Detroit River." In B. Bryant and P. Mohai (Eds.), *Race and the Incidence of Environmental Hazards: A Time for Discourse.* Boulder, CO: Westview Press, pp. 96–99.

West, P.C. 1992b. "Health Concerns for Fish-Eating Tribes?" *USEPA Journal* 18(1): 15–16.

West, P.C., et al. 1989a. *Michigan Sport Anglers Fish Consumption Survey.* A report to the Michigan Toxic Substance Control Commission. University of Michigan, School of Natural Resources, Natural Resource Sociology Research Lab. Technical Report #1.

West, P.C., et al. 1989b. *Michigan Sport Anglers Fish Consumption Survey: Supplement I—Non-Response Bias and Consumption Suppression Effect Adjustments.* A report to the Michigan Toxic Substance Control Commission. University of Michigan, School of Natural Resources, Natural Resource Sociology Research Lab. Technical Report #2.

West, P.C., et al. 1992. "Minority Anglers and Toxic Fish Consumption: Evidence from a Statewide Survey of Michigan." In B. Bryant and P. Mohai (Eds.), *Race and the Incidence of Environmental Hazards: A Time for Discourse.* Boulder, CO: Westview Press, pp. 100–113.

West, P.C., et al. 1993. *1991–92 Michigan Sport Anglers Fish Consumption Study.* Final Report to the Michigan Great Lakes Protection Fund, Michigan Dept. of Natural Resources. University of Michigan, School of Natural Resources Research Lab, Technical Report #6.

Chapter 11

American Indian Policy Review Commission. 1977. *Final Report.* Washington, DC: Government Printing Office.

Americans for Indian Opportunity (AIO). 1986. "Survey of American Indian Environmental Protection Needs on Reservation Lands." Report for the U.S. Environmental Protection Agency. Washington, DC.

Angel, B. 1992. "The Toxic Threat to Indian Lands." A Greenpeace Report. San Francisco: Greenpeace.

Blue Legs v. United States Bureau of Indian Affairs, 867 F.2d 1094 (8th Cir. 1989).

Bresette, W. 1992. "Treaty Rights." Presentation made at Bemidji State University. Unpublished. Bemidji, MN.

Bryant, B. and P. Mohai (Eds.) 1991. "Principles of Environmental Justice." *Race and the Incidence of Environmental Hazards.* Boulder, CO: Westview Press.

Bureau of Indian Affairs (BIA). 1986. *Report of the Task Force on Indian Economic Development.* Washington, DC: Government Printing.

California v. Cabazon Band of Mission Indians, 480 U.S. 202, 214–216 (1987).

Cherokee Nation v. Georgia, 30 U.S. (5 Pet.) 1(1831).

Chicago Indian Treaty Rights Committee Newsletter. 1991. Chicago: Indian Treaty Rights Committee.

Churchill, W. 1992. "The Earth Is Our Mother: Struggles for American Indian Land and Liberation in the Contemporary United States." In A. Jaimes (Ed.), *The State of Native America: Genocide, Colonization and Resistance.* Boston: South End Press: 143.

Cohen, F. 1971. *Handbook of Federal Indian Law.* Albuquerque, NM: University of New Mexico Press.

Earth Summit: United Nations Conference on Environment and Development (UNCED). 1992. An international conference held in Rio, Brazil. For a report on the summit see *United States of America National Report: United Nations Conference on Environment and Development.* 1992. Washington, DC: Council on Economic Quality.

Environmental Protection Agency (EPA). 1984. *EPA Indian Policy, William Reilly, Administrator.*

Gover, K. 1992. "Commercial Solid Waste and Hazardous Waste Disposal Projects on Indian Lands." A presentation at the Indian Law Support Center Conference *Developments in Federal Indian Law.* October. Albuquerque, NM.

Grinde, D. A. Jr. 1977. *The Iroquois in the Founding of the American Nation.* San Francisco: Indian Historian Press.

_____. 1991. *Great Lakes Indian Fish and Wildlife Commission: A Guide to Understanding Chippewa Treaty Rights.* Odanah, WI: GLIFWC Public Information.

Institute for the Development of Indian Law. 1973. *A Chronological List of Treaties and Agreements Made by Indian Tribes with the United States.* Washington, DC: Institute for the Development of Indian Law.

International Tribunal of Indigenous Peoples and Oppressed Nations in the USA. 1992. A tribunal organized by the San Francisco chapter of American Indian Movement. October. San Francisco.

Jennison, K. and J. Tebbel. 1960. *The American Indian Wars.* New York: Harper and Brothers.

Kickingbird, K., et al. 1977. *Indian Sovereignty.* Washington, DC: Institute for the Development of Indian Law.

LaDuke, W. 1992. "We Are Still Here: The 500 Years Celebration." *Border/Lines* 23 Winter 1991/1992: 5–7.

Lee, C. 1992. "Principles of Environmental Justice." In C. Lee (Ed.), *The First National People of Color Environmental Leadership Summit.* New York: Commission for Racial Justice, United Church of Christ.

Lone Wolf v. Hitchcock, 187 U.S. 553 (1903).

Lying v. Northwest Indian Cemetery Protection Association, 485 U.S. 439 (1988).

Montana v. United States, 450 U.S. 544 (1981).

Morris, G. 1992. "International Law and Politics: Towards a Right to Self-Determination for Indigenous People." In A. Jaimes (Ed.), *The State of Native America: Genocide, Colonization and Resistance*. Boston: South End Press: 65–67.

Native American Rights Fund. 1992. *Fact Sheet: Native American Sacred Sites Under Assault*. Boulder, CO.

Royster, J.V. and Fausett, R.S. 1989. "Control of the Reservation Environment: Tribal Primacy, Federal Delegation, and the Limits of State Intrusion." *Washington Law Review* 64(3) July: 587–590.

Schaaf, G. 1990. *Wampum Belts and Peace Trees: George Morgan, Native Americans and Revolutionary Diplomacy*. Golden, CO: Fulcrum Publishers.

Schusky, E. 1970. *Political Organization of Native North Americans*. Washington, DC: University Press of America.

Snipp, C.M. 1989. *American Indians: The First of This Land*. New York: Russel Sage Foundation.

U.S. Constitution, Article I, Section 10.

U.S. Constitution, Article VI, Section 2.

United States v. Winans, 198 U.S. 371 (1905).

Washington Department of Ecology v. United States EPA, 752 F.2d 1465 (9th Cir. 1985).

Webster's New Twentieth Century Dictionary of the English Language. 1957. Cleveland and New York: The World Publishing Company.

Wenzel, L. 1992. "Environmental Risk in Indian Country." Report for the U.S. Environmental Protection Agency. Master's degree practicum. Natural Sciences Library: University of Michigan, Ann Arbor.

Worcester v. Georgia, 31 U.S. 515 (1832).

Chapter 12

Anthan, G. 1993. "Mid-size Farms Feel Squeeze." *The Des Moines Register*, August 10.

Boschwitz, R. 1985. "Farming's Future." *Time Magazine* March 18. Letters.

Federation of Southern Cooperatives/Land Assistance Fund. 1993. "26th Annual Report: 1992–1993." Atlanta, GA: 56

Goodwyn, L. 1978. *The Populist Moment*. New York: Oxford University Press: 316–318.

Krebs, A.V. 1992. "America's New 'Centrally Planned' Food Economy." *Prairie Journal* 3(2) Summer. Des Moines, IA: PrairieFire RuralAction: 6–7.

_____. 1993. "Return to Equity." Unpublished analysis by PrairieFire Rural Action. Des Moines, IA.

Number of U.S. Farms Drops Below 2 Million. 1994. *The Chicago Tribune.* Section 3. p. 3.

Office of Technology Assessment. 1986. *Technology, Public Policy, and the Changing Structure of American Agriculture.* Summary. Congress of the United States. Washington, DC: U.S. Government Printing Office.

Pennick, J. 1992. "Turning the Tide on Black Land Loss." *Prairie Journal* 3(2) Summer: 10. Des Moines, IA: PrairieFire RuralAction.

PrairieFire Rural Action. 1993. "Hog Tied: A Primer on Concentration and Integration in the U.S. Hog Industry." Des Moines, IA: PrairieFire RuralAction: 5.

Project 21. 1993. *Greater Des Moines Business Climate Profile & Competitive Assessment.* Des Moines, IA: 102.

United States Commission on Civil Rights. 1982. "The Decline of Black Farming in America." Washington, DC: U.S. Commission on Civil Rights.

United States Department of Agriculture/Economic Research Service (USDA/ ERS). 1991. "Owning Farmland in the United States." Agriculture Information Bulletin 637, December. Washington, DC: USDA/ERS: 1.

_____. 1993a. "Trends in Numbers, Sizes, and Ownership of Farms." Agriculture Information Bulletin Number 664–27.

_____. 1993b. "Off-Farm Income Is Critical to Most Farm Operator Households." Summary of Report Number 8. February. Washington, DC: USDA/ERS.

Werfelman, L. 1983. "Block to Poor Nations: 'Buy, Don't Grow Food'." *United Press International* April 8.

Chapter 13

Allen, P. 1991. "Sustainable Agriculture at the Crossroad." *Capitalism, Nature, and Socialism* 2(3): 20–28.

Beckenbach, F. 1989. "Social Costs of Modern Capitalism." *Capitalism, Nature, and Socialism* 1(3): 72–91.

Bullard, R.D. 1990. *Dumping in Dixie: Race Class and Environmental Equity.* Boulder, CO: Westview Press.

Bultena, G. and F.L. Leistritz. 1992. "Introduction: Socioeconomic Impacts of Sustainable Agriculture. *Impact Assessment Bulletin* 10(2): 3–5.

Buttel, F.H. 1990. "Social Relations and the Growth of Modern Agriculture." In C.R. Carroll, J.H. Vandermeer and P.M. Rosset (Eds.), *Agroecology.* New York: McGraw-Hill, pp. 613–628.

Capra, F. 1975. *The Tao of Physics*. Berkeley, CA: Shambala.

Center for Investigative Reporting and Bill Moyers. 1990. *Global Dumping Ground*. Washington, DC: Seven Locks.

Feher, W.R. (Ed.). 1984. *Genetic Contributions to Yield Gains of Five Major Crop Plants*. Special Publication No. 7. Madison, WI: Crop Science Society of America.

Haraway, D.J. 1988. "Situated Knowledges: The Science Question in Feminism as a Site of Discourse on the Privilege of Partial Perspective." *Feminist Studies* 14(3): 575–600.

Lage, C. 1992. "Comparecencia de Carlos Lage en el Programa Hoy Mismo." *Granma*, November 10.

Levins, R. 1990."The Struggle for Ecological Agriculture in Cuba." *Capitalism Nature Socialism* 1(5): 121–141.

Levins, R. and R. Lewontin. 1985. *The Dialectical Biologist*. Cambridge, MA: Harvard University Press.

Lewontin, R. 1982. "Agricultural Research and the Penetration of Capital." *Science for the People* 14(1): 12–17.

Lewontin, R. and J.P. Berlan. 1990. "The Political Economy of Agricultural Research: The Case of Hybrid Corn." In C.R. Carroll, J.H. Vandermeer and P.M. Rosset (Eds.), *Agroecology*. New York: McGraw-Hill, pp. 613–628.

Martínez-Alier, J. 1987. *Ecological Economics: Energy, Environment and Society*. Oxford: Basil Blackwell.

Mohai, P. and B. Bryant. 1992. "Race, Poverty and the Environment." *EPA Journal* 18(1): 6–8.

National Research Council. 1986. *Soil Conservation: Assessing the Natural Resources Inventory*. Vols. 1 and 2. Washington, DC: National Academy Press.

_____. 1989. *Alternative Agriculture*. Washington, DC: National Academy Press.

Needham, J. 1956. *Science and Civilization in China*. Cambridge, England: Cambridge University Press.

Peréz Marín and Muñoz Baños, 1991. Agricultura y Alimentacion en Cuba. Editorial de Ciencias Sociales, Habana.

Perfecto, I. 1992a. "Pesticides and the International Connection." In B. Bryant and P. Mohai (Eds.), *Race and the Incidence of Environmental Hazards: A Time for Discourse*. Boulder, CO: Westview Press pp. 177–203.

_____. 1992b. "Pesticide Exports to the Third World." *Race and Class* 34 (July–September): 107–114.

_____. 1994. "The Transformation of Cuban Agriculture after the Cold War." *American Journal of Alternative Agriculture* 9: 98–108.

Perfecto, I. and B. Velázquez. 1992. "Farm Workers: Among the Least Protected." *EPA Journal* 18(1): 13–14.

Phipps, T.T. and P.R. Crosson. 1986. "Agriculture and the Environment: An Overview." In T.T. Phipps, P.R. Crosson and K.A. Price (Eds.), *Agriculture and the Environment: Annual Policy Review*. Washington DC: The National Center for Food and Agricultural Policy, Resources for the Future, pp. 3–31.

Pimentel, D. and W. Dazhong. 1990. "Technological Changes in Energy Use in U.S. Agricultural Production." In C.R. Carroll, J.H. Vandermeer and P.M. Rosset (Eds.), *Agroecology*. New York: McGraw-Hill, pp. 613–628.

Pimentel, D., et al. 1992. "Environmental and Economic Cost of Pesticide Use." *BioScience* 42(10): 750–760.

Redclift, M. 1987. *Sustainable Development: Exploring the Contradictions*. London: Methuen.

Repetto, R. 1992. "Accounting for Environmental Assets." *Scientific American* June: 94–100.

Robinson, J.C. 1991. *Toil and Toxics*. Berkeley: University of California Press.

Rosset, P. M. 1994. "The Greening of Cuba." *NACLA Report of the Americas*. Vol. XXVIII: 37–41.

Schneider, K. 1986. "Erosion Is Called Small Threat to Crop Yields." *The New York Times* May 16.

Shiva, V. 1988. *Staying Alive: Women, Ecology and Development*. London: Zed Books.

Soule, J.D. Carré and W. Jackson. 1990. "Ecological Impact of Modern Agriculture." In C.R. Carroll, J.H. Vandermeer and P.M. Rosset (Eds.), *Agroecology*. New York: McGraw-Hill, pp. 613–628.

U. S. Department of Agriculture. 1984. *Inputs—Outlook and Situation Report*. IOS–6. Washington, DC: Economic Research Service.

――――――. 1986. *Agriculture's Link to the National Economy: Income and Employment*. Agriculture Information Bulletin No. 504. Washington, DC: Economic Research Service.

――――――. 1987a. *Agricultural Resources—Inputs—Situation and Outlook Report*. AR-5. Washington, DC: Economic Research Service.

――――――. 1987b. *U.S. Irrigation: Extent and Economic Importance*. Agricultural Information Bulletin No. 523. Washington, DC: Economic Research Service.

――――――. 1987c. *Measuring the Size of the U.S. Food and Fiber System*. Agricultural Economic Report No. 566. Washington, DC: Economic Research Service.

――――――. 1987d. *Agricultural Resources—Cropland, Water, and Conservation Situation and Outlook Report*. AR-8. Washington, DC: Economic Research Service.

Wallerstein, I. 1989 . "Culture as the Ideological Battleground of the Modern World-System." *Hitotsubashi Journal of Social Studies* 21(1): 5–22.

_____. 1991. *Geopolitics and Geoculture.* Cambridge, England: Cambridge University Press.

West, P.C. 1992. "Invitation to Poison? Detroit Minorities and Toxic Fish Consumption from the Detroit River." In B. Bryant and P. Mohai (Eds.), *Race and the Incidence of Environmental Hazards.* Boulder, CO: Westview Press, pp. 96–99.

Williams, W.M., et al. 1988. *Pesticides in Ground Water Data Base: 1988 Interim Report.* Office of Pesticide Programs. Washington, DC: U.S. Environmental Protection Agency.

Chapter 14

Brown, L.R., et al. 1993. *State of the World 1993.* New York: W.W. Norton.

Bryson, R.A. 1990. "Will There Be a Global 'Greenhouse Warming'?" *Environmental Conservation* 17: 97–99.

Buttel, F.H. 1992. "Environmentalization: Origins, Processes, and Implications for Rural Social Change." *Rural Sociology* 57: 1–27.

Buttel, F.H., A. Hawkins, and A.G. Power. 1990. "From Limits to Growth to Global Change: Contrasts and Contradictions in the Evolution of Environmental Science and Ideology." *Global Environmental Change* 1: 57–66.

Canak, W.L. (Ed.). 1989. *Lost Promises.* Boulder, CO: Westview Press.

Center for Science and Environment (CSE). 1990. *Global Warming in an Unequal World.* New Delhi: CSE.

Daly, H.E. and J.B. Cobb, Jr. 1989. *For the Common Good.* Boston: Beacon.

The Economist. 1994. "Aid and the Environment—Outlook: Cloudy." *The Economist* February 12: 42.

Ehrlich, P.R. 1968. *The Population Bomb.* New York: Ballantine.

Freudenberg, N. and C. Steinsapir. 1992. "Not in Our Backyards: The Grassroots Environmental Movement." In R.E. Dunlap and A.G. Mertig (Eds.), *American Environmentalism.* New York: Taylor and Francis, pp. 27–38

Gilpin, R. 1987. *The Political Economy of International Relations.* Princeton: Princeton University Press.

Gore, A. 1992. *Earth in the Balance.* New York: Plume/Penguin.

Lipietz, A. 1992. *Towards a New Economic Order.* Beverly Hills, CA: Sage.

Lipschutz, R. D. 1989. *When Nations Clash: Raw Materials, Ideology, and Foreign Policy.* New York: Ballinger/Harper & Row.

Mann, C. C. 1991. "Extinction: Are Ecologists Crying Wolf?" *Science* 253: 736–738.

McMichael, P. 1992. "Rethinking Comparative Analysis in a Post-Developmentalist Context." *International Social Science Journal* 133: 351–365.

Meadows, D.H., et al. 1972. *The Limits to Growth.* New York: Universe.

Mitchell, R.C., A.G. Mertig and R.E. Dunlap. 1992. "Twenty Years of Environmental Mobilization: Trends Among National Environmental Organizations." In R.E. Dunlap and A.G. Mertig (Eds.), *American Environmentalism.* New York: Taylor and Francis, pp. 11-26.

Myers, A. and B. Myers. 1982. "From the 'Duck Pond' to the Global Commons: Increasing Awareness of the Supranational Nature of Emerging Environmental Issues." *Ambio* 11: 198-201.

Pearce, D., et al. 1989. *Blueprint for a Green Economy.* London: Earthscan.

Pearce, F. 1992a. "American Sceptic Plays Down Global Warming Fears." *New Scientist* December 26: 6.

_____. 1992b. "Mirage of the Shifting Sands." *New Scientist* 12(December): 38-42.

Peluso, N.L. 1991. *Rich Forests, Poor People.* Berkeley: University of Cal. Press.

Portney, L.E. 1992. *Controversial Issues in Environmental Policy.* Beverly Hills, CA: Sage Publications.

Reich, M.R. 1991. *Toxic Politics.* Ithaca, NY: Cornell University Press.

Repetto, R., R.C. Dower, R. Jenkins, and J. Googhegan. 1992. *Green Fees: How a Tax Shift Can Work for the Environment and the Economy.* Washington, DC: World Resources Institute.

Schnaiberg, A. 1980. *The Environment: From Surplus to Scarcity.* New York: Oxford University Press.

Schneider, S.M. 1976. *The Genesis Strategy.* New York: Plenum.

Stern, P.C., O.R. Young, and D. Druckman (Eds.). 1992. *Global Environmental Change: Understanding the Human Dimensions.* Washington, DC: National Academy Press.

Sunderlin, W. 1992. "In the Shadow of Ideology: Instrumental Environmentalism." Paper presented at the VII World Congress for Rural Sociology, Pennsylvania State University, University Park, PA, August.

Taylor, P.J. and F.H. Buttel. 1992. "How Do We Know We Have Global Environmental Problems — Science and the Globalization of Environmental Discourse." *Geoforum* 23(3): 405-416.

Turner, B.L. II, et al. 1990. "Two Types of Global Environmental Change: Definitional and Spatial Scale Issues in Their Human Dimensions." *Global Environmental Change* 1: 14-22.

United Nations Development Program (UNDP). 1992. *Human Development Report 1992.* New York: Oxford University Press.

World Commission on Environment and Development (WCED). 1987. *Our Common Future.* New York: Oxford University Press.

Yearley, S. 1991. *The Green Case.* London: Harper/Collins.

Summary

Boggs, G.L. 1993. "Preparing People to Work for Social Change." An unpublished paper presented at the Steering Committee, Neighborhood Academy, June 7.

Brown, L.D. and R. Tandon. 1983. "Ideology and Political Economy in Inquiry: Action Research and Participatory Research." *The Journal of Applied Behavioral Science* 19(3): 277-294.

Brown, P. 1992. "Popular Epidemiology and Toxic Waste Contamination: Lay and Professional Ways of Knowing." *Journal of Health and Social Behavior* 33 September: 267-281.

DiPerna, P. 1985. *Cluster Mystery: Epidemic and the Children of Woburn, Massachusetts.* New York: The C.V. Mobsby Company.

Freudenberg, N. 1984. "Citizen Action for Environmental Health: Report on a Survey of Community Organizations." *American Journal of Public Health* 74(5) May: 444-448.

Gregory, R. and H. Kunreuther. 1990. "Successful Siting Incentives." *Civil Engineering* 60(April): 73-75.

Lewin, K. 1946. "Action Research and Minority Problems." *Journal of Social Issues* 2(4): 34-46.

Index

Belgium, 109
Berkowitz, Farkas, 95
Biological agriculture, 155–56
*Blue Legs v. United States Bureau of
    Indian Affairs* (1989), 146, 147
Boschwitz, Rudy, 159
Brazil, 159
Britain, 199
British Columbia, 89
Browner, Carol, 5, 187
Browning–Ferris Industries, 39
Bryant, Pat, 69
BTU tax, 120
Bureau of Labor Statistics, U.S., 92
Bush, George, 58–59, 150, 188, 198

California, 59, 62, 77–78, 99
*California v. Cabazon Band of Mission
    Indians* (1987), 146
Canada, 88, 89, 109, 143
Cancer, 45
Capitalist world economy, 177–79
Carbon taxes, 201
Cargill, 166
Caribbean, 109
Carter, Jimmy, 156
Causality between toxics and human
    illness:
  cancer, 45
  community groups as decision makers,
    12–15
  complexities involved, 9
  cultural variation, 61
  health-based information, 47–55
  participatory research, 19–20
  political economy of scientific
    inquiry, 15–19
  pollution prevention and issues of
    certainty, 21–23
  recycling, reduction, and reusing, 20–
    21
  regulatory agencies, 60
  toxic substances, ubiquitous nature
    of, 46
  uncertainty, social/psychological
    impacts of, 10–11

Center for Disease Control (CDC), 58
Centers for the Reproduction of
    Entomopathogens and Entomopha-
    gous Agents (CREE), 181
Central America, 109
Cerrell Associates Inc., 78
Chavis, Benjamin, 69
Chemical Council of New Jersey, 88
Chemical industry, 23, 152, 190
Chemical Waste Management Inc.
    (CWM), 39, 43
Cherokee Nation v. Georgia (1831), 141,
    145
Chronic toxicity, 48
Cigarettes, 10
Citizen action, *see* Community groups
Citizen's Clearinghouse for Hazardous
    Wastes (CCHW), 22, 41
City Care Conference (1979), 68
Civil Rights Commission report, U.S.
    (1982), 165
Clean Air Act Amendments (1990), 89
Clinton, Bill, 187
  administration analyzed, 2–3
  economic growth and job creation, 87
  election platform, 188
  environmental activism stirred by, 86
  environmental community pressuring,
    204
  Executive Order 12898, 218–26
  Indigenous peoples, 148
  National Service Program, 20
  trade agreements, 198
Cloning, 29
Club of Rome's Project on the
    Predicament of Mankind, 108
Coal, 143
Coalitions constructed by environmental
    community, 205
Cohen, Felix, 140
Cold War, 1, 172, 199
Colorado, 162
Commerce Department, U.S., 95
Commission for Environmental Protec-
    tion in Cuba, 184
Commodity-exporting corporations, 152